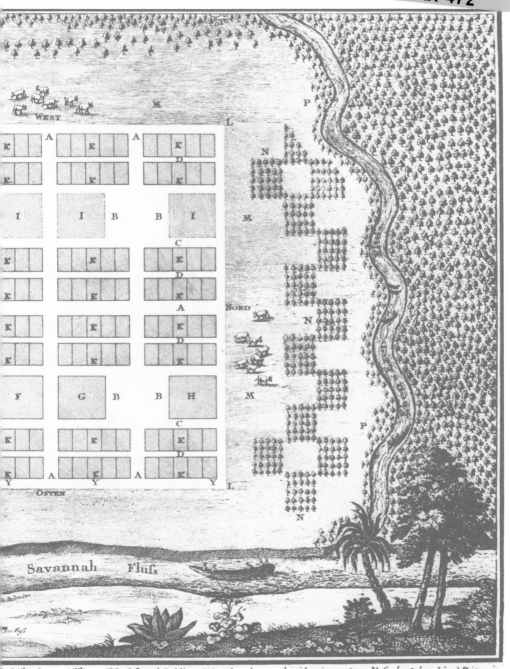

WEST

OSTEN

NORD

Savannah Fluß

...aß Waysen auch Witwen Hauß. I auch Publique Plätz aber dato noch nicht eingeräumet K Sechs Zehen ...
...t steht, u. von ferne der Statt ein ansehen macht als wäre sie verpalisadiert M Vieh Weyde. N Gärten O ...
...lt Eben-Ezer zwey Stund von dem Neuen Eben-Ezer. Ueine See. W Burgbury zwey Stunden von Eben Ezer N...
...nende Vornehme u Reiche Leuthe aufbehalten. Z Maaß Stab von 300 Fuß wornach der Plan der Statt ...

...achrichten, 13te Continuation, Erster Theil (Halle and Augsburg, 1747).
...ollection, University of Georgia Library.

Detailed Reports on the
Salzburger Emigrants
Who Settled in America . . .
Edited by Samuel Urlsperger

The Imperial City of Ulm on the Danube from whose territory most
of the Georgia Swabians came
(COURTESY OF THE CITY OF ULM)

Detailed Reports on the Salzburger Emigrants Who Settled in America . . . Edited by Samuel Urlsperger

VOLUME SIXTEEN

1753

Translated by
GEORGE FENWICK JONES

1754

Translated by
RENATE WILSON
and
GEORGE FENWICK JONES

1753 and 1754
Edited by
GEORGE FENWICK JONES

THE UNIVERSITY OF GEORGIA PRESS
ATHENS AND LONDON

The paper in this book meets the guidelines for
permanence and durability of the Committee on
Production Guidelines for Book Longevity of the
Council on Library Resources.

Printed in the United States of America

95 94 93 92 91   5 4 3 2 1

Library of Congress Cataloging-in-Publication Data

(Revised for vol. 16)
Urlsperger, Samuel, 1685–1772.
  Detailed reports on the Salzburger emigrants who settled in America.

  (Wormsloe Foundation. Publications, no. 9–   ) Translation of Ausführliche
Nachricht von den saltzburgischen Emigranten, die sich in America niedergelassen
haben, which covers the period 1733–Mar. 1751, and Das Americanisches Acker-
werck Gottes which begins with April 1751.
  Vols. 1–5 issued in series: Publications
(Wormsloe Foundation)
  Includes bibliographical references and indexes.
  1. Salzburgers—Georgia—History—Sources. 2. German Americans—Georgia—
History—Sources. 3. Lutherans—Georgia—History—Sources. 4. Ebenezer (Ga.)—
History—Sources. 5. Georgia—History—Colonial period. ca. 1600–1775—
Sources. 6. Stockbridge Indians—Missions—History—Sources. 7. Indians of North
America—Georgia—Missions—History—Sources. I. Jones, George Fenwick,
1916–   . II. Urlsperger, Samuel, 1685–1772. Americanisches Ackerwerck Gottes.
English. 1968. III. Title. IV. Series: Publications (Wormsloe Foundation); no. 9, etc.
F295.S1U813   975.8′00436   67–27137
ISBN 0–8203–1329–7 (alk. paper : v. 16)

British Library Cataloging in Publication Data available

Volumes 1–5 were published as part of the Wormsloe Foundation
Publications Series.

  *Contents*

Introduction

1 7 5 3 – 5 4

To understand the circumstances and activities of the Georgia Salzburgers in the years 1753 and 1754, one must be familiar with their origin and previous condition. For this reason, the following six paragraphs are repeated here from previous volumes for the benefit of newcomers to the series. Readers who have read the earlier volumes or are otherwise familiar with the story of the Salzburgers are advised to ignore them.

When the Lutherans were expelled from Salzburg in 1731, not all the exiles went to East Prussia and other Protestant lands in Europe: a small number, some two hundred, were taken to the colony of Georgia, then in its second year. Georgia, the last of Britain's thirteen North American colonies, was founded according to the grandiose schemes of a group of benevolent gentlemen in London, called the Trustees, who wished to provide homes for impoverished Englishmen and persecuted foreign Protestants, to protect the more northerly colonies from the Spaniards in Florida, and to provide raw materials for English industry.

The first Salzburger transport, or traveling party, consisted of recent exiles who had been residing in and around Augsburg, a Swabian city just northwest of Salzburg. This group arrived in Georgia in 1734 and settled some twenty-five miles northwest of Savannah, where they founded a settlement which they named Ebenezer. By the time the second transport arrived a year later, the land that had been chosen had proved infertile and the stream on which it was built, Ebenezer Creek, had proved unnavigable. When a third transport arrived in 1736, composed mostly of Upper Austrian and Carinthian exiles, the survivors at Ebenezer joined them at the Red Bluff on the Savannah River, bringing the name of the earlier settlement with them. The original site, which became the Trustees' cowpen or cattle ranch, was henceforth called Old Ebenezer.

A fourth and last Salzburger transport, consisting of exiles who had been sojourning in Augsburg and other Swabian cities, arrived in 1741. The Salzburgers were joined by Swiss and Palatine settlers from Purysburg, a Swiss settlement a short way down the Savannah River on the Carolina side, and also by some Palatine servants donated by the Trustees. Finding insufficient fertile land on the Red Bluff, many Salzburgers moved their plantations to an area along Abercorn Creek where the lowland was flooded and enriched each winter by the Savannah River. This explains the terms "the town" and "the plantations." After some gristmills and sawmills were built on Abercorn Creek, it was usually called the Mill River (*Mühl-Fluss*).

Despite appalling sickness and mortality and the hardships incident to settlement in a wilderness, the Salzburgers were the most successful community in Georgia. This relative success was largely due to the skill, devotion, and diligence of their spiritual leader, Johann Martin Boltzius, the author of most of these reports. This young divine had been trained at the University of Halle in eastern Germany and had taught there at the Francke Foundation, a charitable institution that was to have great influence on the development of Ebenezer.

Although Boltzius was at heart a minister, his secular responsibilities in Georgia molded him into a skillful administrator, economist, and diplomat. A few of the reports were written by Boltzius' admiring younger colleague, Christian Israel Gronau, who officiated whenever Boltzius was away, in Savannah or elsewhere, until his untimely death in 1745. After that, some of the reports were written by Gronau's successor, Hermann Heinrich Lemke.

Boltzius' journals were edited contemporaneously by Samuel Urlsperger, the Senior of the Lutheran clergy in Augsburg. Comparison of the original manuscripts surviving in Halle with Urlsperger's published edition shows that he took considerable liberty in deleting unpleasant reports and suppressing proper names, which he replaced with N. or N.N. So far as we know, the original documents for 1753 and 1754 no longer exist, so there is no way to know how much Urlsperger changed or deleted; but there is reason to believe that Boltzius made an entry for every day, as he had been instructed to, and that Urlsperger made major deletions for both diplomatic and economic reasons. In some cases he simply consolidated the material for two or more days into one. Urlsperger's deletions are very illogical: he often deletes a name in one passage even though it appears in another and can be easily recognized. His deletions for 1754 seem to have been even more drastic than in previous years.

Beginning in April of 1751, for reasons unknown, Urlsperger had abruptly changed the title of his edition to *Das americanische Ackerwerck Gottes*, or *God's American Husbandry*. The symbolism is clear: in John 15:1 Christ says, "I am the true vine, and my Father is the husbandman." In other words, God's American husbandry is His spreading of His word in North America through the Halle missionaries. Despite the change in the title of the original, the title of the *Detailed Reports* has been retained since the content is almost unchanged, unless Urlsperger has taken even more license in abridging the work. Because of Boltzius' chronic illness and eye ailment, the entries for 1754 were mostly by Lemke and the new minister Rabenhorst. Both schooled themselves so well in Boltzius' style that it is not always possible to distinguish between them, except when the writer mentions himself or the other minister by name.

The years 1753 and 1754 were more or less a continuation of the period 1751 and 1752, which had been a turning point in Ebenezer's history. By now all the major transports had arrived: four Salzburger transports in addition to a mini-transport in 1739, contingents from four Palatine transports in 1737, 1738, 1746, and 1749, and three Swabian transports in 1750, 1751, and 1752. After that only free individuals joined at their own initiative.

By 1752 the emphasis upon small self-sufficient yeoman farmers had changed to emphasis on production of silk and lumber for foreign export, and this policy continued and was urged from the pulpit. Also, the Salzburgers' long opposition to slavery had ended, and even they were beginning to acquire slaves because they were unable to find loyal white servants. The beginning of the change from family farms to slave-operated plantations can be seen in the efforts during 1753 and 1754 to develop the "minister's plantation" to support the third minister, for whom no salary had been provided.

In general, the years 1753 and 1754 were uneventful and merely continued the routine of previous years. Paul Mueller, a lad from Purysburg who had been educated in Ebenezer, returned there after living among the Indians for many years, Boltzius' surviving son, Gotthilf Israel, departed for study at Halle, and the oldest Schubdrein girl was drowned in the Savannah River, in which she was found six weeks later. We also meet, for the first time, Johann Caspar Wertsch, an indentured baker's apprentice, who was eventually to become one of the two leading men of Ebenezer. Boltzius' few remarks about Briar Creek and Halifax reveal the failure to establish the third Swabian transport there, as had been planned.

The incidence of sickness remained high in 1753, and malaria was even worse than previously. Boltzius had always been able to praise the Lord that either he or Lemke had been well enough to tend to divine services; yet now, even though the two had been reinforced by Christian Rabenhorst, there were times when no minister was strong enough to perform his duties. Because malaria was not usually an outright killer, the mortality was not as high as in some other years, unless possibly Urlsperger saw fit to delete some mentions of death. For unknown reasons, the year 1754 was healthier, malaria was less severe, and Boltzius could claim on one occasion that only two parishioners were sick.

Early in 1753 Boltzius made a journey to Charleston, where he made many, and often amusing, observations especially about slavery. Although now convinced of the necessity of slavery, he still believed that Blacks are as intelligent as whites. This did not, however deter him from making a large purchase of slaves for the new minister's plantation or from justifying the use of slave labor. Many of the entries for 1754 concern the slave-operated minister's plantation, which was not only to maintain the third minister but also to create funds for other purposes.

ACKNOWLEDGMENTS

I wish again at this time to thank Alice Ferrell for laboriously reading the proofs to this volume and to thank Pastors Hermann Winde and Hartmut Beck for help in identifying hymns and Biblical passages.

The funds for publishing this volume were borne by four loyal members of the Georgia Salzburger Society, who have dedicated it as follows:

> We, the undersigned, dedicate this volume of the Detailed Reports to our ancestors who immigrated to Ebenezer in the Colony of Georgia. These ancestors were: George and Anna (Gress) Gnann, Jacob Gnann and his son Jacob, Jr., Conrad and Anna Barbara (Paulitsch) Rahn, Mary Judith Heintz, wife of Andrew Lebey.
>
> We also dedicate this volume, with deepest love, to William George and Pearl Rahn Gnann, and to Louise Gnann LeBey, beloved wife of John C. LeBey.
>
> John Courtenay LeBey
William George Gnann, Jr.
Charles Andrew LeBey
Amy Gnann LeBey.

Detailed Reports on the

Salzburger Emigrants

Who Settled in America . . .

Edited by Samuel Urlsperger

Daily Reports Of the Year 1753

JANUARY 1753

The 1st of January 1753. Highly praised be God, Father of our Lord Jesus Christ: In His graciousness, He not only permitted me and my two highly esteemed colleagues, Mr. Lemke and Mr. Rabenhorst, to end the past year with His blessing but also to start the new one with new blessings! May He mercifully accept our poor private and public prayers for ourselves, our ministers, the entire congregation, the whole country, our future rulers, all Christendom, and all our dear known and unknown Fathers, benefactors, and friends, for whose salvation through Christ, our source of redemption, we are praying with today's opening verse Isaiah 12:3. However, we are also asking the God of Peace with all our hearts for everything we have prayed for in yesterday morning's sermon from 1 Thessalonians 5: "And the very God of peace sanctify you wholly; and I pray God your whole spirit and soul and body be preserved blameless until the coming of our Lord Jesus Christ. Faithful is he that calleth you, who also will do it."[1]

Today I started to give some dear old listeners a blessed and edifying reminder from Senior Urlsperger, our dearest Father, and from Senior Riesch, the true friend of the Salzburgers from Lindau and other places.[2] These listeners have suffered many trials and tribulations during this pilgrimage and, in many respects, have become like our Lord Jesus in His state of humiliation. I will continue with this gradually and wisely. This valuable gift, which is worth more than gold, consists of the beautifully bound volume of Good Friday and Easter Sermons delivered by the dear Samuel[3] of our Evangelical churches, who was instructed and trained by God. He has sent a large number of copies to us as yet another proof of his fatherly love. The complete title of this handsome octavo book, which comes in more than one alphabet, is as follows: *Words on the Death and Life of Jesus*

Christ, as Divine Power and Wisdom, Discussed in Ten Lenten and Two Easter Sermons.[4] At the end of this handsome book there is an appendix on the power of Jesus Christ's resurrection, based on the blessed example of a pious, learned, and keen-witted candidate of theology named Breuer, who died peacefully in Augsburg.

The other welcome gift to the Salzburgers who have been in Lindau and have enjoyed many benefactions from the late Senior Riesch is entitled *Trifolium Rieschianum*, i.e., the life of the late Senior Riesch and two of his sermons. Since we did not have sufficient time, I read only the short, but very inspiring, and to me impressive, foreword in which Deacon Buerkmann, the late Senior's righteous friend, promises the public another edifying *Trifolium Rieschianum*, i.e., three important sermons by the deceased, which we would also like to have. As the foreword indicates, this hard-working Senior,[5] who loved Christ with all his heart, gave 3,543 sermons during his work in Lindau. I have given other useful books and treatises to some other people for New Year's, and may our dear God bless them!

Although we had very cold weather during the past few days, this did not deter us from attending our public church service. Tonight we held a repetition hour instead of a prayer meeting; and we sang with great pleasure the very enjoyable New Year's hymn composed by our dear Court Chaplain Ziegenhagen: *Mein Vater, Du hast mich erwaehlt* . . . etc., which is appropriate at any time of the year when we receive spiritual and material benefactions.

After the prayer meeting I read from the above-mentioned *Trifolium Rieschianum* the first beautiful sermon about God's reward to pious people. The sermon is very detailed, clear, and comforting; and one cannot read it without feeling a sense of healing emotions. Indeed, dear Lindau and the Evangelical Church had a worthy minister and leader in the late Mr. Riesch! I regret that the *Trifolium* does not describe his life in more detail, particularly the final hours of his final lingering illness.

The 2nd of January. Today our hard-working and very able carpenter Joseph Schubdrein was married to the eldest daughter /Maria/ of the Salzburger Brandner; and for the ceremony I drew on the late Professor /A. H./ Francke's magnificent booklet on the *Philanthropia Dei*, especially the two first verses: "Yea, he loved the people," and "God so loved the world," etc.[6] We have every reason for doing this. Because our dear inhabitants of Ebenezer, too, should call out to one another, full of amazement: "How much our Lord loves us poor people!" The numerous spiritual and physical good deeds He has showered on us from time to time instead of on many other people in this country and in Christendom are ample proof of it; and I could not refrain from talking about them on this occasion. It is true that the Lord imposes many burdens on us and subjects us to many temptations.[7] However, interpreting this as an indication of God's lack of love for us would be not only a childish, but a satanic conclusion, as we find it in Christ's temptation in Matthew 4.

It is not a good sign if parents believe that their ill-behaved children are unworthy of punishment and that punishment is lost on them, or if God allows people to pursue their own ways. It is better to sing: "Children whom the Father should draw to all that is good" and "If then I am God's child, why should I flee? . . . etc."[8] To explicate my sermon I referred to the noteworthy 73rd Psalm, which describes very clearly and succinctly the thoughts and words of many people who are not well disposed toward us and consider themselves happy when they are physically well off and consider us unhappy with our abundant preaching of God's word, our Evangelical teachings, and our many beautiful books and welcome opportunities that inspire both our children and adults, etc. Verse 11, in particular, reflects their thinking: "And they say, How doth God know? and is there knowledge in the most High? Behold, these are the ungodly, who prosper in the world; they increase in riches." Also, there is a noteworthy word in Verse 15: "If I say I will speak thus; behold, I should offend against the generation of thy children. When I thought to know this, it was too painful for me; Until I went into the sanctuary of God." That means, all those who draw such wrong conclusions about our burden and misery, as people did at Assaph's time, condemn not only all of God's children, but Christ himself as the leader of the believers. They have never entered God's sanctuary and they have no idea of, and have never experienced, the secret of the cross. Alas, souls who sin against God and His children and forego so much good deserve our pity.

The 3rd of January. Important business matters require me and Artillery Captain Krauss to travel to Charleston; and the currently temperate, dry, and not-too-cold weather seems to favor such a trip. Some years ago, our dear God let fall to me and my dear colleagues, in an unexpected and unsolicited way, 1,000 acres of unusually fertile land in a good location that must be cultivated lest we lose it or invite all kinds of accusations. Also, in view of our economic circumstances, we have to grow all kinds of crops and raise some cattle since ministers in America depend on it because of their very small salaries. The secretaries of our Lord Trustees indicated that 12 pounds 10 shillings per year are to be deducted from our salaries. To make up for it, they have given a certain amount of money which we are to use in a way that would compensate us every year for the lower salaries.

In this country the only possible and safest way to accomplish this is to establish a plantation on good soil and to raise cattle. We cannot get any white servants, as our experience and also the unsuccessful attempts of our dearest friends in Europe have demonstrated; and, because of their high wages, they would be of little use to us. So far our mills, and also several members of our congregation, have had a lot of expenses and troubles with these white servants and little or no benefit. As much as we would like to settle only white people in our community, this is impossible for the stated reasons. For that reason we had to decide in favor of buying and using some Negroes or Negro slaves; and we truly want, and have, the Christian intention to lead them to our Lord Jesus Christ, the Savior of all mankind, through Christian teaching, a good example, good deeds and moderate, yet sufficient, work.

If it were up to the white people, including those of the lowest social extraction, they would even abolish the article in the *Haustafel*,[9] which is based on God's word, concerning the status, duties, and good deeds of farm-hands and maid-servants; yet without it a bourgeois society and even the Christian church itself could not exist. There have always been masters and servants, and it must stay that way. And since, for almost 21 years, it has been impossible in this country to establish such an order, because everybody in this free land wants to be a gentlemen, master, and householder, and almost nobody wants to be a servant, apprentice, or hired hand, most people are poor and physically ill; they die prematurely and have little to eat.

In view of these circumstances, we have to resort, whether we like it or not, to taking on black servants instead of white ones. Through God's providence, they now not only have the honor to do what the Christian *Haustafel* demands in its Catechism; but, as a result of their conversion, they may also expect and enjoy what it promises, as Colossians 3:22-24 says. What the Lord Trustees are expected to give us would not be enough to buy a sufficient number of Negroes to warrant a Christian and hard-working supervisor for them. For that reason we have been waiting, on the one hand, for our Fathers and European benefactors to approve our plan and, on the other hand, for several signs of God's providence. We are glad to have received both in the most recent letters.

Not only has our plan to set up a plantation been approved, but our wondrous God has found some sympathetic hearts that will give us significant help at the beginning. At the same time, we got some very advantageous proposals that enable us to have a manager and overseer on the plantation. As part of God's particularly gracious providence in this important matter, which we had tackled with much fear, we got, contrary to our thoughts and expectations, the honest, hard-working and prudent Hans Schmid and his pious wife as overseers and housekeepers. They are thoroughly reliable, and we do not have to worry about them, and that was our greatest concern.

To be sure, we will not be entirely able to start this plantation and its initially difficult installation without going into debt since food is very expensive as a result of the bad harvest, and especially since the money the Lord Trustees sent us cannot yet be paid out. Also, many unexpected expenses may come up. However, we hope God will continue to lend us a helping hand through His known and unknown tools, in accordance with what they are able to do and without depriving others. May our gracious God give them His blessings and, hopefully, also the joy of hearing that we and our families are now enjoying better living conditions and that the Negroes and Africans in our service have turned, through God's word and Holy Baptism, from poor slaves into free followers of Jesus Christ. This is our and our pious overseer's goal. Some of the few Negroes in our community are looking forward to my teaching them.

The 4th of January. This afternoon the surveyor came down from the new land[10] and told us that he had surveyed 3,000 acres for so-called gentlemen and for some people of the most recent transport,[11] who were with him; and that his work had been interrupted because the other colonists did not come with him and choose their land themselves. He indicated, however, his willingness to come back as soon as they and Mr. Krauss want him to. By order of the Council, he surveyed 300 acres of very good and well-located land close to the plantation center. He said that the newcomers, or in some instances some people on their behalf, wanted to go up there ten days ago at the surveyor's request, but could not get beyond Briar Creek, which they were unable to cross because it had risen so much. Also, it seems that some of the new people will not be able to move to their land because they are too poor to do so, and some would rather be near the church and school and fellow-countrymen at Ebenezer, at least for a time.

Our dear brother and colleague Rabenhorst discussed with us his given profession before the Lord, and we all agree (and the entire transport is also convinced of it) that he should stay, work, and suffer with us as a third minister who has been called to Ebenezer to preach in God's name, and that he should see and taste with us how friendly our Lord is toward those waiting for Him and toward the souls asking for Him. He helps us preach and catechize once every two weeks, delivers the weekly sermon on the Blue Bluff, and teaches the catechism to our school children, with Mr. Lemke conducting the preparatory lessons for the older children and taking over much of my other work when I am traveling. He also does me the special favor of teaching my only boy for a few hours, as my dearest colleague and brother-in-law, Mr. Lemke does, without affecting their other duties. I can report to our Fathers and friends: we stand together as one before the Lord. Praised be the Lord!

The 5th of January. For several reasons and because of obvious signs of God's providence, our dear colleague, Pastor Boltzius, accompanied by Captain Krauss and a trustworthy Salzburger,[12] has been persuaded to take a trip to Charleston, as he has reported in his diary. Hence, last evening, he said good-bye to Mr. Rabenhorst and me, Lemke, as much as his short time permitted him to do, and we wished him well. May the Lord be with him and his dear traveling companions for the entire trip, and may His angel accompany them so that they, God willing, may soon be back with us.

In the meantime we will take care of some of his work; and therefore we have started today to read Senior Urlsperger's latest letter in both the Zion and the Jerusalem Churches. In doing so, our good God has given us an opportunity to preach to those among us, who, despite their unsettled hearts, look upon themselves as having been good Christians for quite some time, and to show how corrupt their condition really is, as they show by their lack of desire for God's works. We always welcome opportunities provided by servants tested by God to convince those in the audience who do not yet believe that they must change before they can enter God's Kingdom. But it is extremely difficult, if not impossible, to make some people, especially older people, understand this. Finally we thanked God for the advice and comfort given us by this blessed letter from our dearest Mr. Senior; and we prayed for him and all our dearest benefactors and friends and wished them much good, in time and eternity, from the abundance of Jesus Christ, as a rich reward for the many good deeds our Lord has bestowed on us through them, although we do not deserve them.

The 8th of January. Yesterday our congregation heard, from dear Mr. Rabenhorst at the Jerusalem Church and from me at the Zion Church, Christ's wonderful gospel, for which our gracious God has mercifully given us strength. While riding my horse to Zion Church, I had the misfortune of having my horse fall to the ground, with me on its back; but God's grace ensured that I suffered nothing but a slight injury to one of my feet. However, after a few hours, the swelling and pain forced me to cancel the afternoon sermon. As Mr. /Ludwig/ Mayer told me to do, I have been applying warm compresses since last night, with the result that most of the pain and the swelling have subsided. I am deeply grateful to our dear God for mercifully sparing me and for the help He has once again given me. In all likelihood, too much work would suddenly have been thrust upon dear Mr. Rabenhorst, had God not averted greater damage. Meanwhile he substituted for me in a marriage ceremony at Zion Church; and he returned from it at noontime today, greatly strengthened, despite the constant rain we are now having.

In the late afternoon, I was once again well enough to meet the request of a sick man in the neighborhood for my visit. As instructed, I talked to him about the words: "Remember therefore from whence thou art fallen, and repent."[13] He listened and agreed with them with tears and sighs, and he asked me to pray with and for him, and I did so. On this short trip, God also gave me much pleasure in another house through a person who had been sick for a while and several times close to death. Since early this year, our dear God has begun to give her renewed strength and get her back on her feet. In addition, He was very merciful toward her soul during her illness; and she praised God for it with her heart and mouth. I agreed with her; and thus our hearts flowed together in praise of God; and we both felt greatly encouraged and blessed by what we had talked about and prayed for.

This incidence demonstrated the effectiveness of God's chastisement. In particular, we enjoyed the words from dear Senior Urlsperger's fatherly letter, and we are now discussing its most notable words in our prayer meeting: "It is true, for them as well as for us, that joy and sorrow always alternate and that it would not be good if it were otherwise."

The 9th of January. We have had steady rain for several days, and this undoubtedly has made the trip much more difficult for our dear colleague and his companion. We have often asked and prayed to God to spare them all harm. Today, the sky has cleared up, and once again it has started getting colder. Last Saturday an Englishman brought me a letter from the President of the province[14] addressed to my dear colleague and asking him to marry some people from Abercorn, whose bans had already been read three times by the preacher in Savannah, but who had refused to be married there. Although I found it difficult to agree to their request, especially since I have never performed such a ceremony in English, I felt it was a good idea to meet this request because the President had outlined in great detail the reasons for which these people surely could be married. Hence, following our weekly sermon, the ceremony took place in our manager's house near the new sawmill, where the engaged couple and some Englishmen had gone. God then helped me both here and, earlier, at the Zion Church, and I am deeply grateful to Him for that.

On my way I met a man who had been given to drinking, and I asked him when he would finally render his heart to God? He sighed and said that it was probably high time for him to do so. I confirmed that, adding that, unless he would do so in the near future, sin would gain more and more control over him; and, since he was already quite old, it might be easy for his conversion never to materialize. He did not say anything else. On leaving, I asked him to make an early decision on what he wanted to do. I asked him not to believe that it would be impossible for him to free himself of his sinful habits and that God could do more than we ask for, comprehend, and believe.

The 10th of January. Mr. Rabenhorst gets much of his encouragement from people who arrived here with the most recent transport.[15] They are telling him of their great confidence in him and saying that they regret his inability to move with them to their land at Briar Creek. Those whose land has been surveyed are getting ready to leave here and hence are taking leave of him emotionally, and in return he is giving them much needed advice and telling them comforting words to follow. He has promised to visit them occasionally if they come to pick him up.

I spent a pleasant hour this afternoon with a man who has been awakened several times; but, unfortunately, every single time it has come to naught. There are now more indications than ever before that he is truly repentant. He told me during my visit how he would gradually overcome his habitual sins. But, since the way he wanted to do it was not according to God's word, he had to be told that he would primarily have to make a true change of heart. He would have to surrender his corrupted, bad heart with all its sins to Jesus Christ and ask for, and accept, His mercy and the forgiveness of his sins and all the strength to lead

a pious life. He then would surely be able to overcome his habitual sinning. I recommended frequent praying, something he
has neglected until now, as he himself admitted; and he said that
since then his condition has increasingly worsened. I read with
him the song: *Es ist nicht schwehr ein Christ zu seyn* . . . etc., and
then we prayed together. Eventually he made amends for some
youthful injustice by helping the poor and showing his love, in
particular, for dear Mr. Rabenhorst, whose sermon, he said,
awakened him during the last day of the old year.

The 12th of January. In Mr. Boltzius's absence and prior to the
weekly sermon I am instructing the children on the plantations
in the catechism, and I am basing my teachings on the *Concise
Order of Salvation in Five Questions and Answers,* as Printed by the
Halle Orphanage,[16] and I hope to finish by the time, God willing, our dear colleagues' return safely. Today we covered the
question and answer: "Who then has mercy on you?" etc., which
leads to the Root and Source of our salvation, who has given us
His eternally merciful love and who, in His wisdom that sur-
passeth all human understanding, has found a way to save us.
The children were very attentive, and to my great edification it
gave me great pleasure to spend the hour with them. Praised be
our Father in Heaven for it! In church we continued with the
letter from Senior Urlsperger, our dearest Father in Jesus
Christ.

My dear colleague Mr. Rabenhorst is discussing with the
town's school children the *Order of Salvation* by Pastor
Freylinghausen.[17] He has a nice way of dealing with children,
and hopefully it will work with benefit under the Lord's blessing.
This evening he also took over the prayer hour, in which he edi-
fyingly presented, from the booklet *Jesus, the True Friend of Sinners,*[18] the sweet truth of "Jesus accepts the sinners, even the dis-
heartened sinners." May this have God's blessings!

The 13th of January. Today has been an upsetting day for us,
my dear colleague and myself. An old man lives with his son and
daughter-in-law in great discord because of some money which
he had given to the son and now wants back, and because of
other things. The matter was to be resolved today. During that
occasion many bad things about the old man have come to light.
May God have mercy on him and may He show ways and means

to save the man's soul, which is already near the edge of eternity. He probably will no longer bother us in the way he used to in the past.

In the afternoon we are expecting the visit of an Englishman who wishes to have his bans read and to be married to Greiner's daughter.[19] I have referred him to the minister in Savannah, but he insists that he has his land at Abercorn and wants to belong to our congregation. Therefore, he hoped that I would not deny his request and that he had been referred here. The woman owes Hirschmann her fare for the crossing and she wants to work it off in his service, but she has left his employment prematurely because she does not like it. In so doing she is abusing this country's freedom as many others do. She has now been told to pay up before the marriage can be performed. Because of that, the matter had to be brought before Mr. Mayer, the justiciary, who early on did not want to let Greiner and his daughter have their way but later said that, since the Englishman had given a written assurance that he would make the payment, the planned marriage could take place.

The 14th of January. Praised be our true Savior, our supreme Shepherd, who has lent His gracious support to us, His poor servants, on this Sunday so that His word could be told in the review meeting this morning, afternoon, and also evening.

We talked about the Gospel John 2:1 on Jesus's love for the faithful poor because we wanted to educate and comfort especially those among our dear old and new listeners who are poor and wanting. At first we discussed Proverbs 28:6. Oh, if only all poor people would become pious from the bottom of their hearts, because God would then surely not let them suffer from want, although that may mean many struggles and tribulations.

I hope that these words have filled some people in their present misery with new courage, as I often tell myself when I am unable to serve this or that person the way I should: "But thou, O Lord, how long?" and the answer is: "For ye have need of patience."[20] They must go with Ebenezer through difficult times, Mr. Rabenhorst is telling those who wish to talk to him about our humble circumstances and who demand to know about one, but not the other, thing. We also sang tonight: *"Even though we pass through many trials, you already see the end," etc . . . "* etc.[21], from

the song "*Alles sei dir uebergeben . . .* " etc., which is part of the
new collection of holy songs sent us from dear Wernigerode on
the most recent ship as a dear present.

The 15th of January. This winter our dear Lord has visited
some people in our congregation with sickness, and we have had
the same experience in our house. Yet I feel strengthened and
also comforted by God's goodness, and dear Mr. Rabenhorst has
contributed much to that. What is there to learn in our Savior's
school of crosses? "O Lord, correct me, but with judgment; not
in anger, lest thou bring me to nothing."[22] It is quite easy to trust
the Lord in good days, but it is much more difficult to keep trusting Him in troubled times and to prove it with actions, although
that is possible through God's grace. My dear colleague brought
me the news today that things are going well for locksmith
Schrempf and his inner feelings. He also told me yesterday that
the law no longer affects him as harshly as before, but that he
could now trust his Savior not to reject him.[23]

A boat with corn arrived today from Savannah Town. It was
sold in no time to our inhabitants at a high price, namely, 2 Sterling 9 pence. Nevertheless, we are very glad that the corn has
come to our place because we are very short of it as a result of
our bad harvest this year. Thus our Lord always helps when the
need is greatest and undoubtedly would do more if everybody
were the way he should be in accordance with God's word.

The 16th of January. Today our Heavenly Father did us some
good deeds which we rightly view as being among His best benefactions. In both the schools and churches I and my dear colleagues delivered God's word to our own and, we hope, our dear
audience's edification. In the Zion Church I have begun to lay as
a basis for our edification our dear Senior Urlsperger's important and thorough contemplation concerning godless unchangeability.[24] I believe that this will assure me in advance of
God's great blessing and make me feel markedly strengthened
by it today.

Until now our mills have had enough water to cut a good
number of boards. Tomorrow some of them will be taken to Savannah on rafts we built today; and we can expect to earn some
income from this, which we need very badly in our current situa-

tion. I was pleased to work on it until late into the night, although I would like to leave such work to somebody else. But so long as nobody else is available and one of us ministers has to do this work, I cannot turn it down. However, it is only a matter of assisting our manager, in whose name everything is done, with bookkeeping and writing. My heart rejoices that Thou art so eager to help us. "My heart shall rejoice in thy salvation. I will sing unto the Lord, because he hath dealt bountifully with me."[25]

The 17th of January. For the most part, those people of the latest transport who wanted to move to their land have now left. Today a boat is leaving at the very time my dear colleague will hold our usual edification hour for the people of the Blue Bluff. An old woman was standing by the bank of the river and was very sad because she could not accompany her only son since her stubborn husband, who is also staying behind, will not permit her to do so. We could not advise these old people to move with their son to his land, primarily because that would deprive them of the ministers' comfort, which they dearly need, and also because they are not in need in material terms; on the other hand, we could not advise them against doing so either, because they will need their son's care.

The fact that these people get the so-called "good" land is a very good thing indeed. However, weighing the difficulties commonly associated with it in both spiritual as well as physical terms, I cannot really be sure what I should tell them. We know for sure that, if we would plow the high-lying land (which includes the pine forest with its shallow layer of loam or clay) the way it is done in Germany and other countries, our harvest here would be just as abundant as there. If this way of cultivating fields had become more popular and if one could be more certain of the good effect, the people would derive still other, not inconsiderable, physical and spiritual advantages, apart from living closer together and in a better way.

The 18th of January. The weather during this winter month is as warm as it usually is in the spring. Hence, one has to take good care of one's health since warm weather at this time of the year, with its thick, foggy, yet sometimes somewhat cool air, seems to be bad for the human body. But it does help the poor people and those who are about to establish themselves on their land, and possibly also our dear colleague and those with him who, we hope, are on their way back home.

Today Schrempf, whose heart is very distraught because he feels and realizes that he has sinned, has requested and received Holy Communion. He had prepared himself by praying and beseeching God, and he freely confessed his sins before Him and accused himself of being the greatest sinner. To comfort him, I talked about the words: "God hath not appointed us to wrath, but to obtain salvation by our Lord Jesus Christ." 1 Thessalonians 3:9,10. May God bless this in him!

The 20th of January. Last night Lachner's pious wife let me know that she had fallen sick suddenly and wanted very much to see a minister. Because it was already late, I did not ride out to her plantation to see her until this morning, and there I found her in a very weak condition. She complained about her great lack of faith, about which she had shed many tears yesterday, and she said that this was the reason why she was so exhausted. I told her about: 1.) what happens to many people when they feel that they lack faith and suddenly want to believe, thinking that they can force the matter. At other times, they do not use faithfully the means of grace, prayers, and God's word; and, by doing so, they are damaging their faith. As a result, they sometimes get into new trouble. She said that this was what happened to her and that this was what is hurting her now. 2.) I showed her God's loving intention when he made her fall sick, how He wanted to use it for cleansing her, and how he wanted to create a basis for her to achieve it. 3.) How she should conduct herself, namely, by accepting readily, willingly, and patiently what God would do to her outwardly and inwardly, and by developing and maintaining great trust in her Savior even though He had caused her pain; because everything was meant well. In this connection I quoted the verses in Deuteronomy 32:4 and Hebrews 12:2: "Looking unto Jesus," etc., and Chapter 10:35,36. Then I prayed with her and commended her soul to the Lord. She gave me to understand that my words of comfort had pleased her.

The 21st of January. Today we were again awakened and strengthened by God's word, and we cannot give enough thanks to our true God for it. Under the present circumstances, while we are continuing to have sickness and other misery in our congregation as well as in our home, the introductory words from Psalm 13, Verse 6, were very sweet to me and perhaps even more so to others. How refreshing to read in the Gospel: "I wish to do it; I will do it; I will come."[26] Oh Lord, strengthen our faith! We talked, from the Gospel, about the heart of our Lord Jesus Christ which is eager to help us. I was rather exhausted, and my visit to the sick Schrempf, following the noon sermon, may have contributed to it. I had to talk to him at great length in order to awaken his heart, with his heavy burden of sins, to take refuge in the wounds of our Savior. For that reason I had to ask my dear colleague, who preached at Zion Church today, to hold the prayer meeting.

The 22nd of January. Today the Salzburger Riedelsperger, who traveled with Pastor Boltzius and Captain Krauss to Charleston, has returned; and he has brought the welcome news that they are well, that they journeyed from Charleston to Port Royal, and that we can expect them to return from there in three days.

Yesterday and today, Mrs. Bacher let me know that her illness had not improved, but worsened. Hence, I immediately rode to her this morning and found her near death, although quite composed and full of joy. She held out her hands to me, telling me in a very weak voice that her Savior had cleansed her with His blood of all her sins and would mercifully welcome her in Heaven. In response, and to strengthen her belief, I called out to her: "For he hath made him to be sin for us, who knew no sin; that we might be made the righteousness of God in him."[27] "Yes," she said, "I believe that," adding: "Jesus Christ is my righteousness; I shall wrap myself in His wounds, and I shall rest in them."

After these words I and the people around kneeled down and prayed with and for her, we put her on and into Jesus Christ's heart and asked Him to help her, through the Holy Ghost, in her last struggle and to grant her complete and early victory over all her enemies, according to His gracious will. I then wanted to take leave of her, saying: "There is nothing I can bring before God, except Thee, my greatest possession: Jesus! I must succeed through Thy rose-colored blood," etc.[28] However, she first asked me to convey a friendly greeting to certain persons, thanked them through me for all their love for her and for all the good she had experienced, and that was how she felt especially about her ministers.

Since I had requested to be informed whether she would live longer, because I wish to visit her again, they told me this noon that there had been no change from this morning. However, on my way to her, I ran into Mr. Thilo, who told me that she had died while he was there. Hence, although her wish was granted, we ourselves have suffered a very great loss because of her experience as a midwife and because of the upright character she manifested in whatever she did. As a result, she was well-liked by all members of our congregation, and it was the wish of many that it would please God to let her stay with us for a longer period of time.

Last night, a boat arrived at our community from Savannah with some of the most recent arrivals, who want to travel to their land in Halifax and requested that we administer the Holy Sacrament to them before their departure because there would be no opportunity for them to receive it up there. We were unable to deny their request in this emergency situation; and, after the proper preparations had been completed, my dear colleague administered it to them this morning at Mr. Boltzius' home, since our Jerusalem Church is currently under repair and work on it started today.

The 23rd of January. Since I had to take care of quite a few outside emergencies and deliver a funeral sermon this afternoon, our dear Mr. Rabenhorst substituted for me in conducting school and our weekly sermon on the plantations. The water of the Savannah River has risen high, but it has not yet affected the mills. Since the new sawmill is now also in almost constant use, we could again take a number of boards to Savannah to sell there. Thus our gracious God has given us new proof of His Fatherly concern for us.

At the funeral of Mrs. Bacher, who died yesterday, I had to deliver the funeral service, as planned. Therefore, a good number of our audience gathered in the new building we constructed for spinning silk. They heard through Hebrews 4:9 the words: "There remaineth therefore a rest to the people of God."

During her lifetime, the late Mrs. Bacher showed virtues which, according to the Holy Scripture, are found in those who belong to that kind of people. I then mentioned some examples for their edification and the benefits they had derived from her having let herself become, at an early time, part of God's people, in God's order. All those present were greatly moved, and this demonstrates that her death must have touched many of them. May the Lord in His grace replace the loss we have suffered through this death, and this is also what we asked Him for in our prayers.

This evening our dear colleague, Pastor Boltzius, let us know that he and Captain Krauss had returned in reasonably good health and in good spirits. We are very happy at that and humbly praise our Lord for having graciously taken care of them. Because it is already very late today, we hope to see and talk to him tomorrow.

The 24th of January. It would have pleased me greatly if one of my dearest colleagues had wanted to continue this diary in the same way I started it during my journey, especially since I recognize that the longer I write it, the less adept I become and that, against my expectations and intent, I have given many misinformed as well as unfair people an opportunity to treat its simple, but true, news as spiders treat flowers. Blind people do not see God's great and small deeds in His congregation, and they stumble on things that edify others. Since both my dearest colleagues are in favor of my continuing to prepare these records (at least for some time), I will once again shoulder this work in God's name; and I pray and hope that He will let me enjoy the help and guidance of His Holy Spirit in this undertaking.

I had started on the attached half-sheets of paper to write down some comments on matters that happened to me during my successful trip. However, because I have to continue this diary on my brethrens' recommendation and with their approval, I will include in this diary whatever remains to be reported, instead of putting it down on a separate sheet of paper, hoping that Senior Urlsperger, our dearest Father, who edits the Ebenezer Reports[29] will—if necessary—publish only what he considers useful news and what serves our edification.

All of Carolina has wide and dry roads, bridges, and ferries across some rivers so that one can travel rather comfortably by day and night. The most recent, extremely severe storm washed away a bridge and damaged others. The distance between Purysburg to Charleston is 100 English miles, and from Charleston to Beaufort (the only town on the Isle of Port Royal) 74 miles. It is easy to walk three miles an hour and ride on horseback five miles an hour. The worst stretch is the 20 miles from Purysburg, through a low, very swampy pine forest, to the Cusaw-Hatchee River, where one can never hope to find a better way because this entire area does not lend itself to farming and is far away from a river. The people of Carolina only take care of those ways that lead through their plantations; and everyone, be it master or servant, white or black, must work six days a year on them without payment. Some roads, all of them 12 feet wide, run through very low wetlands, which are laid out but are hardly ever passable during the rainy season.

I was told that a Swede, whom I consider my relative by religion,[30] was living in a large house along the way. I visited him and received a warm welcome, and I benefited a great deal from our conversation. He used to live on a Dutch plantation in the West Indies and had come to Carolina some 22 years ago with much money. However, he lost most of his fortune in unsuccessful projects. He built a rice stamp in order to brew beer from rice, then he turned to growing grapes and silkworms, and he planted many trees of all kinds. He started a large plantation all at once in a fertile, yet unsuitable location, with many Negroes, and he failed miserably. Although he is Lutheran, he seems to have a mind of his own in religious matters, yet Dr. Tillotson is his family preacher.

A planter gave me some sesame seeds from which he squeezes, with a poorly working machine, some sweet oil which is believed to be similar to olive oil. One bushel, or 32 English quarts, of seeds yields 10-12 quarts of oil, which keeps better in this climate than olive oil. Old seeds yield the best-tasting oil. It grows well and in great abundance on good corn land. Currently there is not much interest in Carolina in oil or indigo because rice is fetching a very good price. Hardly anybody devotes himself to sericulture or viticulture except for the people of Purysburg, because the former brings in too little and the latter does not do too well. Because of the large numbers of ricebirds and

other birds,[31] it is almost impossible to grow grapes. Some plan-
ters did not plant their wheat until now, and some will plant it
even in February. They plant it in very fertile and well fertilized
soil, and I was assured that it would mature already by the end of
May. There are a lot of sheep in Carolina, which can be raised
very easily and safely on Port Royal Island because there is no
evidence there and or other neighboring islands of wolves,
bears, or tigers (which, here, are only some type of lynx).[32]

In a tavern I found a Carolina newspaper, which reported,
among other things, that 293 Negroes or Moorish slaves from
Africa and the West Indies, 124 big barrels of rum or sugar-cane
brandy, 13 large casks of wine, 518 barrels of flour and 4,762
bushels of salt had been brought to Carolina since last September. A large number of ships are anchored off the coast of
Charleston, and some small craft are off the coast of Beaufort on
Port Royal. The new Negroes, who cost 25-30 pounds Sterling in
past years, now cost 37-40 pounds each, regardless of whether it
is a man or woman. Also, many small children are brought over
from Africa, and they can be bought for 12-14 pounds. I wish I
had the money for these children, whom I would distribute
among worn-out pious Salzburgers, provided they raise them as
their own children and as Christians and keep them in the future as servant boys and girls under stable and bearable conditions. This would be a truly lasting benefit not only for the masters and their offspring, but also for those heathen children.
May God guide the hearts of our European benefactors to such
a laudable undertaking! I think 100 florins would be sufficient
for one child. Even the Englishmen who believe it is impossible,
too dangerous and harmful for the country to convert adult
Negroes (although this contradicts common sense an the Scriptures), think that this would be a way of bringing Christianity to
the Negroes.

In the winter, it is dangerous to buy new Negroes. They are
not used to the cold weather or to our clothes and blankets and
they easily catch cold; and this leads to fever, stitches in the side,
and dysentery, etc.; and, because it is hard to make them take
medicine, they die. Some are homesick and run into the woods
when they are told to work and obey some rules, and they get
sick from one night out in the cold. Negroes from Guinea, Gam-

bia, and Angola are considered to be the best and most easily
managed ones, whereas the Ibo Negroes are the most stubborn
ones. However, once the latter have been subdued and, in a
sense, broken, they make good artisans and can be used for any
job. They have a proud, arrogant, and militant disposition; and
they like to drown or hang themselves out of despair and in the
ridiculous belief that such a violent way of dying would enable
them to return to their native land where they lead a lazy life,
just like highwaymen.

Unfortunately, among the many uses of poor Negroes, none
are more important than work and reproduction. Therefore, a
Negro man is permitted to have as many women and a Negro
woman as many men as they like, which is a loathsome horror;
and one hardly ever reads of honorable heathens doing this. For
the following reasons, we have been advised against old Negroes
who were born in this country or are used to our customs: 1. The
neighbors buy the best among them for themselves. Whenever
they hear that good Negroes are for sale in the neighborhood,
they are the first to buy them, even though they already may
have 100 or 200 and more of them. 2. They do not like to be
separated from their friends and relatives and frequently run
off from Georgia to Carolina. 3. They are full of malice and usually know how to handle poison, which they use to take revenge
on white people and Negroes. For this malice, they are burnt
alive in Carolina.[33]

A merchant at Beaufort showed us how to build solid and low-
priced housing. There they have many oyster shells from the
ocean, which they process into lime; they break the oyster shells
into small pieces and mix them with the lime into mortar. With
the help of a wide club, this mixture is stamped into a long box,
about one foot wide, which is easy to disassemble; and this is a
quick way of building a four-sided wall that is firmer than
stones.[34]

A Negro barber shaved me and my companions. He said that
he was a Christian, but he did not behave like a Christian when
he charged us both a lot of money for such a small effort. In
Charleston, a baptized Negro learned to play the violin very
well, and he earned so much money playing at social gatherings

that he was able to buy his freedom for 100 pounds Sterling. He leads a wild life.

An English acquaintance of mine who trades among the Indians told me that an Indian, who had murdered a white man, was to die. But since he did not want to die, another Indian died for him in a heathen act of daring. After giving a speech, he thrust a knife into his chest, while cutting his throat. This shows what ambition is and what the heathen rule is all about: *Viva et fama pari passu ambulant!*[35]

The Indian trader had kindly offered to show Captain Krauss all Indian towns and installations far and wide if he would come to Augusta where he will be for a while and from where he will visit the Indian nations to trade with them. The Indians are said to be very hospitable towards strangers.

To be sure, we saw many mulattoes and mustees (these are children of a Negro mother and a white or Indian father, and their skin and color look almost like those of Indians), but we met no Indians. It is safe to travel everywhere and it is difficult to lose one's way. A few years ago, some merchants built a costly sugar refinery, where brown West-Indian sugar is boiled and turned into white loaf sugar. It is, however, not nearly as good as the sugar from Europe and therefore they will not be able to survive for very long. We found a man in that factory who considers all religions the same. There are many like him in the old and new world. I also visited the library there, which has a good number of fine books. The bishop's church, with its two preachers, has a fine organ, graceful pulpit, and, besides many other ornaments, a noteworthy epitaphium, put up by the inhabitants of Charleston and Carolina only recently in honor of the brave first royal Governor Johnston.

Every Sunday morning between 7:00 and 8:00 o'clock a pious merchant in Charleston teaches a number of adult Negro men and Negro women how to read, and then they sing and pray. A Christian Negro teaches the Negro children. For Christian children, Charleston has some schools where they learn how to write, do arithmetic, and sew. But there is nothing like this in the rural areas. Also, some years ago, a society was founded, which now has some 90 members, who assemble every week; and each member deposits 4 pence a week.[36] The money has grown so much that they now want to lend out 140 pound Sterling at interest. This society cares for the widows and orphans of their membership. It keeps the orphans in school and either lets them study or lets them learn a craft. It also receives some legacies. The society collects from its 90 members and their seemingly small contributions some 78 pound Sterling a year, which grows into a fine sum of money in 10 years.

May God awaken the hearts of Christian patrons in our German fatherland to such a laudable society, whose members would contribute 9 or 10 kreutzers a week—how much good could then be done in the East and West Indies, especially if an annual sum could be spent on buying Negro children, as I mentioned earlier. God is able to see to it (because He can boundlessly do beyond anything we ask for or understand) that all kinds of grace abound among our dear benefactors in Europe, that they have enough of everything, and that they are rich enough to do all kinds of good works.

In this city, there is also the Society of the Freemasons. There are many merchants and shopkeepers, most of whom own large, beautiful homes and live in grand style both in terms of clothing and expensive household effects and dine lavishly with Negro servants. This is particularly noticeable on Sundays. Many come to church in their carriages; and in both winter and summer the female members of their families wear black masks on their faces in the streets. This looks beautiful to them, but quite horrible to a stranger, especially if he has never seen anything like this before. It shows what fantasy, fashion, and custom can do!

People are called to church by many bells. In Independence Church, the Holy Sacrament was offered sitting down, and two vestrymen handed out the bread in two bowls and the wine in two pitchers to the men's and women's pews, and everybody took his share. The minister delivered long religious sermons before and after the offering.

The town has a couple of companies of soldiers, who do not cause any trouble. A captain, who knew me, invited me over for lunch; and everything went in an orderly way. They beat the drum at 9 o'clock at night and in the morning at daybreak. Every day they have a meat market, and the goods are brought in from the countryside. Also, the Negro women sell all kinds of things for cooking and also sweets. On Tuesdays and Thursdays all kinds of dried and liquid goods are auctioned off to the highest bidder, and sometimes one can get a good bargain. Even Negroes are sold in this way. Hand-written and printed flyers were posted in the public squares, informing people where they could buy German servants for three or four years. A despicable woman had killed her own child soon after its birth and then wilfully died in her own blood.[37] Such suicides are buried in the Negro cemetery, but not by the hangman.

I left two packets of letters and the diary with a friend for forwarding to London, and I would have liked to arrange with the ship captains not to surrender the heavy parcels until their arrival in London. However, they do not do it this way; rather they deliver them and other mail to the first post office in the first port their ships land at, and they get some sort of reward from the postmaster. I am therefore very much concerned that, in the past, I have caused our dear Court Preacher Ziegenhagen very great expenses with our and the congregation's letters. And that almost keeps me from sending as many parcels as I did in the past. This friend in Charleston still had one of my previous parcels because he had not had an opportunity to send it. Similarly, in Port Royal, Captain Isaac[38] had received from me some weeks ago a parcel for delivery.

Rice is scarce and hence the ship captains have to wait a long time to get a shipment. These are about the most important things I noticed during my rather tiresome and costly trip and wanted to report to our friends, since I know that they would like to be informed about external things, institutions, and conditions here.[39] I have no desire to take another journey like this one, but will gladly spend the short time left to me in Ebenezer, which has become dear and valuable to me, in solitude and on my official duties, according to God's will. May our merciful God be praised with humility for His shielding me and for His comforting kindness, which envelops me at all times. May He abundantly bless the word I am preaching to the Germans and some Negroes and prepare me for doing His will and create within me that which pleases Him for Christ's sake!

The first news I heard in Purysburg about Ebenezer was

about the dangerous illness of locksmith Schrempf and the widow Bacher. On my arrival at the first plantation, I was told that our dear Mrs. Bacher had died and had been buried, and the people had just returned home from the burial. With this first news, our wondrous God also wanted to give me a good lesson that I, too, should put my house in order and prepare myself to depart. I suffered from fever attacks during the trip, and it would have been a harsh punishment for me to fall sick away from home, without doctor or care. However, God heard my sighs, and He blessed some doses of my own medicine for my early recovery. As I said when I left: "Know ye that the Lord he is God,"[40] So I say now, "Thank the Lord, my journey is over!"

The 25th of January. The widow Bacher, who passed away some days ago, not only rejoiced in going home, but has also left to our entire community a very edifying and blessed example to follow. We are happy about that and praise the Lord. She has been a true jewel in our community and has done a great deal of good with her prayers and her friendly ways of dealing with other persons of the female sex and as an experienced and prudent midwife. Now we say of her: "Their works do follow them," "Say ye to the righteous, that it shall be well with him, for they shall eat the fruit of their doings."[41] For several years, but particularly in recent times, she had thought a lot about dying; and only recently she had told Mrs. Mayer that she would die soon. She had asked me quite some time ago to sing at her funeral her favorite song: . . . *Jehovah ist mein Hirt und Hueter* . . . etc. She had shown a great desire to see me in her last days, and I am very troubled that I did not come home until the evening after her burial. How great is our heart's delight if one can think of the late inhabitants of Ebenezer with a feeling of edification! They make up a nice number in Heaven. May God take all of us there!

The truly pious wife of our schoolmaster /Georg/ Mayer has been suffering for some years from a severe physical weakness, but she is a patient and contented lamb of Jesus Christ. He has made her quite special in the furnace of misery. Now her illness has very much gotten the upper hand, and it appears that she has come very close to the end and to peace, for which she is longing so very much. She sent for me today and provided a careful and uplifting confession of her religious belief and hope. She is one of those people at Ebenezer who experience what the words of Jesus say: "What I do thou knowest not now, but thou shalt know hereafter."[42] Oh, how they praise God for giving them this peace and for letting them find the way to life through the Scriptures!

Our locksmith Ruprecht Schrempf is a very strange example of the richness of God's goodness, patience, and forbearance; and here again one can see proof of how true His words are: "Christ Jesus came into the world to save sinners, of whom I am chief." "The Son of man is come to seek and save that which was lost."[43] He had an irresponsible, angry, and pleasure-loving disposition. Because this could not bring him the blissful change in healthy days, our wondrous God has repeatedly, and now again, visited dangerous illnesses on him, and, by so doing, has prepared the way (in a sense) for the Holy Ghost's effects of grace through the word. He has experienced much the repulsiveness and bitterness of sins, including his bosom sins; and he is divinely distressed and now believes in Jesus Christ with all his heart and has been assured that his sins will be mercifully forgiven. The world disgusts him, and he feels like leaving it and being with Christ. He talks extremely sincerely and with experience of the treasure of grace and its spiritual advantages in his humble house, which he does not wish to trade for the most beautiful palace and for all the treasures in the world.

I was called to him close to nightfall because he was dying. We prayed and sang a short song; and I blessed him. He did not show any sign of life, and all his limbs turned cold and stiff. Therefore all those present thought that he had died. But I had hardly left when he regained consciousness, sent again for me, and talked again quite cheerfully. He said he had heard our prayers and songs and that I had blessed him. This was a miracle that occurred right in front of our eyes. We talked about the story of Lazarus's illness, his falling asleep, and his awakening; and he talked cheerfully and with much joy. I again prayed with him and commended him to his Savior's wounds. He liked the pithy and powerful saying: "It is a faithful saying . . . to save sinners, among whom I am chief." This he enjoyed day and night, and it delighted him. He called out several times: "See, our saving God makes saved children out of the horde of the most miserable sinners."[44] He said among other things that he now knows God's children at Ebenezer whom he had not known before, and he thought it was a great blessing that two dear souls, Zimmerebner and Carl Flerl's wife, became his godparents and that they pray for him and praise the Lord. He is genuinely happy and praises God that God's children are sitting with him and praying with him and that they encourage him with God's word and their experience.

When I told him how greatly impressed I was when the pious Rottenberger kneeled and tearfully prayed at the bedside of his wife while she suffered from severe convulsions, and that I believed that God had given her back to him in response to his prayer, he asked me whether I thought that his pious wife had helped his conversion by praying for him; he was sure of it. I confirmed it, saying I knew that she had asked God with tears in her eyes for his salvation. He sometimes thinks of the late Mr. Gronau and is looking forward to seeing him and his late mother soon in Heaven. He also said that if he could, he would write to his brothers and tell them that, if they wanted to get to Heaven, they would have to become like their mother.[45] Although she was considered one of the best Christians because of her quiet life in her village, she probably knew here that piety and righteousness alone are not enough to go to Heaven. He could not write about himself because they would interpret this as arrogance on his part.

The 26th of January. A pious old man from the Savannah Town area has written me a very friendly and Christian letter through his son, who brought grain here while I was away on my trip. In that letter he recognizes the divine grace God has shown toward our community by way of its servants, adding: "Even if those who have been blessed by that good deed for a long time do not see and feel it, it nevertheless is and remains true that whatever the world does not recognize, God recognizes. May our Supreme Lord reward you for whatever good deeds you have done to me and others."

I had given a man, at his request, some edifying sermons for his own use and that of others in the wilderness there, for which he thanked me cordially. That same old friend is now asking me for similar edifying papers for himself and others, to whom he lends and reads them. He says as follows:

> There are some people here who would like to have some good scripts, and I would very much like to help them; however, I have already given away most of the ones I received. I myself am short of good and not-too-short formal sermons. The two I am returning (they were two books by Bogatzky) are convincingly written; yet we need here books about the words (as noted in the preface): Awake thou who sleepeth,' etc.,[46] because I and others are still sleeping deeply in sin, and even though some few appear to be waking up, they must still be called.

Today I again sent him some very inspiring books, sermons, and treatises, which may our merciful God bless in that very dark area!

A Christian woman in Purysburg complained to me that she had not received her small, particularly her printed, sermons because of her illness and asked me for others, which I sent her today. She also reads from them to others. For 19 years, Ebenezer has distributed among people nearby and far away a good many selected German texts, which have been sent to us from time to time. May they, in some instances, serve as a good seed for eternity, as Jesus Christ promised in Isaiah 55:10,11. Therefore Ebenezer might as well be named Bethlehem: not only does it enjoy abundant bread of life, but it can also share it abundantly with others. Praised be our Lord!

In the above-mentioned letter, I found the following news item in the area of nature:

> This summer we had a lot of wind, which flattened much of our corn, particularly a terrible storm on 15 September. We ourselves were not affected, except for corn that had been planted late. However, down in the country, the storm was horrible and caused much damage to our homes and buildings. The trees were either severely damaged or they were knocked down altogether. In Charleston the damage is almost indescribable. The wind whipped the sea so high that big ships and

other vessels were thrown far inland onto the land. Almost all
goods stored in vaults spoiled. Also many people lost their
lives.

In early October we had high water, but it was about three
feet less than a year ago, so that it did not cause any damage
here, except that it flooded the lower-lying corn fields. The
people living at Carolina's Santee River had more water than
last year and they suffered much damage from it. Despite the
dry and hot summer, the corn here (praised be our Lord) has
turned out well so that we have a good harvest. However, because there is a great shortage further down south, a bushel
fetches somewhat more than 2 shillings Sterling, and wheat
over 4 shillings; and both have to be shipped there. Otherwise,
almost all areas are complaining about the bad harvest. Sweet
potatoes did very well; most of them are fed to the pigs. This
fertile growth weather has continued halfway through
November, without frost, and many of the rice plants that had
been burnt by the sun's heat sprouted again and ripened.

Most sweet potatoes were picked in early November—at a
loss, because they did not grow as a result of the dry and hot
summer. However, those who let them grow for most of the
extremely fertile month of November had a very good harvest.
Usually, one acre of land yields 100 bushels of potatoes; but I
have harvested more. As for corn, I have harvested more than
1,000 bushels on 17 acres during this bad year. Strong winds
during the summer did more damage to the good land than
the drought did because they flattened much of the corn which
had not yet ripened. At present everybody is busy plowing and
sowing wheat. Mine is already a finger high this November.
With these warm temperatures, the seeds germinate within a
few days. Some people do not start sowing until February and
March; and, in most instances, that wheat grows as well as the
earlier sowing. But it must be sowed more densely since it does
not yield as much as the other seeding.

The 27th of January. This morning I received the news that
our locksmith Schrempf passed away at 4 o'clock in the morning, gently and blessedly, leaving behind in this pilgrimage a
pious widow with three young children. However, she will be
well taken care of, because she is God-fearing and leads the children to Him by her words and example. They have a nice home
and many beautiful mulberry trees; and they own some worldly

goods in the form of money and other belongings which the deceased has earned, with God's blessing, by being an industrious and skilful worker. He was a very good locksmith and able to do almost anything that was put before him, and hence we have lost a very able and useful artisan as well as a righteous Christian; and we will no doubt meet him again in Heaven.

Yesterday morning he told me that he had enjoyed all night the beautiful verse: "This is a faithful saying and a dear etc. . . . to save sinners, . . . " etc.[47], and it made him feel good. I gave him another verse for the night which delighted his soul. Then we prayed, and while we were praying the verse became sweet and dear to me: "Come unto me, all ye that labor and are heavy laden, . . . " etc.,[48] which he embraced eagerly and which I again sought to commend to him warmly in the evening. And with Christ's gentle voice calling him, he fell asleep and passed away. He felt like a troubled and burdened man and again confessed his sins; in doing so he wept heartily and very loud, praising God for his illness, which God had blessed for the sake of his soul, and he was happy about the many good things my dear colleagues and I said about him. Should God give him the strength, he said, he would write everything down so he could remember and enjoy it. He had already started writing some things down.

The late Schrempf's stepfather,[49] whose plantation is close to the minister's land at Goshen, came early on Sunday for the church service; and he was pleased to hear that God had shown mercy on Schrempf. He himself had been fatally sick some years ago, but our merciful Lord had restored his health and the life of his soul. He acknowledges this with humble thanks and wishes everybody would realize how very wonderful it is to live here in our solitude, in complete freedom, with all kinds of suffering and trials, and yet in the green and healthy pasture of God's word. Some Salzburgers live in the same area, and they all meet every week in the evening to read and pray together, and our Lord blesses them for doing so. They derive much benefit from the clear and edifying book of sermons by my dearest and beloved father-confessor, the late Pastor Freylinghausen.[50] For the same reason I gave the man the recently received, very important Good Friday sermons of our dear Senior Urlsperger,[51]

which we use to help many souls longing for God's word and
which we have in many copies.

The 28th of January. Work on our dear Jerusalem Church is
finished, and last night we were able to conduct our prayer hour
there; and on this fourth Sunday after Epiphany we could hold
our regular church service. Praised be our Lord for this dear
blessing! Our dear colleagues, Mr. Lemke on the plantations,
and Mr. Rabenhorst and I in town, have preached the word of
our living God about the Gospel and the reading of the Epistle.
We had the opportunity to do in both churches what the late
Schrempf had expressly asked for, namely, we asked the congregation, on his behalf, to forgive him for all annoyances he
had caused before his conversion and we wholeheartedly
warned all and everybody about any persistent unwillingness to
repent and about delaying their conversion until they are on
their sickbed or deathbed.

In our sermons in the morning and in the afternoon we sometimes included impromptu some necessary and important
words through which this notable example of a late, yet true
penitent and believer might serve the congregation members as
a warning and as encouragement, and as comfort to his mourning family and other pious burdened people. He was buried after the afternoon service, attended by many people, with blessings and much emotion in our audience from town and the
plantations. Schrempf's father-in-law, the old Kieffer, also attended the church service and the funeral with great benefit, as
his words showed. His wife preceded her son-in-law in death at
Purysburg on their plantation, following a very painful illness
that lasted 10 weeks and three days. He told me some inspiring
things, which convinced him that she died believing in the dear
rewards of Jesus Christ. He wants to move here as soon as possible to live with his children and spend the few remaining days of
his life quietly and with God's word, in preparation for eternity.
This is also my heartfelt wish for him; and, as a sign of my love, I
gave him dear Senior Urlsperger's Good Friday and Easter sermons, which he liked very much.[52]

The 30th of January. I noticed in several people who came
with the most recent transport that they would very much like to
stay on, if only they had some fertile land here and knew how to

feed themselves. It is very hard for them to move away from God's word, church, and school, of which they and their children had so much here and which they liked so much. There are some fine and adaptable people who are eager to be saved. I have consoled them with the hope that, if God and our Fathers in Europe wish it, they may still get a Christian and experienced man as their pastor after the Halifax congregation has grown. As of now, only a few families have settled there.

A sensible God-fearing servant girl working for a pious family has received a proposal of marriage. She has asked me to ask her pious mistress whether she would continue to keep her in her service: she would be prepared to live and die with her and not ask for anything more than what she needs for food. She said she had enough clothes for many years to come. Never before in her work as a servant had she felt so much inspiration and blessings as in this house. She said she does not want to take any other service, that she would be forced to accept the marriage proposal unless they would keep her in her present employment.

We are having very warm weather. If the warm temperatures continue, the plum and peach trees will soon show their blossoms. So far the winter has been quite bearable and the weather has not been too cold, too wet, or too dry. The wheat is coming along very nicely everywhere.

The 31st of January. Our almighty and merciful God be praised with our hearts and humility for permitting us to come to the end of this month! He has shown us again this month much spiritual and physical kindness; and He has not left unblessed our work for our healthy, sick, and dying parishioners. Also He has commenced his acts of grace in several souls among our most recent transport, and most of them show much love for His word, church, and school; and they are therefore very sorry that, in their new, very fertile and well-situated land, they have to do without these dear benefactions, which the Ebenezers receive in such abundance. Had the entire transport stayed together and settled at Briar Creek or Halifax, there might have been a greater likelihood that one of us might have lived among them and taught them. However, since they are so scattered— despite our warnings—with some living in Savannah and some at Ebenezer, etc., and some of them moving to Halifax, it is, of

course, inappropriate for a minister to spend all his time among
so few people, since we have enough work here and also have to
look after the Germans at Goshen and Savannah. We are sorry
and sad that the people of the last transport are having such a
hard time. May God protect them in these trials from impa-
tience and unhappiness, and thus make them part of His community so that they may experience His special caring and not
want for anything (Isaiah 43, 1-3).

FEBRUARY

The 3rd of February. With the end of this week we have, with
God's grace, also finished reading and repeating or holding
highly important discussions in our evening prayers concerning
the words that were sent to us from Augsburg: "They will not
change and do not stand in fear of God."[1] Through them, our
gracious God has given many blessings to our dear listeners, and
we have praised Him for it.

The 5th of February. Today our gracious and righteous God
has given us both joy and sadness. Maurer's wife, a very upright
follower of Jesus Christ, suffered sudden abdominal pain which
caused her soul much difficulty. She had previously been sure of
her salvation through Christ's atonement; but last Friday her
soul was in such darkness that she believed there would be no
mercy left for her. Hence she drew nearer to Jesus through tears
and prayers, merely asking for mercy, of which she was then assured so strongly that it came as a great surprise to her. She
thought she was in heaven, seeing many of the people she had
known here in the Lord: she once again is full of hope that God
will give her all her family and lead them to His glory in such a
way that no claw, as she herself called it, would be left out.

As edifying as this has been for all of us, just as distressing was
the news of Joseph Schubdrein's sister and her unfortunate
death, after she and two other people had a boat accident yesterday after church and she drowned, while one of the men and
her sister barely escaped. Right after the afternoon service she
had come to our dear Mr. Boltzius, putting her name and that of
her husband down for communion; and to him she seemed
rather cheerful and in a great hurry to catch a ride to her planta-

tion. She is leaving a small child behind. Thus we are like her who was in a rush to leave; may the good Lord teach us to be careful.

The 6th of February. The pious widow Schweighofer asked Mr. Boltzius, much to his pleasure, to come and see her in her house because she wanted to talk to him confidentially about her request, rather than at his house where he hardly ever can be by himself.

The 8th of February. More than three years ago, our dear God sent us a very fine young man. His name is Caspar Wertsch. He is from the Anspach region and has worked as a man servant for a very pious family from Salzburg, who treated him very well. Because of his skills and true devotion to God he was selected to be schoolmaster on the plantations, where he has discharged his duties to the great satisfaction of the parents and to the heartfelt love of the children. Now that his years as a servant are coming to an end, we must think of his situation in a different way, because he is unable to live on 6 pounds Sterling, two of which he pays to his master. Although our dear Boltzius is adding another pound Sterling, this is not enough in this country. Our Lord, who has given us the children and them a schoolmaster who loves them, knows where and how to find a solution so that this worker will win his wages.

There is some spiritual blessing among the artisan journeymen who came to us three years ago. They are becoming useful although they were wild and unruly when they first arrived here. May God also change newcomers, who will consider our solitude here very strange.

The 9th of February. We would very much like to serve the Germans in and near Savannah, if only they would take the small trouble of picking us up. As long as the Lord Trustees were the rulers, we ministers were able to ensure, through a request to General Orglethorpe and the Council in Savannah, that they would cover the expenses for all our trips there and back again when we had to go to them with our office every eight or nine weeks. This benefit has now come to an end since these people would rather forego the ministry than expend some efforts. But today people want to have the Gospel for nothing and without exerting themselves, or else not at all. Often enough they use

our mill for their crops, but in most of them the hunger for
God's word is not yet great. Alas, may God help us with this
misery!

The 10th of February. In spite of all search efforts in the river,
it has been impossible to find the Schubdrein brothers' eldest
sister; and that makes the pain the relatives, especially the old,
almost inconsolable mother, feel about this saddening death
even worse. The children have learned, and we adults want to
learn with them: "Let God's spirit lead you to timely repentance
and prepare you well for death."[2] The Christian burial of the
drowned woman would have been a good opportunity to
awaken some people who are used to living in security[3] if only
we had found her. The mention of it on Wednesday during the
weekly sermon on the Blue Bluff stirred up a lot of emotion
among them, which our faithful God may have used in order to
effect a blessed change in one or the other.

The 13th of February. After repeating his Sunday sermon in
school, Mr. Boltzius has started to give Christians advice on all
kinds of situations they are encountering. The printed advice
was sent us by Master Sommer in Schortwitz; and, like his
printed little rhymes, he caused much edification and joy among
children.

The 15th of February. Today it said: "For the Lord taketh pleasure in his people: he will beautify the meek with salvation."[4]
However, people who do not find here what they are looking for
and who do not wish to accept what they may have for free, leave
us and scream wildly. That, however, will not harm us if, with
God's grace, we keep leading as upright a life as we are doing
today. We are happy together that we have a Father to call on,
who sees the hidden things, and that we are able to follow Him
safely through many trials and difficulties on the path, our Lord
is showing us the way. Now then, praise Him, do not complain so
much—praise Him, praise Him daily!

The 16th of February. We have received news from
Charleston, via Beaufort, that a ship with 400 Germans aboard
arrived there and that they felt our dear God's hand protecting
them during their voyage. The ship was about to sink when they
set sail from a certain, faraway place, but our wondrous God had
known how to save them in their distress and how to get them

out of this dangerous situation. Our Lord is our friend, and His goodness lasts in all eternity.

During our evening prayer hour, a very edifying letter from our very dear Court Preacher Albinus to our congregation caused a great deal of emotion in some souls. In that letter he wrote about the great ingratitude displayed by some people of the latest transport with regard to the good deeds they have received and continue to receive. Oh, may the Lord cleanse all hearts of all secret malice and insincerity, and may He not make us suffer because of these ungrateful people.

Today on the plantations I had to marry some Englishmen from Abercorn, who submitted a paper showing that their bans had been read three times by the English preacher. At the same time I received a package of letters from our dearest Court Chaplain Albinus and two letters from our dear Father, Senior Urlsperger, which will provide us with much material for praising God, for interceding with Him, and for giving comfort. Our highly respected Fathers also have to deal with joy and sorrow and with good and bad rumors, which in part are similar to those we ourselves are confronted with. However, my heart hurts deeply that they suffer from the Ebenezer congregation not only much work and expenses, but also dismay, ingratitude, and badmouthing. We just heard of some new saddening examples.

Many people who have come here from Germany were told many times and very clearly in Augsburg and London (and some have acknowledged it), and they could also read about it in the diaries, that they must not expect an easy life in Ebenezer, but that: "In the sweat of thy face shalt thou eat bread." Also: "In sorrow shalt thou eat of it all the days of thy life" (off your land which is damned because of sin)."[5] From the very start the members of our congregation did not leave their homeland for material things, a good life, and earthly advantages, but they came here to win freedom of conscience, a church and a school, and the freedom to adhere to, and enjoy, their Evangelical religion. As for their worldly welfare, they were willing to content themselves with some hot soup once a day and with wearing the simplest clothing.

He gave them the gospel and its seals, the Holy Sacraments,

during their journey by land and by sea, once they had been offered and had accepted their calling to Georgia, the asylum of
hard-pressed Protestants. Since the first transport arrived at
Ebenezer almost nineteen years ago, He has provided them
purely and abundantly through their ministers, during their life
and in death, with church and school buildings, with mills and
other good institutions from the benefactions sent from Europe
in order to feed their bodies and make their lives as pilgrims
easier, although they themselves contributed little with their
own work. They have enjoyed for so long, and continue to enjoy,
the care of a doctor and a surgeon, very costly medicines, Bibles,
hymnals, and many other edifying books.

And not only the Salzburgers have shared in these benefits,
but also others who arrived here from various places in Germany. Now, since neither our all-knowing and most gracious
God nor His dear tools, our dear Fathers and benefactors, intended for our inhabitants to enjoy physical benefits and good
days, and since He has given us, in His wise and gracious providence, an abundance of spiritual food, although little nourishment for our bodies (if only we would be satisfied with what is
absolutely necessary!), it is not only a serious, multiple sin, but it
is also unfair to whine about the physical trials at Ebenezer and
to grumble and complain in words and in letters.

He who walks in fear of God, who strives primarily for the
Kingdom of Heaven and His righteousness, who works hard,
asks his family for advice and accepts it will find here, through
God's grace, all he needs; and he humbly thanks God for the
good opportunity to take care of his soul and he gradually learns
to accept all tribulations that are very necessary in Christianity.
Quite a few people who come here have committed their full
share of sins. They have come here for worldly reasons, continue
here with their non-repentance and old habits, and do not wish
to serve and learn first. They marry soon and start their households and plantations either with empty hands and debts or with
obstinacy and as they see fit. They have never learned how to
plow the land and what it means to live in the country. Hence,
this lifestyle is very difficult for them; and, if the ministers here
are unable to help them with money and other things as they

want them to do, they get upset, grumpy, use bad language, and blame other people here and in Europe for their moving here.

These rude people believe that nobody is better suited than the ministers, who are expected to give all the time and, in a sense, serve at the table, although they neither know how, nor are able to do so. Certain benefits are expressly meant for the Salzburgers, and this is why the other people who cannot participate in them, consider us unkind and biased, although they know, and there are enough witnesses who can attest to it, we have tried to further the spiritual and physical welfare of all and each parishioner by word and deed, not merely to the extent that we were capable of doing so, but beyond. If they nevertheless condemn us here and far away, it hurts, but we take solace in the example of Christ and all His servants, those of the past and the present, and particularly in the main promise in Matthew 5:11-12: "Blessed are ye, when men shall revile you for my sake, . . . " etc.

The 19th of February. An unmarried woman came to our community not without God's extraordinary providence and had to overcome many difficulties. Since then she has felt the urge to return to her family in her homeland. However, this is why she changed her mind. One night, she thought a lot about the verse: "Listen, daughter, see to it, . . . " etc.[6] In the morning, when she opened the Bible, the first words before her eyes were these same words, and on the very same day, this very same verse was read to the congregation and to her. Since all of this seemed strange to her, she talked about it to a Christian woman, who admonished her not to ignore this request but to stay with God, who had a reason for bringing her to Ebenezer and to trust His Fatherly care that would not leave her wanting. She also offered her a home if she did not know where to go. Thou art indeed working in secret ways, Thou God of Israel, Thou Savior! Our Lord continues to live among us and it pleases Him to do good things to the people of Jerusalem and Zion.

On 20 February I sent a small package of letters and the diary, including my special diary;[7] and on 21 February I dispatched again some letters in response to the pleasant note I received from Senior Urlsperger and Court Chaplain Albinus on the

15th, which also included a piece from the ordinary diary and of my special diary. My God protect everything and may He ensure that some good comes of it, to His glory, to our fellowmen's edification, and for the well-being of our congregation!

In late February the Savannah River rose much higher than it usually does. As a result our relatively high bridge is now almost impassable. A German from Savannah Town, who had brought corn here for sale, complained to me about his loss of fifteen big pigs during the flooding last fall and, recently, of a Negro in another incident. His land is in the low-lying area and is usually flooded by high water. Since this sometimes happens all of a sudden up there, every thing is destroyed if it cannot be moved quickly. He would like to sell everything, he said, and move down to our area and to his co-religionists,[8] but he cannot get his English wife to do so. He knows the danger his soul is in, and he is very worried about it. So many people are suffocating internally and externally as a result of the deceit of sin and of the world that later on it is almost impossible for them to get out of it. Oh, how fortunate are our inhabitants, despite their poverty!

The late Mr. Kraft spent much effort in getting well established at Ebenezer. Hence he bought some Negroes in order to build a plantation, he increased the many goods he brought with him by trading them for many he purchased here, and he made plans to build a spacious house and store. However, since our wondrous God called him away to an early death seven months ago, that is, during his first, still unfinished efforts, his dear widow has suffered much grief, upsets, and trouble, and more harm than benefits. But she has not given up the one necessary thing; and she included all her misery in her prayers and entrusted them to Jesus, our Savior, who, in His loving kindness, omnipotence, and wisdom, made everything well and made her into a true friend and lover of Jesus Christ and thus a blessed example to the entire community. She soon freed herself from the difficult Negro household by selling her black maid, and our dear Lord took away her baptized Negro child. But she could not do without one Negro for her business and the construction of her house and had to keep the Negro servant girl for housekeeping, although the latter had been giving her a hard time.

In this country a widow is among those who suffer and are

distressed, who need help from our Lord and good advice from Christian people. She is thoroughly tired of trading and its prolixity, and our dear God has heard her sighs and freed her unexpectedly from trading and other difficult matters. Because, in His wisdom and goodness, He has seen to it that, in accordance with God's will, our dear colleague and brother, Mr. Rabenhorst, got engaged to this very pious and sensible widow in a Christian way and had his marriage to her sanctified and blessed by God's word and prayer.

The attached paper describes how the reading of the bans was handled. It also states: "I have to announce something to your Christian love, which undoubtedly will lead to joy and praise of God in the hearts of all our righteous listeners. That is the engagement, ordained by our Lord, of our dearest colleague, the esteemed Mr. Rabenhorst, to our and our congregation's upright friend, Mrs. Kraft, whose engagement in the Lord, God willing, will take place in the Christian and, for us, customary way. Her planned sacred marriage will be blessed with God's word and with prayer because the engaged couple is asking for the Christian congregation's heartfelt prayer since they consider such devout intercession and good wishes to be the most important proof of the love and kind feelings of our Christian congregation toward them, and they will use them to sincerely return their love and intercession.

We are now praying to our Lord that He shower the dear bridegroom and his beloved bride with a large measure of His spirit, abundantly fulfill all the dear promises He has given to the Christian married couple, and to let them feel clearly His gracious delight in starting and continuing their new sacred matrimony, so that they can say to His glory: "Our Lord considers everything well and makes everything, everything all right, praised be our Lord."[9] May He do so for Christ's sake, He who is the bridegroom of our soul. Amen.

I also have to report that there are some other Christian persons who are planning to enter holy matrimony and marry next Tuesday, God willing. They are Christian Buerck and Ursula, the eldest daughter of the widow Kalcher. I have no doubt that Mrs. Kalcher and her late husband have many upright friends in this community who will help them pray for their and their children's well-being. I will also ask them to include this planned marriage in their heartfelt prayers so that it may redound to God's glory, their fellowmen's edification, the mother's joy and relief in her sad widowhood, and to the spiritual and physical well-being and salvation of this young betrothed couple. May our faithful God grant this for the sake of Christ, who is the bridegroom of our souls!

The marriage text was from Isaiah 61:10: "I will greatly rejoice in the Lord, . . . " etc.; and I spoke with God's marked assistance about the state of joy, happiness, and glory in God's children while we sang from the new Wernigerode hymnal the beautiful song: *Kind des Hoechsten lebe, lebe,* etc. Before the ceremony we assembled in the house where the marriage was to be performed and we read the 84th Psalm; and the bridegroom prayed with his friends and guests from the bottom of his heart and with great emotion. The wedding meal was eaten during friendly and useful conversations and it was concluded with singing and praying (as we usually do).

My house is crowded, Mr. Lemke's house is very little, and our means for taking care of Mr. Rabenhorst's needs are so small that this might have caused us and him some worries because we and the congregation have no money to build him a house and take care of him. Our dear Senior Urlsperger wrote in his most recent letter of 14 September of last year the following words: "Since Mr. Rabenhorst is still receiving such a small salary, Mr. Kraft, for example, could give him his meals in light of the words: 'Ye gave me meat.'"[10] There is no doubt that our Father, who so lovingly takes care of us, would be pleased to hear how wonderfully our dear Lord has taken care not only of the upright, young and cheerful Mrs. Kraft but also of our dearest colleague, who now has food and a house and, most importantly, a devoted wife.

When he accepted the call to Ebenezer, he left his father, mother, inheritance, and all kinds of physical benefits and arrived here empty-handed, trusting in his God and master. Who could have thought that Jesus would fulfill his promise in Mark 10:30 so soon and noticeably on this his servant: "He shall receive an hundredfold (or at least manifold) now in this time, houses, brethren, etc." It was hard for Mrs. Kraft to marry before a whole year was over, because she did not want to offend anybody. However, after her friends also assured her of God's merciful and benevolent will in the matter of her marriage, she did not let herself be influenced by what the world or other unnamed friends might say if she did not mourn an entire year over her very dear husband's death but remarried.

At the end of this month I have to reveal again my concern and worries about the outward lifestyles of many of our inhabitants. Who knows what it may lead to through God's providence? In my humble view this country with its complete freedom of conscience and its outward freedom is one of the blessed countries where many people, who would toil and moil elsewhere, could easily feed themselves, if only they would fear God and adapt to the characteristics of the country. For instance, how much employment could a tanner of red or white leather provide in light of the readily available hides, barks, limestone, boards, etc. to help feed himself and others? How much money could a skilled brickmaker earn for himself and with others if only he pursued his trade properly, without getting involved in other things? In our colony, 1,000 bricks, each eight inches long and four inches wide, cost from 18 to 20 shillings at the kiln; we have an abundance of timber, clay, and water; and they cost nothing.

The home planned by our late Mr. Kraft would be almost finished, had it not been for the lack of bricks. Now we have to send two large boats with ten men to Savannah in order to get bricks. That means not only that so much cash must be sent to Savannah for transportation, but also that our masons will lose out on these earnings. This is because the mason who sells the bricks sells 1,000 for 20 shillings Sterling on the spot, provided he is hired to lay them. Our community has much more and better clay and the opportunity to make bricks. We have some brickmakers here, but we cannot do anything with them, as we know from experience, much to our detriment.

The same is true for the wheelmaker or cartmaker, cooper, and carpenters: they are busy farming and raising cattle and they forget themselves and their fellowmen. Also, not a single man wants to take up making barrel-staves and shingles, although we obviously need them very badly. I do not want to talk

about other means and possibilities for improving our physical
well-being, since I have left no stone unturned to further the
common good by making suggestions and providing true encouragement; and this is probably why I am judged and crit-
icized unfairly.

The first Salzburgers admittedly are exhausted; and they live
on farming and cattle-raising. Still, others are young and
healthy and could pursue other necessary and useful activities.
It is impossible to improve one's living conditions by pursuing
only one way of living and one type of work. If people listened
and accepted good advice, many could feed themselves in our
community and they would not have to stray so far from God's
word, from its sacraments, and from our other advantages,
much to their own spiritual detriment and that of their families.
In my weekly sermon on the Blue Bluff that I gave today for
dear Mr. Rabenhorst, I dispensed at the end, with the help of the
First Epistle to Timothy 6:6, some good advice to those who
would like to get ahead.

The letters from dear Senior Urlsperger show new signs of his
fatherly love and concern. Once again, they have been a physical
blessing not only to us ministers but also to the poor, sick, de-
prived, widows, and orphans; and we thank our Lord for them
and pray wholeheartedly for our dear benefactors. Our Lord
knows them. May He reveal in both physical and spiritual ways
that He has not forgotten their works of love!

Today our Heavenly Father sent us a boat with about 150
bushels of corn for a low price. There is nothing to be had for
money in Charleston and probably in some other places. But the
Lord is looking out for us, and He also has seen to it that our
settlement is situated in a place that is much more convenient for
trading with Augusta and the Savannah Town than, for instance, Savannah.

The 24th of February. The old widow Schubdrein, whose
daughter recently drowned and could not be found, is now able
to live with her great loss. She claims that her daughter had already been a true lover of God's word and true piety in Germany, and that this is why she has no doubt about her salvation.
Meanwhile this old woman continues to believe that, just as she
had consoled herself during her journey across the ocean that

the ocean would release its dead, she would eventually meet her daughter again in soul and body in her resurrection.

The 25th of February. Because the river has risen unusually high and flooded the swamplands everywhere, the people with plantations farther out could not attend today's service in the Jerusalem Church. For that reason we preached the Lord's word in both churches. At Ebenezer in the morning, we talked about God's complaint about the unfortunate lack of change in so many people, "They will not change," etc.;[11] and we showed why so many, many people would not change. Our Savior has clearly explained it in His parable about the sower. May the Lord open our ears and hearts so that we can hear and take it all to heart and remember it!

The weather is very pleasant. The crops on our plantations are promising and we hope for God's blessing. The peach trees are turning green and blossoming so that one cannot look at it without joy and edification about God's loving kindness, which renews everything. "Wherever I cast my eye, I find what feeds and keeps me."[12]

The 27th of February. Yesterday, a German man from the area close to Savannah Town asked our dear Mr. Boltzius whether we would build a new, more spacious church in view of the fact that our congregation had grown so much larger, as he had learned recently. Noticing now how beautifully the present building had been repaired, he doubted that we still intended to do so. However, he and a good friend in his neighborhood, whom our dear God had blessed, would be willing to contribute 100 pounds[13], or 14 pounds Sterling, to the construction of such a new church. With three times 14 pounds, its exterior could be redone. Such an unexpected offer gives us great joy and draws our attention to God's gratifying and careful providence. True, the present church was built in such a way that we could do without, and have continued to do without, a much-needed school-house. If our faithful God provided the physical means to make it possible for us to make such a change, we would have space to teach our dear young people, a home for a teacher, and room for our library. May the Lord do whatever pleases Him!

The 28th of February. After enjoying several days of pleasant and very fruitful weather, we now have rather cold weather once

again, and it would be a miracle if this did not damage our mulberry trees and other fruits on the trees and in the fields. We
conclude this month appropriately with the words: "Our Lord
has done everything well," etc.[14] He does well with us when He
distresses us, and He does well by us when he rejoices us. We
have experienced much during this important time period; we
have been pressed but not suppressed. Today our pious Mrs.
Maurer passed into eternity. We are still alive. May the Lord see
to it that we preach the Lord's glory every hour.

MARCH

The 1st through 6th of March. We know how disillusioned
many people of the most recent Swabian transport are and how
suspicious and disgruntled they are in their speech. This has led
me, with God's guidance, to base my sermon at the anniversary
of our memorial and thanksgiving celebration on the Lord's
words in 1 Corinthians 10:10: "Neither murmur ye, as some
. . . " etc., and, at the beginning from the Lamentations of
Jeremiah 3:39, to call this sin unfair and unjustified. How can
people recognize God's kindness and benefactions and praise
Him for them if their mind is filled with dissatisfaction and im-
patience, and their mouth with murmuring? My two dear colleagues, Mr. Lemke at the Zion Church and Mr. Rabenhorst at
the Jerusalem Church, have studied texts that attest to God's
kindness and hence provide material for praising God. We have
now been at Ebenezer for more than 19 years. Oh, how much
kindness has the Lord shown me and others during that period!
    Among the books a dear benefactor from Leipzig had sent us
as a welcoming gift, I found shortly before the festival Doctor
Carl Gottlob Hofmann's *Christian Memorial* etc.[1] where I discovered two thorough and edifying sermons he had given in public
to a group of emigrants from Salzburg and again two years later
in memory of the noteworthy emigration of the Salzburgers.
They not only pleased and edified me, but they also strongly reminded me again of the great works God performed in our days
before the entire Christian church; and they strengthened and
increased my love for the Salzburgers. Oh, how much I would
like to be of spiritual and physical help to them during the last

years of my life and office, since most of them are now old and
worn out and in need of physical assistance in matters concerning their households![2]

There is much I did not understand during the past 19 years
about matters concerning food and housekeeping;[3] and hence I
was unable to advise and help them, as it was necessary in this
strange land from the very beginning. As one gains greater insight into many things, one finds that one is too late and it is impossible to achieve one's objectives of improving the physical
well-being because of the many obstacles one faces from the inside and the outside, as the very well-built and useful mills and
other congregational matters have shown. It is impossible to list
all obstacles; also it is best to be quiet and view everything as
from God's hand. Ministers, in particular, must be very careful.

Since my memorial and thanksgiving text in 1 Corinthians
10:10 has led me to the history of the old emigrants and exiles,
the children of Israel, I have started to read up quietly on this
most remarkable story for my own edification and renewed recognition of the ways God pursued with His own people and
church from the very beginning. With this, God will also give me
something I can use in my official duties.

The expenditures for our community are so manifold and
their annual amount is so large that they are beyond the imag-
ination of our friends and benefactors, as experience has demonstrated. Most members of our congregation are not wealthy
enough to make any contribution, even if they wished to, for
maintaining our public institutions and for supporting those
who spend their time and efforts to contribute something. We
therefore continue to need the help of our dear benefactors,
who never tired of sending us their benefactions. May our merciful God compensate them abundantly for their good deeds!

On 6 March I was with Captain Krauss in Savannah to attend
to some important business. We found the President and the
other council members quite willing to agree with us on what we
wanted. Our inhabitants, former servants, and members of the
most recent transport had asked me to clarify some things relat-
ing to the plantations they will operate. But I could not comply
with their request because it was Ash Wednesday, and hence a
half-holiday, and the Council did not attend to any business af-

fairs. I had two opportunities to preach to the assembled Germans the dear word about the cross, which through God's grace did not remain unblessed. I much enjoyed the upright ways of some people I visited and had contact with. Also God has given me to understand that the cross and misery we live with at Ebenezer are not the worst, but that others are worse off, although they may enjoy some advantages during their lifetime on earth. There are always the words after the fall: "In sorrow, shalt thou eat of it, etc.," "If they be fourscore years it is labor and sorrow," "Man that is born of woman is of few days, and full of trouble," "much labor was created for every man, etc."[3]

On the way back from the mill to my home, I met a pious woman, who was riding a horse on her way from the town to her distant plantation. She told me with great emotion and tears in her eyes that our dear Lord had given her new edification and comfort through the song in the new songbook: *Ich quaele mich mit keinen Grillen,* . . . etc.

Last week an unmarried Swiss man from Pennsylvania came to our settlement via Augusta, claiming that he was looking for his brother. He told me what I had also heard from others, namely, that the country is very crowded with people and that servants must hire themselves out for many years in order to find a master who will pay the ship's captain for their release. With people living so crowded in such a free country, where everything, even Roman Catholics and their churches are tolerated, injustice, theft, murders, and annoyances are rampant and there is almost no way to control them. I wanted to hire this man for one month at 20 shillings Sterling and good food, but he felt that that wage was too low. Hence he left for Savannah. He had neither an axe nor a hoe, and yet he wanted more pay than he was offered.

A Christian man from the Savannah Town area returned the books he had asked me to lend him for reading. He wrote me that he had received many books from his homeland, but without a single edifying prayer book among them. He very much enjoys the Passion sermons delivered by Senior Urlsperger and the sermons of Court Chaplain Ziegenhagen about Christ's great and grave spiritual suffering,[4] and he would also like to have the first sermon since I had been able to only send him the second. He conducts Sunday services at his home, which his housemates and neighbors attend, and I am glad to lend and give him all kinds of edifying books. This upright man heard Senior Riesch preach in Lindau, and that is why he appreciates so much more the *Trifolium Rieschianum* I have given him. Our gracious God bestows much kindness on us and our German neighbors through good books, treatises, sermons, and songs. Oh, that everybody recognize these signs of God's grace!

At our 4th[5] of March evening prayer, we sang, to the great awakening of our hearts and with joyful and well-harmonized voices, the fine song from the new Wernigerode hymnal *Auf, o Seele, preise deines Schoepfers Guete* . . . etc. I felt as if I were in heaven, and my colleagues and others shared that feeling, as I was told afterwards. We sang this beautiful birthday song because our most beloved and esteemed Father, Court Chaplain Ziegenhagen, will celebrate his birthday tomorrow and we humbly wanted to remember together, and thank Him in advance for, the great spiritual and physical blessings the Holy Trinity of our Father, Son, and the Holy Spirit has so amply rendered unto him and us, as this illuminating song says. May it convey to His dear and proven servant our sighs, wishes, prayers, and praise!

I asked the members of our congregation to bring to tomorrow's evening prayer hour the edifying song written by the court chaplain: *Mein Vater, du hast mich erwaehlt* . . . etc., because we are planning to sing it at his birthday, to our new melody, for God's praise and our edification. May God let him and us see many returns of this joyous day! We are now directing our thoughts on how to celebrate our approaching annual memorial and thanksgiving service; and we remember with humility and gratitude from the above-mentioned, very edifying song, the blessings God has bestowed upon us over the past 19 years we have lived in this country. This is how our Lord works in the hearts of His children, and it is a clear sign that He appreciates, for Christ's sake, our praise and demonstration of gratitude for our dearest Court Chaplain Ziegenhagen and us pilgrims. Because nothing pleases Him as much about us, in us, and through us, as His own work.

The 7th of March. The Spaniard who was in the Savannah jail has been released at the request of some people. That his con-

version ended during his prison stay is probably a good guess.
He came back here pretending that he was planning a trip to the
Indian country. However, since he left, we are also missing a
young boy, and we are afraid that the latter may be with nobody
else but him. We do not yet know whether he encouraged the
boy to come with him or whether the boy ran after him. He has
already caused much fear and heartache to many people here
and threatened some with bringing ruin upon them. May our
gracious Lord protect us against all malicious attempts by this
poor man. We are not used to this kind of excess here, and we
are therefore all the more upset about the bad example he may
set for others.

The 8th of March. Today we had the pleasure of the safe return of our very dear and esteemed colleague and his companion.[6] Our dear Lord has faithfully helped him in so many difficulties both in Savannah and during the journey which they
made in unhealthy weather. As a result, everything there went
well and he has been able to start the work he enjoys here.
Praised be the Lord, we live here together in unchanging love
and harmony and I share the earnest and sincere prayers of my
other very dear colleague that our true spiritual leader may continue to give us and take care, for us to enjoy, of this tireless,
experienced servant who has proven himself in many distressing situations. Amen!

The 9th and 10th of March. During these two days we had
very harsh weather. Torrential storm winds alternated with
heavy rain, hail and also some snow that may set back our trees,
especially our mulberry trees, which are just about ready to bud.
In instances like these, true Christians are waiting for Jesus
Christ and His almighty hand.

The 11th of March. On this Sunday, Invocavit, our loving God
has given us new strength so that, despite the very cold weather,
we three could preach the word of how much our Savior suffered for our sake. This gospel is particularly suitable to comfort
us and to strengthen our hearts in our pain. Hence we have
taken this opportunity to talk in our morning sermon about
Jesus, our often-tested and hence compassionate high priest.
Highly praised be He who, out of love, involved Himself in such
weaknesses because He wants to know about our hearts and take

us into His heart so that we will come closer to Him despite our inward and outward misery. He is also aware of the feelings of those who are in the desert and have no food. For this reason, people continue to believe in Him and see that it is possible to be happy in Jesus, despite poverty and a lack of food.

The 14th of March. Some letters have arrived from Savannah Town or that region in which we are asked to send some uplifting books to a man who lost all his good books in a raging fire, and we have complied with much joy. Our dear Lord has blessed us with a good number of useful books and sermons so that we put them to good use. And the Lord shows us how much blessing these writings we gave or lent have brought to some souls. Although we do not succeed with everybody, our efforts will silence those who are looking for an opportunity to envy and talk badly about us. May God bless His word with victory everywhere!

At the birthday of our dearest Father, our dear Court Chaplain Ziegenhagen, we and some pious members of our congregation had several opportunities not only to thank God from all our hearts in their homes for the manifold kindnesses He has shown this loyal servant of His, and through him, to his church both in Europe and in East and West India, but also to think of him in public during today's evening prayer by praising Him. We also sang the song he has written: *Mein Vater, du hast mich erwaehlt . . .* etc., which has given us much material and encouragement for praising the Lord. Tomorrow, God willing, Mr. Boltzius will have it sung in the Zion Church prior to the weekly sermon, and we will ask God to take care of this servant of His in his old age and, because he is waiting for Him, our Lord, to give him new strength so that he can continue to walk without weakness and fatigue in spite of his worries about his own community and other congregations in Europe and the two Indias.

The 16th of March. We hope that an upright Salzburger, with a very pious wife, will take care of our school on the plantations. Our dear God has given us the pleasant hope that this will be the case. We therefore beseech Him, whose children they are and Who desires them to be sent to Him as a work of His hands, that He select somebody whom we can joyfully entrust with such an important task. We hope there will be fewer changes of this kind

among us, as this is our very sincere wish. We would be prepared
to do everything possible to take care of the physical needs of
such a man. If we only had people who are experienced in carrying the yoke of our dear Savior and ready to share our suffering
under God's guidance, our heavenly Father would not let us
want for anything. Oh Lord, give us faith, faith!

The 17th of March. The widow Heinle, who works in the
mills, is seriously ill and is given abundant spiritual and physical
care. She seems to feel like a great sinner and looks to Christ
alone for righteousness and salvation. Our dear God has blessed
His word among us on her soul by taking her away from her own
righteousness and making her recognize that the only way for
her to achieve everything is from grace through being saved by
Jesus Christ.[7] Her eldest son, who is in Glaner's service, is one of
those servants we would like to have more of.

The 19th of March. One of us visited a man today who came to
our community with the most recent Swabian transport and has
since taken over a plantation near town. The man has proven
himself to be a good person, both during the entire journey and
also here in this country. His wife was so depressed in Heilbronn
that it would not have taken her much effort to let her husband
leave by himself, while she returned to her village. But now she
very much enjoys attending our beautiful church services and,
together with her quiet and honest husband, cultivating their
land. She brought along some European seeds that are growing
well. Perhaps our inhabitants would do far better if they concen-
trated more on garden crops, as people in Europe do, instead of
growing only Indian corn for their food.[8]

The 20th of March. Although the frost destroyed the first
tender leaves of our mulberry trees some days ago, enough were
left for the silkworms because the weather after the frost has
been extremely fertile and pleasant so far. Silkmaking has provided our inhabitants with a good harvest and income, and we
therefore praise our dear God for His gracious guiding of the
wind and weather. At present, some people are afflicted with
dangerous stitches in their sides, which was also the cause of the
death of our late Schrempf's apprentice. By the diligent use of
the means of grace, he had developed into a very orderly and
modest person and, over time, would have become a Christian

and useful member of our congregation. He did much for his
late master during his last illness and derived much benefit from
his last edifying conversations. We hope this helped him in his
last hours, although we do not know any details about it because
he died in Purysburg where he recently had gone to visit his
parents.

The 21st of March. This has been a very noteworthy and
blessed day for us because we celebrated it as a memorial and
thanksgiving for the numerous benefactions our merciful God
bestowed on the first inhabitants, and especially our dear colleague Mr. Boltzius, throughout the nineteen years. We held services in both churches and chose the texts from God's word and
with His guidance to suit the nature of our listeners and other
things, and we spoke about them in such a way that we hope
every one of our listeners who wanted to hear it got what he
needed. In the morning, we talked about murmuring, according to the words in Jeremiah's Lamentations 3:39 and in 1 Corinthians 10:10, and we demonstrated with these texts how irresponsible and inappropriate such murmuring is.

This teaching against murmuring against God and his instru-
ments was all the more necessary since people who have arrived
here subsequently have not experienced the hardships the poor
Salzburgers had to bear and have not witnessed the many tribulations here before conditions became as they are today. Therefore they violate this point more and more often, as if God's word
does not forbid them to do so. May our Lord continue to bless
His word! The Lord's will must be done, regardless of whether it
makes sense to us. Our hearts must be full of the recognition of
how wonderful God, our Father, is, how much He has done for
us, and particularly of His goodness toward His servant, the eldest among us, whom He has strengthened in his weakness for
nineteen years and wisely guided in so many ways, and boundlessly filled him with new eagerness to be loyal in His house like a
householder. Praised be the Lord, our refuge, forever and in all
eternity!

The 23rd of March. Because Mr. Boltzius wanted all our dear
listeners to know which quotations we had chosen from God's
word for our reflections on our day of thanksgiving, we thought
that it might be a good idea for me (Rabenhorst) to conduct to-

day's Friday sermon in the Zion Church and to repeat here the sermon held with God's gracious assistance in the afternoon of the 21st. Praised be the Lord, not only for leading me, an unworthy man, here and for guiding me to this hour in what He wanted me to teach, but also for helping me to preach His word to our children in school and to the adults and young people in church. The opening words were from Jeremiah 17:17 and the text from Psalm 146:5-10, which I chose because I wanted to show how important it is to reach the stage in which one can place one's hope in the Lord, our God, that is, how we can escape the curse and win eternal blessing and true happiness. May our merciful God show us that it pleases Him to live with us, in us and in this community, that it is forever true: "Here I want to live because it pleases me and we can say with all through His goodness: Ebenezer!"

The 24th of March. Our wondrous, merciful and righteous God has tried many ways to make the ill-famed N.N. think, repent, and improve his life, but to no avail. Several times his life was in obvious danger; and, after he was rescued, he continued with his ill-mannered behavior without changing. Some days ago, fire broke out in his house; and, before he knew it, his house, cows, stables and almost all his household effects went up in smoke. However, even this sharp punishment by God has not changed him for the better. His honest, pious wife said that, much to her distress, he later got drunk again. Neither punishment by the church nor punishment by the secular authorities have affected this tough man. We are therefore worried that he may set an example for others and receive even harsher punishment. Oh God, take mercy on him!

Our pious miller Zimmerebner is suffering from a strange illness, which cannot be described in detail. For us it is another example of God's Fatherly punishment of those of His children who are dearest to Him because of their strong faith, love, and patience. And often this is hard to understand. If our people were to choose an illness for him, they would select the smallest and easiest one because of the love he enjoys among God's upright children, his honesty before God, and the high respect the people in the mill have for him in view of his loyalty, caring, and helpfulness, although they are only ordinary people. But God knows better that, to Him, a big one is better than a small one. He does not let us be tried beyond our endurance.

The 25th of March. The sermon our dear Mr. Boltzius preached on the 21st about murmuring should have been heard by the people on the so-called Blue Bluff, who arrived here a year ago. Yet very few of them attended; and thus the morning sermon this Sunday, Oculi, about 2 Timothy 2:25-26 was a repetition of, and a renewed admonition about, what they were told before. Like all those who do not know God and His ways, these people have a particularly hard time. My dear colleague has again been told that the people on the Blue Bluff are very badly off with regard to food. As much as he feels pity for others in distress and would like to help them in their needs as much as he knows how to and can, his hands are bound by these people. They have owed him so much money for over a year that he himself is in debt and under great pressure, and our dearest friends in London had the same experience with them with respect to their journey to Georgia. But this does not bother these people in the least.

Our almighty God, who created heaven and earth, the sea and everything that is in it, and who is unchanged in His love as He remains loyal and maintains His loyalty and faith forever, continues to have enough ways and means to help His servant in everything. We, on the other hand, want to stay quiet and wait. Perhaps our gracious Father will keep His small fountain flowing in Europe for our benefit. Since our dear benefactors frequently want to know about our needs, we obediently report in our childlike trust in God's heart-swaying power that He, of whom we are part, use it as He pleases. We wish to thank Him for his willingness to help us. If God blessed the mill installations and allowed them to be put in good condition, then we would not be such a burden on our dear benefactors and would have the opportunity to help the needy members of our congregation. May our Lord be gracious and make our listeners repent and have faith; we then could hope with greater certainty that their physical needs be met.

The 26th of March. A Salzburger, Martin Lackner, has now come to the plantations as our schoolmaster; and we hope that God will support the work in his new position as well. Today he was shown the teaching method which the ministers have been following from the very beginning. The problem with such a change is that the children have to get used to a new person and that cannot be done through regulations, despite all efforts and assistance. School is only in the morning from 8 to 10 o'clock; on Tuesdays and Fridays Mr. Boltzius, or whoever delivers the weekly sermon, teaches the catechism. His salary is 6 pounds Sterling,[9] and he would be unable to live on it unless he pursued some additional work. Oh, that God would give us only workers as the Apostle Paulus had in Timothy, who was so much to his liking.

The 27th of March. Praise to our merciful God who gave us such good souls in our congregation and multiplied them: they accept God's counsel on their salvation, follow the order of salvation, and live in dignity with the word of truth. A man, an ex-soldier and, as he admitted, a bad person, as well as his wife, have turned to God, after our dear Savior visited on him a dangerous chest illness last year. Since then he has followed the good way of life and benefited from many physical and spiritual blessings. This married couple are also industrious workers and they are raising their three children in a Christian way to be good people. Our dear Lord is also with this man's neighbor and all those who have eyes can see His blessings. He established his plantation on pine land and equipped it so well that he would not trade places with anybody who has good land, but lives quite a distance from our settlement.

There is much land left around our town that has not yet been surveyed, but people would rather move away from their church and school to a distant area than settle on such land. We cannot do anything about it because they would otherwise say that, although we take care of their souls, we let their bodies rot, or that it would be our fault that the people have to live in poverty. It is an unspeakable blessing for both grownups and children alike to be close to the sermon in which God's word is preached on Sundays and workdays, and to be able to take advantage of school.

The eldest sister of the Schubdrein brothers, who drowned six weeks ago, was found last night. She was hanging from a tree, one mile down from where she drowned and did not show the slightest injury. All her limbs, and also her face, were unharmed and her body did not smell more than if she had been dead for only two days. We have taken this opportunity to encourage our congregation to prepare for their departure from this world and to bury the body of this person in a Christian way.

The 28th of March. We already reported that, sixteen years ago, we accepted, together with other orphans, the son of a poor widow from Purysburg; but, as it often happens in this excessively free country, bad people persuaded him to run away rather than let himself be restricted like that (Jeremiah 2:20).[10] Subsequently, he also ran away from his mother to live with the Indians, and he became quite like them in their ignorance and customs and forgot the German language while living among them. Some years ago he got married and intended and promised to receive instruction and start an orderly life. However, he found it very difficult to stick with it, especially since he was a poor beginner on a new plantation who, because of his land, has not even done the most necessary things. Today he reported to Mr. Boltzius for the Holy Communion, and the latter discussed many necessary things with him and gave him Master Schuetze's simple and easy-to-understand catechism tests,[11] afraid that he might back out unless we accepted him. He was instructed from Psalm 127:1-2 that no matter how hard you work, you will not win anything without God's blessing.

The 29th of March. The widow Schrempf, who has been richly comforted by God and lives the life of an honest widow in pleasant solitude, while trusting the one who is her real husband, was visited today and was strengthened by God's promises in her faith in her Savior. About her late servant she said that he had been very sad shortly before his departure for Purysburg, that he had committed many sins in his youth and that one would have to change in order to be saved.

Young Thomas Zuebli, son of our recently deceased David Zuebli, was also afflicted by stitches in his side in Purysburg last week. He died five days later and was buried on Sunday. Thus both father and son, one after the other, said goodbye to this troublesome world. The mother lives modestly, though cheerfully, on her husband's plantation. She expressed her heartfelt wish in Savannah to die in Ebenezer in order to enjoy the frequent visits by the ministers to her deathbed.

APRIL

The 5th of April. While being awake, a certain woman in our congregation had a terrible fantasy of Satan, who suddenly blew into her the most terrible thoughts against our good God and His gracious work; and she almost fainted. She told her husband, who continues to commit his usual sins despite good gestures and intentions, about this bad incident and the thoughts blown into her. He then joined her in praying. She now seems to have rendered her heart unto God, which helps for various reasons, especially in faithfully following the means of grace. Our pious God is also helping her through special indications of His Fatherly care; and she recently told us two beautiful details of signs she experienced last Sunday, shortly before the sermon started, of God's goodness in taking care of His friends, and they were very welcome to her. This is how the Lord makes people repent through love and seriousness.

God's mercy also showed itself clearly in a servant girl whom a pious landlady had brought up to believe in God. She grew so fond of Ebenezer that, when her parents, who do not live in our community, took her back to their house, she kept pleading with them until they let her come back here. She is now one of the people who are studying the catechism. May God continue to give His blessing for planting and watering!

The 6th of April. A young Christian man who, two years ago, had surveyed a plantation for himself at the Black Creek,[1] complained that he often has to wade in water during wet weather and that he would completely lose his already poor health as a result. He therefore asked Mr. Boltzius to help him get a plantation again in our town, which the latter, of course, cannot do. Like others, he knows only too well, for they are told publicly and often enough, that it would be better to settle, with God's word and other advantages, on not-so-good land than to move to faraway good land and to overlook many other important and indispensable matters. At first that is easy for them; and such people are amazed at what they enjoy. But then they are sorry, as it happened to somebody who went to N.N.[2] and regretted leaving here and would very much like to come back. However, that is not easy to do after one has settled in a faraway place.

Our gracious God has sufficiently strengthened us so that all three of us can preach His saving word. We held confession in both churches, with songs, prayers and God's word. In the Jerusalem Church Mr. Boltzius used the Christian interrogations as the basis of preparing those who want to go to Holy Communion. He also instilled in the listeners', hearts much that was important and edifying for their trials and encouragement. In the Zion Church, they dealt with the verse in Luke 19: "The Son of man has come to seek and to save which was lost." They described to the assembled congregation not only the great intention or wondrous final purpose of the future of man's Son, but they also called on their listeners to examine their past behavior in view of such a wondrous final purpose, etc., etc. May He, of whom we are and under whom we serve, accept what we discussed and bless it to save their souls and continue to strengthen the solemn covenant they have made with God.

The 8th of April. Today we spent a wonderful day with our listeners. We received many presents and, thank God, also could accept many, indeed all of them. The weak, simple souls, whose spirits live in true poverty, were richly served by our faithful Shepherd who reminded them of His all-gracious will that "God, our Savior, will have all men to be saved . . . " etc., (1 Timothy 2:4), and also administered the Holy Sacrament to them. And those who are and wish to stay so far away were told that they, too, are to be helped. We unbelievers have lost the freedom to think, not to mention to say: "God does not want to." Nobody should dare to stay away from those whom God will call to come and recognize the truth. The Holy Sacrament was held with 127 communicants who, because of their innermost condition, are better known to our Lord, who looks into their hearts, than to us. But we can be very sure that many derived great benefits from it.

The 9th of April. Botzenhardt's wife continues to be in poor health,[3] and she is not able to do her work nor can she attend church services here. However, she likes it very much when we visit and encourage her with Christian conversations, God's word, and prayers. She and her husband prefer staying here close to the church and school, instead of moving to Halifax,[4] and so her husband has applied for a good piece of land here nearby. However, we understand that the authorities in Savannah continue to insist that the most recent colonists go to Halifax. Although some families are there, they easily could be persuaded to move farther north to Savannah Town because the lower-lying land continues to be covered by the heavy floods in Halifax. And such a change could be harmful to their souls because they live farther and farther away from their co-religionists.[5] We would, of course, like to support the idea that the people could stay close-by; and, if wishing would help, the stretch of land from Halifax down to us would gradually be settled by our co-religionists so that we could preach God's word to them as well. And how we would rejoice in that! But we must be quiet about the way the authorities do it. Nevertheless, God rules the earth.

The 10th of April.   It is a very common obstacle, also in other places where God's word is preached according to instructions for ministers, hence particularly in our community, that one frequently has the opportunity to learn more about the spiritual state of one's listeners when the grace of the Holy Spirit touches and persuades them. This is because they then have the best of intentions although they do not specifically look for the persuasive power of God's word. Thus it happened to a man in the N.N. congregation, who has a very upright wife, that the sermons often convinced him of his unsuitable condition and he heard this so vividly in his heart and conscience that he told himself: "You are also one of those." He then believes that others have reported him and told the ministers about his thoughts. Then, without turning his eyes inward and surrendering his heart to our true calling God, he becomes even more hardened, blaming his wife or others, as if they had reported him. He then gives up his good intentions and convictions. If God would only give us the wisdom to deal with people like him, too! His good wife told Mr. Boltzius some details about how her soul has been feeling in the recent past and about her experiences, which have proven to her that she is under the gracious regimen and guidance of the

Holy Spirit. After much internal and external suffering, she is turning into a chosen vessel of God's teachings. She not only makes diligent and good use of the means of salvation, but also encourages her children to do likewise. Her eldest son has been in heaven for more than two years.

The 12th of April. Our wondrous God has stricken our community with many hailstones which hit, in particular, the fields and gardens surrounding the Zion Church. The rye, in almost full bloom, suffered great damage and the leaves of many mulberry trees, which were fully covered by foliage, due to the nice spring weather, were damaged or knocked off the trees. How very hard it is to understand His decisions and how unfathomable His ways are! Nevertheless, it is said that: "When everything seemed to melt away, I was still aware of Thy help. Thanks be to Thee, great King, thousands and thousands of times."[6] There is a great shortage of food in other communities, but we have enough to eat even though corn is expensive.

The 15th of April. Praised be the Lord who has seen to it that all three of us were able to start our Savior's Passion Week by preaching God's word. In the morning sermon soon after reading the gospel, we covered, time permitting, the true understanding of Jesus Christ, after introducing the question: "Who is He?" But in the afternoon services, we held a catechistical sermon in both churches about our Savior's deathwalk.

The 16th of April. It is very regrettable that some people hold God's word and the Holy Sacrament in such low esteem that they subordinate God's great blessings of preparing for and strengthening their absolutely necessary spiritual life to their stomachs and, by doing so, move away from the places where they can enjoy the good and go where they have to do without the spiritual pleasures and where, contrary to their expectations, they cannot satisfy their physical needs either. We could cite some examples, if necessary.

The 17th of April. Today our dear colleague, Mr. Boltzius, left for Savannah to take care of some important matters which he is best suited to handle. Such trips by this dear man are always important to us. He travels only in matters of great urgency, but to us, his trips seem frequent and very long, although they occur in intervals of several weeks and he does not stay for more than a

few days. Our Lord has bound us together so much that we like
to be together in heart and soul and enjoy one another. Praised
be our Lord!

The 19th of April. I, Mr. Boltzius, spent part of this Maundy
Thursday at Goshen, where I preached to the assembled listeners about Holy Communion. After the sermon an educated
and Christian man showed me a song from Pastor Stark's *Little
Communion Book*,[7] which exactly fitted in with my sermon, and
this is why he and others liked it so much. One has to try to support our co-religionists with this comforting passage from the
Bible against the hypocritical assertions of corrupt reasoning because we have in this country many people who like to contradict
and dispute.

Our dear people want us to preach more often and they offer
to make a contribution to the support of a third minister to the
extent that they are able to do so. Who knows how God will show
us what to do, so that we do not have to worry about it. Last evening I preached in Savannah about the words: "Thou hast wea-
ried me with thine iniquities."[8] Although it was a very difficult
day, I felt many signs of God's caring.

The 20th of April. I had wondered why our dear God
brought my manifold official matters in Savannah to such an
early end and made me rush back to Ebenezer via Goshen. Soon
the reason became clear to me when I heard that dear brother
Rabenhorst's dear wife was seriously ill and that he was so exhausted from staying up and suffering with her that it would
have been difficult for him to take my place in conducting the
Good Friday morning and afternoon sermons in the Jerusalem
Church on the death and burial of our dearest Savior. On
Wednesday, I felt weak in Savannah and stronger on Thursday
at Goshen; and on Good Friday at Ebenezer I felt so well that I
was able to preach with joy both in the morning and afternoon.
God be praised for answering the intercessions of His children!
Mr. Lemke is also working tirelessly and both colleagues assist
me to the best of their ability.

The 21st of April. Highly praised be the Lord, our refuge, for
permitting us to spend the blessed Holy Week in happiness,
good health, good order and peace, and for giving us during
this period many a blessing by meditating on His word and for

also doing much good for our physical welfare. This year the
Passion story according to St. Mark was the basis of our edification during the Lent Sundays. But in the mornings we reflected
on the regular Sunday gospels. May God see to it that we all benefit from this in eternity!

The 22nd and 23rd of April. Our good Lord gave us much joy
during these two Easter holidays and let us end them with His
blessings. Our dear listeners came eagerly to hear God's word,
and we were able, through the power of our dearest and living
Savior, to preach to them the comforting gospel: "He has
risen."[9] On the second holiday our very dear Mr. Boltzius served
our dear people at Goshen, who are very eager for the means of
salvation, with a sermon on God's truth and administered Holy
Communion. Praised be the Lord who lets us enjoy such beautiful church services! We are singing and praying, teaching, and
preaching; and nobody prevents us from doing so. We can adapt
our sermons to the needs of our listeners, and there is nobody
who sets up any special rules for it. Meanwhile, whatever our
true spiritual Leader instructed us to do in His dear word, that is
our uppermost rule, which we appreciate very much and which
the three of us, through our Savior's mercy, will continue to observe ever more precisely. May the Lord help us in this! Our
Lord was gracious enough to let the third share in our pain during the days of the Passion Week and to be happy again at the
beginning of the Easter day.

Because my dear helpmeet fell so sick on Monday, she believed on Thursday that she surely would be completely free on
Good Friday and able to follow our late Mr. Kraft to her eternal
peace. For me, who have no experience with this type of illness,
this was almost unbearable. However, our dear God does not
tempt us beyond our endurance and listens to the prayers of the
poor and weak. May we record it for our descendants that we
have a God who is true to us in His actions and who does not
withdraw from us when we call him. We praise Him for helping
us in our pain, for all His grace to let us preach His word, and for
all the superabundant good deeds He has assured us of through
Christ's resurrection!

The 24th of April. During the recent holidays, our Savior who
has been resurrected for our salvation has, in the abundant

preaching of His gospel, richly fulfilled His word: " If I be lifted up from the earth, I will draw all men unto me."[10] A man from Savannah attested his joy at our services here, and another man from our congregation said he could not tell how he felt at our ceremony. And how much is still hidden in souls who have experienced the power of the convincing spirit of God in a quiet heart, even if they do not say publicly what they are privately experiencing. God be praised for letting us know that the Lord has His seed among us that is serving Him and that there will be no sorrow as long as it does not run out. God will help us through everything. But woe unto the people from whom the Lord must withdraw.

The 25th. The silk harvest may not bring in as much this year as last year. In addition to the fact that we had fewer worms, many of them perished even though there were enough leaves and even though many people did not fail to tend them and care for them. Meanwhile, however, the silk is in part very fine and beautiful. The Lord, our House Father, well knows how to replace what is lost in any place.

The 26th. Our dear colleague, Mr. Boltzius, has again traveled to Savannah via Goshen, where he preached on the last Easter day to the inhabitants there. To this he was driven by his love of being useful to his neighbor in every way. On this occasion we have been greatly delighted by letters from Europe, from which we know that the Old God is still living and revealing Himself to us in a friendly and gracious manner by keeping our dear Fathers and benefactors alive and in health. He has strengthened them while they were weak and while they were providing for us when we were about to lack in physical things. At the same time we sympathize with them when they suffer tribulations and sorrow. May our dear Father in Heaven reward them for their love, care, and effort for us and our dear Ebenezer with spiritual and physical blessings! Amen!

The 27th. Our very dear colleague has returned to us again today hale and hearty. Our dear God richly blessed him on his journey by opening wide the doors in Goshen and Abercorn, as well as in Savannah, for proclaiming the gospel and for saying words of admonition and comfort here and there. From a ship that had arrived before Savannah we received a crate of books along with very pleasing letters that are full of evidence of God's fatherly providence over Ebenezer. The two crates with medications and books, as well as the packet of letters that arrived in Charleston two months ago, have not yet arrived.

In Goshen and Abercorn and on Black Creek live many people of the Lutheran faith. If our dear God would grant the means for us to cultivate the glebe land, which lies right in this area, we could very appropriately build a church and school there.

Our marvelous God has planned something, as we see with amazement from the present letters. Even high dignitaries are becoming guardians and nurses of the Lutheran Church in Georgia. He is also letting us know more and more that He has sent a third person here for important reasons, for whose support He has especially cared for from a distance.[11] Oh, may we observe these signs of the times and apply everything well! May God give us wisdom and loyalty so that His marvelous and loving counsel not waver. The German people in and around Savannah have come up in a boat to pick up Mr. Lemke so that he can preach to them and administer Holy Communion. May God accompany him on this important journey, which is dangerous because of the many trees that lie in the Savannah River and hold back the water, which rushes over them all the stronger; and may He bring him back to us with His full blessing.

For some time the weather has been very dry and windy, and at night it has been extraordinarily cool. The thirsty earth is refreshed by the heavy night dews, which are now very cold. However, the wheat again appears to be suffering great harm in that much of the usual rust is settling on its stalks. As mentioned, the silk has not turned out well. We could have made four hundred pounds more silk than last year if there had not been a lack of worms. Our inhabitants have been urged from far and near to exchange their silkworm seeds for foreign ones, as has been done with wheat, flax, etc. But, to all appearances, they have made a bad exchange. The worms from our seed have turned out well: those from the Italian seed hatched but gradually died out. This year there is a great quantity of mulberries on the white and black Spanish trees, which are so large and beautiful that their likes have never been seen here. They are very easy to collect for sowing and eating. Usually the birds eat them; however, we now see very few of them in the trees. Perhaps there are not too many of them here, or they get enough other food elsewhere so that they do not need these mulberries. God takes abundant care of all creatures, would He forget and leave us? Our Savior says: "No!" Wherever we are wanting, it is because we have no faith.

The 29th of April. Our listeners have little for their physical well-being, but ample in spiritual terms, and so they have everything our friendly God has promised them in His word. Whenever they complain and murmur, these people have no right to do so and are punished for it, because they themselves or their discontent are the reason for their trials and tribulations. Many people have no other worries except those they create for themselves. If all our dear inhabitants believed that Jesus' actions are friendly toward the wretched people, as they have been told during last Sunday's sermon, they would soon be free of anything that produces fear. The world cannot believe those who are and continue to be like Thomas. They do not want to believe, but they only want to see and feel at all times. How small is the group of saved people who do not want to see, but literally trust the word! Oh, Lord, we pray to You to give us and heighten in us, in the entire congregation and all our dear friends, the true faith we speak of! Amen!

The 30th of April. A young man by the name of Kreuter, a barber by trade, came to us one-and-a-half years ago and seemed almost unable to adjust here. However, he now seems to be doing well and will be a very useful and helpful man, able to earn a living. We do not hear good things about other young people who left for other places in search of larger material gains. He who is willing to work and obey good order can make a living here, is protected from many temptations, and has plenty of opportunities to save his soul. What else is there to be wished for in this short life? People of both sexes who did not learn much in Germany and do not want to learn and endure anything here either are complaining about Ebenezer and they are sorry to have come to America. We feel sorry for them, but since they do not want any advice, they often cannot be helped.

M A Y

The 1st of May. In praise of God and for the congregation's edification, we have told our listeners in both churches on this first day of the new month what the letters we received said about the special proofs of God's caring for our congregation. May God let this have benefits! Whenever the season or month changes, we remind ourselves publicly in church of the manifold spiritual and physical blessings our Lord has bestowed upon us during the past month and ask Him to forgive us our sins, to give us His blessing for our usual or special work, and to pray for our dearest friends and benefactors, as we also have done today. Even now we are calling out to each other: "It is of the Lord's mercies that we are not consumed, because his compassions fail not. They are new every morning." etc.[1]

The 2nd of May. We now have very fruitful weather. Although the soil was dried out earlier, our almighty Father and Ruler of all things is now richly refreshing it with fertile rain. Not only are the thunderstorms here much more frequent than in Germany, but they are also unusually heavy. The flashes of lightning are so frightening that everything seems to be on fire. Unlike in Germany, where lightning stops as soon as it starts raining, storms here become more violent. However, our Lord also protects us in the midst of fire. Although His words come out of flames and heavy thunder, to His children they are soothing and sweet.

The 5th of May. The day before yesterday, on my trip to the Zion Church, I ran into a Salzburger who was on his way to get the doctor for his young sick son. He asked me to visit the child, but because I did not believe from his description that he was seriously ill, I attended to other necessary business matters and postponed my visit to the 10-year-old boy. Today, two hours before sunset, my horse came to my house door, without my having called it, and I felt an inner urge to drop all planned work and rush to see the sick boy. He had such a serious *Asthma convulsivum* that it was much worse than I and the doctor had expected on the basis of what the father had said; otherwise we would have come to help the poor child more and earlier. After comforting the dear boy from the Bible, especially its present main passage: "Jesus is coming as a righteous and helping man,"[2] and after praying wholeheartedly with him and his distressed parents, I reported the sad circumstances to the doctor, who then rode to him immediately. Some time ago I had given him and other schoolboys Pastor Sommers's short rhymed prayer about Christmas and Whitsun,[3] which his fearful mother had to pick out for him from among other books; and he drew renewed benefits from them. The child was in great pain and that aroused my profound sympathy. However, his patience and his wish to die and enter Heaven were admirable and gratifying.

Since our dear colleague Rabenhorst's arrival, I have been allowed to preach only in the morning and to conduct, instead of the public prayers shortly before nightfall, the very popular repetition service which always closes with pleas, prayers, intercessions, and thanksgiving.

On this second Sunday after Easter, our dear brother came down with fever; and, because I was also holding the afternoon church service for him while Mr. Lemke was preaching in the Zion Church, we again held the public prayer hour instead of the repetition service before nightfall.

Some days ago, there was among the most recent letters and news items we received from Europe much material for praising God and for Christian intercession, which we have now (as we had done in our previous evening prayers) brought before God's throne of grace on behalf of our godly intermediary. We have also given adequate thought to God's servants and His work in Pennsylvania[4] and the East Indies,[5] since we received and saw very noteworthy and stimulating news from both these regions. The devotion of these dear missionaries, country preachers, and catechists is admirable; and so is their unity and Christian subordination. Wherever this happens, our Lord promises life and blessings forever and in all eternity.

How important this well-grounded unity is among the teachers of the New Testament for saving their own souls and for building God's kingdom is also shown in Christ's dear, worthy, and sacerdotal prayer (John 17), where there were undoubtedly no tautologies when Christ so ardently prayed for unity among His apostles.

When I have some more time, I will mark for myself those

passages in this continuation that may be useful for the edification of our adult listeners and our children. Some days ago, cit-
ing the example of the unchanging heathens, I warned them in
two prayer meetings and the weekly sermon of their sins and
their punishment with the words in Romans 1. Although they
did not pay attention to the need to recognize God, etc., see 2
Thessalonians 1:8. Based on the example of the converted heathens, I now have the welcome opportunity to encourage them
to work for their salvation. We are now dealing in our weekday
assemblies with the proper use of the means of salvation.

The 7th of May. In the chest of books we just received from
Halle, there is a letter to the esteemed Pastor Muehlenberg in
Pennsylvania and a long list of books intended for them. That
led me to write some letters to the esteemed brother himself and
to the esteemed Pastor Brunnholz, in which I not only told them
again of my heart's desire to enter into a brotherly and edifying
correspondence with them, but also gave them the reasons for
my belief that such a correspondence, started and continued
with God, could result in our joint edification, help strengthen
our brotherly love to one another, and expand God's kingdom in
their and our congregation. The dear missionaries in East India
make it part of their work to correspond not only with their dear
European fathers and friends, but also with the English and Dutch
missionaries. This *Vinculum christianae fraternitatis*[6] is particularly prevalent among the dear teachers of the heathens in Tranquebar, Madras and Cudulur. I will also send a small chest of
books and uplifting treatises from our supplies to our dear
brethren in Pennsylvania.

The 9th of May. Because dear Mr. Rabenhorst is ill, the people
on the Blue Bluff have asked me to conduct their weekly sermon, and I told them something from the important and comforting words: "The Lord is my shepherd, I shall not want." Neither should there be too few burdens and too little distress for
Christ's sheep, since they would then miss in and among their
shepherds an indispensable major part on the way to salvation.
Anyone who comes to Christ, our Shepherd and Savior, down-
trodden and heavily laden will, to be sure, find refreshment and
peace for his soul but also a light burden and soft yoke. Whatever a man brings upon himself on his own volition, by distanc-

ing himself from Christ when he worries about food and many other kinds of sins, is difficult and hard. This is why we have in Christianity so many complaints and even damage.

Finally I took something from the fifth continuation of the noteworthy Pennsylvania reports,[7] which can teach us much. Many Germans there are much worse off than in Germany, and this is evidently God's holy judgment for them, about which I warned my audience seriously and truly (Romans 1). Because they did not pay attention to recognizing God, He permitted them to do that which is not good, fully unjustified, as the subsequent verse relates all the horrors which, also in that country, go unpunished.

The people on the Blue Bluff surely need such warnings: many of them do not love God's word, are likely to continue living in their old sins, thus going too far and inviting God's displeasure more and more. It has been a long time since they asked for one of us to hold the weekly sermon. Some of them are honest people who are unhappy with the bad situation. The man who took me up there in a small boat remembered with humility and gratitude the Lord's goodness which had healed him from a serious deep-seated illness. Because our gracious God is feeding him and his family three times a day, they follow the example of the prophet Daniel and praise Him for His spiritual and physical blessings three times a day, namely, in the morning, at noon and in the evening.

The 10th of May. This evening I got a letter from a young German man in Charleston, who is the son of a schoolmaster from the Wurttemberg area and has to serve a merchant to pay for his passage. He heard that Ebenezer is looking for two schoolmasters and applied for the jobs provided we obtain his release for 7 pounds Sterling. However, we do not need him. We rather select schoolmasters from our own congregation so that we will not get into trouble. A schoolmaster here must till the land besides teaching school, or he must know a trade; otherwise, he cannot live on his small salary. If God made it possible for us to increase the salaries of our two teachers so that they would pay for a modest life, then these men would spend all their time for the best of the congregation and help us with many necessary things. As we already said, much good could be accomplished in our community, to God's glory and to serve our brethren.

We have to praise God for bestowing upon us many physical benefits from Europe for nineteen years; without them, the Ebenezer congregation could not have done as well as we did, to the joy of our friends and to the displeasure of our enemies and others who envy us. Praise to the Lord! But since the benefactions come one at a time, they have been used every year in the best possible way for the congregation. I was reminded today: "O Israel, trust thou in the Lord, he is their help and their shield. Hallelujah!"[8]

The 12th of May. N.N. wanted to have a letter written from his youngest son to his godfather, a famous cotton printer in Augsburg, because he was hoping for a gift from him. He asked my advice as to how the letter should be written. I advised him to, first of all, send his children to school and Christian instruction, because something could then also be written about their learning and their increase in goodness. This would please Senior Urlsperger and the child's godfather more than hearing something superficial about his children. He promised to do so. But seeing is believing. I have been after that man and his wife for several years to persuade them to, at least, send their children to catechist instruction, but I have been unsuccessful in accomplishing it with love or seriousness. They would not have to pay for school.

We have a good school here, and it should and could be improved if we had a larger number of children. It is good and important to hear in the letters from East India that they have lured so many heathen children in Tranquebar and other parts of the country to school in a Christian way and have carefully educated them. One has to admire the diligence of the dear missionaries, the dear country preachers and catechists, and praise God for it and help them ask the Lord for new courage, joy and strength. The most recent 73rd continuation bears witness to some beautiful blessings they derived from working with these heathen school children, which would probably put many Evangelical children to shame. Our Ebenezer congregation is also remembered in it and I acknowledge this properly and with humble gratitude. In the appendix to the foreword on benefactions received during 1750, it says on page 13: "Wernigerode sent us 35 Reichsthaler, which Her Highness the late Princess of Stolberg-Geudern left to the work of the missionaries and the Ebenezer congregation, with each receiving half." God be praised for this blessing, since this helps us pay our debt in Halle, which we have incurred by purchasing costly, and therefore prescribed, medicines and books for us and others.

On this third Sunday after Easter our dear colleague Rabenhorst continued to be sick with fever. May the Lord, in His gracious will, make him recover soon. On this Sunday Jubilate I have to praise our Lord's mercy for giving me great strength for an important matter, which is part of my duties and which I approached with fears and a sad heart, and for giving me the wisdom to tell the entire congregation about it at the meeting. A couple of young fine people, who had not been without grace, started their marriage in a disorderly way, as the birth of their child, who was born too early, showed. God's children among us were genuinely saddened by it, but the world was angered and pleased.

This disorder, which to our knowledge is the first of its kind in our community, was also disseminated to other communities by ill-disposed people who despise our order and institution. This makes it so much more necessary to deal with in a Christian fashion, according to God's word and for the benefit of the fallen, as a lesson and warning to the members of our community and the secret sinners among us that they examine their conscience and refute those who speak evil of us and slander us, which these two married people also thought needed to be done. God had truly forgiven them, and so it was easy to deal with this sinful and objectionable affair before the people so that the entire congregation could benefit from it.

Earlier, I delivered a sermon on the sinful pleasure of the world at the suffering of believers. At the beginning we reflected on the words from Micha 7:8: " Rejoice not against me, O mine enemy, . . . ," a reminder for the benefit of those who lie in wait for us, slander us, speak evil of us, and are our enemies. I do not want to go into details about this solemn undertaking, during which I distinctly felt the gracious presence and support of my shepherd and bishop Jesus Christ, because it would take too much time and not be for all readers. Without church discipline, our congregation could not remain a Christian and orderly community because this country provides so much freedom and its inhabitants are so impudent. We also had people from Goshen and Savannah who will probably say that we do not tolerate public sins and annoyances. I hope some people felt pangs of conscience, and that was also a purpose of this undertaking.

Afterwards the mother was churched with her small child like somebody who was at peace with God and mankind, and she was unexpectedly joined by another woman, who had given birth six weeks ago, and her small child. That was in error, but was not to be looked on as a matter of chance because it probably gave the person who earlier had been disgraced with some edification and comfort to see that she was not alone in stepping to the altar with her child, I could not adapt the usual words to this special situation but, for the sake of the other woman who was being churched, had to stick to what our dear God had blessed on this truly repentant, religious, and forgiven sinner.

The custom of churching, which aims at edification and the blessing of mothers and children, always takes place on Sundays or holidays, either before or after the sermons. Sometimes two or three people are blessed together; the entire congregation rises and, with its prayers and good wishes, seeks to give support to the churching mothers and their small children. Every mother must give the officiating minister advance notice of her planned church visit; one of the women, who had come today and had borne her child six weeks ago, had asked her brother to do so on her behalf, but he forgot.

The 15th of May. Whenever I visit our people on their new plantations (as I often must do at the beginning), the inhabitants of Goshen get together to hear God's word, which they have been eager to hear for some time. This time I preached to them about the first words of last Sunday's epistle in 1 Peter 2:11 "I beseech you as strangers and pilgrims, abstain . . . ," etc.

About our N.N. I heard the sad news that he had wanted, in the manner of the world, to honor somebody on a certain occasion by firing a round of shots, but that he shot the powder in his face and hurt himself badly. I visited him in his misery and found that in this hard but just punishment he recognizes the hand of God, who had to deal with him in a stern manner, since good deeds had not worked. He also has much trouble with his eldest daughter who has been sick for several months and must lie in the same position, in misery. She is a nice girl, whom God is preparing for His glory by making her suffer. God also is taking the same way with her pious mother who, after much sorrow, will enter God's kingdom.

The 16th of May. A week ago it was the first time, and today the second time, that I was taken to the Blue Bluff to hold the weekly sermon, since our dear colleague Rabenhorst continues to be sick. They had stopped doing so for some weeks at the instigation of some ill-mannered neighbors, who pretended that they would pick me up again provided we resumed our Sunday sermon every two or three weeks. Since almost everybody had come, this was a very welcome opportunity for me to talk to them about the unreasonableness of their selfish request, our well justified reason for disagreeing with them, the harm they suffered by not having a weekly sermon, their ungrateful behavior, and our sincere wish to make our work ever more useful to them. I could also speak with much love on their edification from God's word. They sang so orderly and showed so much devotion that I hope God blessed these spiritually and physically poor people. Oh, how we would thank Him for that!

The 18th of May. A few weeks ago the young Lackner was chosen as schoolmaster on the plantations, but he quit this job today. His plantation is two English miles from the school so that he loses much time by walking back and forth and hence must neglect his work at home. His salary, which largely comes from European alms, is 6 pounds Sterling a year. For that, a schoolmaster teaches on four days for three, and on two days (when the weekly sermons are held) only two, hours a day. For a man who lives nearby, this money provides a good supplement to cover his living expenses: if he is loyal and works hard, he gets something else in addition or we pay him a salary of 7 pounds Sterling. May God send us a hard-working man!

The 20th of May. On this Sunday, Cantata, we administered the Holy Sacrament to 126 people, including some from Purysburg and the Goshen area. We have reason to believe that our

dear God has blessed the preparatory sermons on several listeners; and from now on this will show itself in a better life for
them. With nostalgia and with a longing to save them, I again
referred some of them to dear Senior Urlsperger's important
sermon about the most wretched unchangeability, which some
of them picked up from me in order to read up on it. The questions in our catechism provide us with a very welcome way to
prepare our hearts in the preparatory sermons for the worthy
use of the Holy Sacrament, and I consider those catechism books
that have no sections with questions to be incomplete.

The 21st of May. Today we buried a young man, the only son
of his mother who is a widow of the third Swabian transport. His
name is Georg Raue, and we have reason to hope that he has
gone from his pilgrimage to God's heavenly kingdom. He was by
nature an honest and industrious man, who loved his mother
like a dear obedient son, used his small earnings to provide for
her present and future livelihood, liked his Bible and songbook
and God's word and church services with all his heart and
willingly accepted all good order. He was one of the first who, by
order of the Savannah authorities, moved to Halifax. However,
since he was poor and without means to make a living, and since
part of the new plantation he was setting up was full of water, he
suffered from hunger, misery, and poor health; and, after working for a short time in our community after his return from
Halifax, he contracted fever and dysentery and died all of a sudden at his dear mother's house. For our edification and the
widow's comfort, the funeral address dealt with the noteworthy
word from Psalm 144:3-4 on the nothingness of man and God's
goodness toward him.

The 22nd of May. Although some days ago the young Lackner
had indicated his unwillingness to teach on the plantations for 6
pounds Sterling, unless I would add something, he said after
today's weekly sermon that he wants to continue teaching, regardless of his salary. He said a knowledgeable man had described teaching as work, and the salary as money, that bring
great blessing. He is still a very inexperienced beginning school
teacher; however, as he gains in experience and becomes very
helpful to the children, he will get an increase. Parents are to pay
6 pence a quarter per child for school instruction. However,

since we do not force people to pay, but are very indulgent, we collect very little money for schooling. This time both schools brought in a total of 6 shillings Sterling. Some children are so poor that we charge them no school money at all and, in addition, give them books for free.

Most poor people who have moved here from Germany or other areas of this country do not sufficiently appreciate how very good God is to them and their children, and they cannot stand being told so. The few things which sometimes (though very seldom) have to be handled for the common good of the community are almost always taken care of by the Salzburgers and honest people who think like them. The rest of them, on the other hand, shirk their responsibility, while secretly complaining and fearful the supervisors might turn this and that worthy arrangement into a right and compulsory labor as they say it happened in Germany. They therefore feel that no time should be lost in opposing it.

The 23rd of May. Although our inhabitants are enjoying very good weather for their harvest and are working hard to cut and gather their wheat and rye, our wheat this year has again become so rust-infested that it is hardly worth our while to cut, gather, and thresh it. Rye and barley turned out very well, and we must thank God for giving one thing while taking away another. Experience has shown that this land is not suitable for growing wheat, but that rye, barley, rice, corn, beans, potatoes, and indigo seldom fail. Spelt and or dinkel do not grow here at all although we have made several attempts to plant them.

Some weeks ago some people on the Blue Bluff caused problems when they were asked to come and get one of their ministers in a boat for the weekly sermon. However, our dear God was gracious enough to resolve these problems in the meeting a week ago today, and I felt much joy and interest in preaching God's word and in singing and praying. In order for me to learn who the unruly people were, I told them that I would circulate a written article on their plantations, in which everybody favoring continuation of the weekly sermon would pledge, by signing his name, to contribute 18 pence a year to cover the expense of picking up a minister—God would do the rest. Today the paper was returned to me and I found to my great pleasure that everybody had signed, except for a former soldier and N. The latter is a very angry man who earned a lot of money about eighteen months ago but managed it badly. He is close to God's judgment.

The 24th of May. Some time ago a certain woman did so much wrong in her anger and in other punishable ways that she inflicted much heartache on her husband and trouble on other people. She suffered so much for her sins that eventually she was unwilling to be seen in church. Thus she kept on sinning by staying away and failing to follow the means of salvation and harmed her soul in the process. Today I found that her annoying behavior made her very sad, fearful, and restless by day and night and that she sometimes fought with despair, that she considered her sins to be too enormous to be forgiven, especially since God had worked on her for so long and so unsuccessfully. My words of encouragement and prayers have been blessed on her, and she has asked me several times to come and see her again soon.

N.'s daughter, who is married to N., had arrived here with ideas that were similar to those of her parents, but soon God's word convinced her that this is not the way to Heaven. She therefore became obedient to the Lord's command, "Go forth and separate from them,"[9] and she has truly turned to God, her Lord. She feels sorry for her parents' misery; and by praying, weeping, setting an example and friendly persuasion she tries to help them change. God does not leave her without blessings on her brothers and sisters although everybody who must live with these very evil parents is in a bad way. How grateful she now is to her dear God for bringing her here and saving her from Satan's blindness and other traps!

The 27th of May. We still had to do without the help of our dearest colleague Rabenhorst during this prayer Sunday because it pleased the Lord to continue his illness. It is true for him and others among Christ's friends and lovers: "Sickness is not for death, but for the glory of God, that the Son of God might be glorified thereby."[10] It is right, as it was for Christ, our leader, for us to devote all our actions and pains to the glory of our Heavenly Father, and to praise God through our death just as Peter and many other saints did.

My dearest colleague Lemke suffered from fever attacks last

week. However, with God's help he soon recovered and today was able to deliver two sermons at the Zion Church. May God be praised with our hearts and in eternity for all the spiritual and physical benefactions He gave us on the last Sunday of this month and this spring and during the time before that up to this moment! This includes His giving us His word in such abundance and, by so doing, not only showing us His will, but also proclaiming, offering, and presenting His invaluable grace from the dear Gospel to all those who let themselves be brought to His order through the proper use of the means of salvation. Thus both the morning and afternoon sermons in the Jerusalem Church drew on the passage in 1 John 5:14 and the Bible concerning the right way of praying to God and the wonderful benefits flowing from doing so. I can rightfully say about today's extraordinarily edifying and comforting sermon what I recently saw inscribed in an otherwise edifying prayer book: "This word is a fortress for me, a sweet gospel, indeed, pure milk and honey." May He bless in all eternity these important, lovely, and comforting words on me and all my dear listeners, including strangers, who attended in the morning!

The 28th of May. The upright widow Kalcher was forced to make another change in her pilgrimage in that circumstances made her leave the inn at the mill and return to live in town, where she can serve the Lord in peace and prepare herself for His call. Here she has a house of her own but, since Mr. Rabenhorst continues to live there, she moved to the so-called silkhouse. So far, our dear God has always provided her and her children with the food and support they need; He will continue to do so in the future as well. She wholeheartedly believes in her Savior and prays very diligently and is well experienced in it. She and her house continue to be blessed as they were during her pious husband's life. I wish I were able to help her. She is needy and worthy. To the extent that my current physical weakness permits it, I will be glad to serve her.

Our dearest colleague Rabenhorst is feeling better now, but his dear wife is very sick, and her illness looks serious to me. The troubles of these two married people, who are so well liked by everybody, affects me greatly and makes me very sad. I stay with Christ's infallible word in yesterday's sermon: "Ask, and ye shall receive, and your joy may be full."[11] I am with them with much edification and blessing and wish wholeheartedly that I may enjoy their edifying and blessed friendship for a long time to come!

Yesterday our dearest colleague Lemke returned home sick from the Zion Church. He feels very weak and has a severe headache. Many people are complaining about that now, and I just heard that our gardener /Johann Melchior/ Oechsle died. He leaves behind a widow, four daughters, and two sons. The two eldest daughters truly love God and His order and means of salvation. The other children lived in their parents' house and had to do without instruction in God's word. May our merciful God take care of them and bless them through His Holy Ghost so that they follow in the footsteps of their older sisters!

Although I also felt a bit feverish today, our dear God gave me enough strength to conduct the funeral service for, and to attend the burial of, gardener Oechsle from the beginning to the end. The funeral service was also a sermon of repentance, for which our dear Senior Urlsperger's beautiful book, *Scriptural Instructions for the Sick and Dying, Preceded by Encouragement to Accept the Order of Salvation.*[12] However, we could only use the title and the important words from the Acts 11:18: "Then hath God also to the Gentiles granted repentance unto life." Whenever I have to hold a funeral service, I am planning to use this thorough and evangelical encouragement which we all need, and I have asked the audience to bring that book with them. Our listeners should accept forever in their ears, minds, and hearts the important words of encouragement on the second page, where it says: "This order can and must not be ignored by those who want to partake here and there in God and His kingdom. Neither can a minister accomplish anything important in his verbal and written sermons without keeping a steady eye on this order of salvation and taking it as the solid foundation and guideline for all his work for the congregation that is entrusted to him or also for others whom he is to help now and then."

A friend in Charleston reported that, some time ago, the cost of a bushel of corn was over 4 shillings Sterling. However, since corn from the northern colonies was brought to Charleston in several wagons, the price dropped by more than half, and it seems to be getting cheaper. We must praise our God (oh, if all would only do so!) because we have no reason to complain about a wide-spread food shortage in our community this year and high food prices. Although we did not grow as much as the people here needed, more corn was brought in for sale than we needed, regardless of the prohibition to export from Augusta (which is located in Georgia) to Carolina. And even the poorest, if they want to work, are taken care of. The bushel started here at 2 shillings 6 pence, and went up to 3 shillings.

I recently heard that, in Halifax, some people of the last Swabian transport did not have enough corn, and it seems to be getting worse because they lack money and other support. They sent a man to me to ask whether I could help them out with 100 bushels of corn until harvest-time; they promised to be more grateful than some other people. But I have no money to help these poor people. Meanwhile, in a letter to Mr. Habersham, they have appealed for help to the President and Council in Savannah because otherwise they will have to move on.

There already has been talk that some of their families have moved to Augusta; however, this is not true, with the exception of two young men who accepted employment there as servants. In Halifax, they have very good land, good meadows for the cattle to feed on, good timber, good water, good and healthy air, and hence it would be foolish of them to move farther north and, in the process, they would get into the hopeless situation of forever remaining without a church and schoolmaster. They could hope to get the latter if other people sharing their religious belief joined them and they formed a congregation. We pity those who left the transport.

The widow Schrempf lives with her three children happily in her solitude and behaves like an upright widow, serving the Lord and bringing up her children to obey and listen to the Lord. I greatly enjoyed her children today, especially with regard to the *Golden ABC*,[13] which the oldest child was able to recite in an orderly way and almost without stumbling, both in and out of sequence. Our merciful Savior fulfills in us His dear promise to bless us and to edify us in our prayers and in God's word: "Where two or three are gathered together in my name, there am I in the midst of them."[14] At the occasion of tomorrow's

Ascension Day festival we called out to each other to think of heaven and the *Golden ABC*, and with this in mind we parted. A Christian friend and her daughter attended. It is a great pleasure here in this incomplete life to be one of God's children. How will it be in heaven?

On this last day of the month we celebrated Ascension Day in both churches. Following the afternoon church service I was overcome by fever due possibly to overexertion in speaking in this heat and because of my weak physical condition.

Today God blessed us with the arrival of a chest of books and medicines that contained Mr. Rabenhorst's eagerly expected books and also an edifying letter from one of my upright academic friends, the Constapellian minister Daniel Mueller,[15] as well as some stimulating commemorative quotations, in fine scripture and on fine paper, from some Christian friends of noble status, whom we do not know. We do not suffer from a lack of books and medication. This is a great blessing. The two chests had been in Charleston for quite some time.

JUNE

The 1st of June. To praise the giver of all gifts and to please our friends in London and Germany, I talked on the preceding two pages dated the first of June about some testimonies of God's goodness toward our small Ebenezer group, as I remembered them in my current physical weakness. However, this most recent description of the past and present tribulations of our dear Salzburgers may, at first sight, not at all fit, and anything else I and others reported in the diaries and letters about the pleasant and contented life of the Salzburgers in Ebenezer as well as about their meager existence and support may make even less sense. This is why I want to make it clear that, first, the description of, and information on, our past and partly continuing trials were not unbelievable and impatient complaints.

Neither do I remember having heard anything like this from the Salzburgers, and nobody has asked me to give a detailed account of the misery and tribulations they have experienced. Most have the income they need to subsist, a rather well-equipped farming and cattle-raising operation and housing and

do not yearn for big things. They are home-centered, econom-
ical, and prudent in everything; and they help their needy fellowmen to the best of their ability, as the three most recent Swabian transports and other Germans that came here keep asking
them to do. Because of this, they have been worn out for a long
time and find it very hard to be in their approaching old age
without servants, who do not do well and are simply not available, to work and produce the necessary food. As long as they
are without loyal servants and their sickly wives cannot be of
much help in the fields, they earn by farming and cattle raising
not much more than what they need for their year-round up-
keep. Hence they can contribute only very little to the support of
the church, school, doctor, surgeon, widows, orphans and to
many other extremely vital expenditures of the congregation.

Indeed, some of the Salzburgers have been weak for a long
time and unable to work, and yet they have to provide for their
wives and children. They would greatly benefit from receiving
once in a while some assistance from Europe, and it is truly well
spent on them.

Secondly, I have mentioned the trials of the Salzburgers so
that Ebenezer's benefactors know the reason why the congregation, like all congregations in Pennsylvania, cannot exist without
their assistance. Of course, God has a hand in it, but there are
also many human errors that He allows them to make. Those
who arrived after us have benefited from our experience or they
still could do so. Our wisest and most gracious God finds it necessary and beneficial to apply to us such wondrous ways, which
belie all reason, as He did to His own people in the desert, while
secretly continuing His spiritual work of grace, as we ministers,
who praise His name, do.

Our Salzburgers did not come to America and run into all
kinds of misery on their own. They were following a call and
God's assurance, and their true friends in Europe, who are also
God's friends, were aware of that. Unlike many, in fact almost all
Germans, they did not come here because they were looking for
their good fortune and better living conditions in the New
World, but to serve their God and fellowman, truly and freely,
content with God's gracious guidance, which would make everything well. Because, from the very beginning, our true God,

with His holy word and the holy sacraments, has provided them with the service of two, and since last November even three, ministers and two schoolmasters, and with a church and school in town and on the plantations, as well as well-equipped mills, they now have what they could not have in Salzburg, but what they wanted when they emigrated; and, despite many trials, they do not complain that they are poor.

Third, besides the Salzburgers, there are many other Germans in Ebenezer, among them very poor people. They may be quite similar to the German immigrants in Pennsylvania, except that they may be poorer and, in view of the hot climate, in worse health than the latter. As members of the congregation, they need the help of European benefactors, if not more, then just as urgently as the Germans in Pennsylvania. On some of them the alms are well spent, on others we have good hope that they will be. The latter usually evade the . . . [1] in the congregation, partly because they are so poor and partly for other reasons; and they let the Salzburgers and other well-disposed people carry the burden. Yes, they have overrun us so much in their poverty and with their illnesses and so fearfully and seriously asked for advances of money and food that we ourselves incurred heavy debts because of them, and there is little hope that we will get anything back.

I am now going to leave this somewhat unpleasant subject (although it probably will always be in my heart and prayers) and, in order to awaken my poor and otherwise troubled heart and strengthen my faith, to the selected Bible verses and blessings in front of me, which some dear friends and benefactors from Saxony sent to our Salzburgers at this time.[2] The first is in Isaiah 5:1 [latter number illegible], and bears the comments: "This is being sent for the dear Salzburgers' comfort and edification, M.J.A.L.L." The second is in Luke 12:32 and signed: "I am sending this wonderful promise by our good shepherd to our dear Salzburgers with my heartfelt wishes and prayers that the great Shepherd of Jesus Christ's flock of sheep fulfil His promise on these dear sheep of His in time and eternity, S.E.F.H." The third verse is from Zechariah 2:5: "For I, saith the Lord, will be unto her a wall of fire round about, and will be the glory in the midst of her." The fourth is from 1 Samuel 7:12, subcaptioned

"As the Lord has helped the Salzburger congregation in the past, may He also help them in the future! This is my heartfelt wish, J.C.Ch.H." The fifth from Ezekiel 34:11,14,15, bears the very hearty and blessed subcaption "May our true and good shepherd Jesus Christ continue to fulfil this wonderful promise to the dear Salzburgers in Ebenezer, and may He continue to help them as He did in the past, and may He glorify His name among them so that they enjoy wholeheartedly the good fortune from which they benefit like sheep in their shepherd's green pasture and rejoice and begin to sing one hymn after the other, in praise of Him. This is my most sincere wish and daily prayer for this congregation of the Lord, Z.L.E.A."

No name came with the seventh verse from 1 Peter 5:9, but the following loving subscript, a clear indication of the lasting grace in the noble writer's heart: "To Minister Boltzius and the dear Salzburg congregation in Georgia, I am sending together with this verse some Bibles and Arndt's *True Christianity* with my children,[3] because I have learned from their edifying reports of their strong yearning for such books. When I read that one member of the congregation was frightened by spiritual temptation[4] and did not want to call the pastor because of the distance, I remembered Goodwin's beautiful treatise entitled *A Child of Light Walking in the Dark*[5] and am taking the liberty of adding this and some other very beautiful verses by the same author. May the Lord accompany this with His grace and blessing! I am commending myself, my husband, and my children to their friendship prayer, and I assure them of same from us."

The 3rd of June. Mr. Rabenhorst's health continues to deteriorate. However, after starting to take the recently received medicines from Halle, in accordance with Richter's book,[6] he is now feeling markedly better.

Although I am not yet entirely over my own weakness, our Lord has given me enough strength to conduct the morning sermon and the repetition session before sundown. Thank God, Mr. Lemke as well is feeling much stronger. Since our arrival in Ebenezer it has happened several times that we received alms from Europe between Rogate and Exaudi, as reported in the Diaries. It was the same this year, as reported on the preceding pages. That was not a mere accident, but we remembered this experience a week ago by what Christ said in the Bible: "Ask, and ye shall receive." This will also encourage us to lay before our Father, in Christ's name, the above-mentioned suffering and trials of our community until He hears us.

Our dear Mr. Rabenhorst chose today as his main epistle on his sickbed: "God has spared not his own son, but . . . how shall He not with him also freely give us all things?"[7] Here it says again: "The verse is for me a fortress, a sweet gospel, sheer milk and honey." It was specifically and lovingly applied to me and my late colleague at our ordination by Pastor Giesen, who assisted during that occasion.[8]

The 5th of June. This has been an unusually hot day; it is almost impossible to get any hotter. In the evening a thunderstorm developed with some rain; however, it did not hit our area in particular, which needs it badly. God will give us what, when and how it is needed, as He has promised us through His dear son, the mouth of truth. Oh, if only we had strong faith, then we would receive much and see God's glory behind all trials! For it will always be true: "If thou wouldest believe, thou shouldest see the glory of God."[9] With the above-mentioned Gospel verses, God has given us much edification and awakening; and He has strengthened our faith during our prayer sessions in the Jerusalem Church, the weekly sermons at the Zion Church, and the assemblies on the Blue Bluff. Through them He has bestowed on us much wonderful blessing, although we will have to do without His blessing for our edification we would have enjoyed from the letters that were lost.

The 7th of June. I started this morning to cover with my dear listeners dear Mr. Ziegenhagen's edifying Whitsun sermon, entitled: "A Serious Admonition by Jesus Christ to Ask our Father for the Holy Spirit,"[10] by selecting the text in Luke 11:9-13. I have truly enjoyed the beneficial sermon, delivered in God's order, which is uniquely suited for sinners who are in guilt and are suffering misery.[11] I like to emphasize through God's grace the blessed contents of the Third Article about the Holy Spirit and sanctification, and I show my audience that the two first Articles about creation, preservation, and salvation will not do them any good without the third.

It is just too bad that most Christians know so little about the dear truths of the Third Article which deal with the person, work and effects of the Holy Spirit. Where should such people gain their knowledge of our Father and His Son, and true Christianity? This sermon by dear and experienced Court Chaplain Ziegenhagen is very wise; and I wish wholeheartedly that God give him the time and strength to gradually go over all the important points shown on page 11, since this sermon addresses only the first point, namely, what is meant here by the Holy Ghost.

The 8th of June. On this Friday, shortly before Whitsunday, our dear inhabitants have worked on suspending the beautiful bell, which our esteemed Mr. Whitefield has recently donated at my request, to our plantation or Zion church in a very tall scaffolding built for that purpose. Many people were needed to accomplish that. Hence, the day of our weekly sermon was particularly opportune for hanging it since many men had come and could lend a helping hand. I appropriately tailored my sermon to this special occasion by including the words in 1 Samuel 7:12, sent to us by an unknown Saxon patron who is truly searching for God: "Samuel took a stone and put it there . . . and called it Ebenezer and said: 'The Lord has helped us so far.'"

I told my listeners what they had already heard in the most recent weekly sermon, namely, that God sent us from far away the aforementioned gospel verse, written on a separate piece of paper, which was among the selected Biblical verses we received. And that was also the reason why our wondrous God had given us this beautiful bell through our frequent benefactor Mr. Whitefield, who had even paid for shipping it to Savannah. The bell was then shipped free of charge from Savannah to here. In his letters to me Mr. Whitefield expressed several times his wish that God strengthen many Ebenezers in Ebenezer! He said that He already had done so in many ways, and was now doing it again by installing this gift of a bell. Samuel set down only one stone and called it Ebenezer. But God gave us the pleasure of installing a bell and putting aside the horn we have used until now to call people to church.

Do we not have many reasons to say: "Ebenezer," and look upon this bell as a sign of the Lord? Surely, I added, this is new proof of the Lord showing Himself in all trials as being a wondrous God, and this is a sure sign that He is in the midst of our congregation: now we can also believe that He will continue to be a wall of fire around us, as stated in the comforting contents of the verse in Zechariah 2:5 that was also sent to us and discussed in last week's sermon. I then impressed upon my listeners that these new dear benefactions carry with them certain obligations towards God and their benefactors, that is, primarily towards God.

First, that, whenever they hear the bell's far-reaching pealing, they should humbly and thankfully remember the graciousness of the Lord who made them into a Christian congregation and gave them churches, schools, and ministers. Otherwise the bell will be of little benefit to them.

Second, that they and their families should praise Him with all their hearts, as always but particularly at the sound of the bell, for the great, entirely undeserved benefaction of hearing the sound of a pealing bell instead of a horn, and let themselves be called to church and school. Psalm 50:23. If it brought them God directly from heaven, or through the angels, or from the earth, etc., they should call it a great miracle. However, the way we got it now, that is also something wonderful since He first had to induce, through His Holy Spirit, the naturally unloving and selfish human hearts, even of strangers, who are neither our landsmen nor co-religionists, to donate their money to buy it. On the way over, on the ship, it was exposed to many dangers, yet God delivered it into our hands. These are proofs of his wondrous kindness, power, and wisdom; and for that He deserves praise and prayers.

Third, our duty towards our dearest benefactors, especially towards dear Mr. Whitefield, must be that, when we hear its sound, we remember the bell's true mission and follow its call and, as members of the congregation, prove our sincere and heartfelt love among and for one another. Otherwise, according to Paul's word in 1 Corinthians 13, we will be like a sounding brass or a tinkling cymbal, although we may speak with the tongues of angels and men. Hence we must pray with all our heart for our dear benefactors and, when we hear the bell's sound, we must diligently think of our approaching death and burial, particularly since the bell will also signal, as it does in town, that a burial will be held.

Then we fell on our knees, thanked God, the kind Provider of this and other good gifts, and prayed for our benefactors, ourselves, and the congregation. Prior to the sermon we sang: *Mein Herz sey Gottes Lobethal,* . . . etc. and, after the prayer: *So kommet vor sein Angesicht,* . . . etc. In the evening, I repeated the sermon in the Jerusalem Church reminding us of the kindness God has extended to us from the beginning through Mr. Whitefield and His other dear tools. He has also given us the bell in town and a large sum of money for the construction of the Jerusalem Church.

The 9th of June. The text of the Whitsunday sermon, Luke 11:9-13, was also my text for today's preparation of holy Whitsun, from which our dear Father in Heaven had provided me with much blessing at home and in a conversation with some sick people. These dear words and the delicious promise I expect to use, God willing, as the basis of my sermon tomorrow, the first holy day of Whitsun, are from Isaiah 44:3-5; and I believe they are necessary and blessed in my current condition, since I will be able, with God's gracious guidance, to send shortly after the holidays my only young son Gotthilf Israel, accompanied by our dear friend, Capt. Krauss,[12] via London to Halle to attend the Latin school of the orphanage. We are praying to Him to send the Holy Ghost; and we have no doubt that we will be heard not only because it says in the promise in Isaiah 44: "I will pour my blessing upon your offspring, . . . " etc., but also because Christ, our Lord, has assured us, "If ye, then, being evil, know how to give good gifts unto your children, how much more shall your Father which is in heaven give good things to them that ask him?"[13]

The 10th and 11th of June. Our dear colleague feels sufficiently better now through God's grace and he can do some walking from time to time. However, he is still too weak to preach during the Whitsun holidays. Hence Mr. Lemke held the sermon on the first day in the Zion Church and I in the Jerusalem Church. On the other holiday, he preached for the entire congregation in the Jerusalem Church, while I preached to the inhabitants of Goshen about the Fifth Book of Moses 32:6 and the Gospel, according to John 3:16. Our merciful and loving God has provided us both with sufficient physical and spiritual strength to preach in the morning and in the afternoon, although the weather was very hot. This evening, after sunset, our dear God returned me home to my family, happy and healthy. Praise to the Lord that our pilgrimage takes us closer step by step to our heavenly fatherland and eternal peace which God's people have been promised and which is ready to receive them. In a little while we will see our Savior and all proven upright people. Come, Jesus Christ!

The 14th of June. This summer God has visited on the new colonists the same fever we had to contend with in past years. Some old inhabitants are also sick and weak. God's hand punishes us in many ways, and we need it and benefit from it. Ignorant people say that the air in Ebenezer is not as good as elsewhere, but this is not true. Where there is Jesus and His spirit, there is also His cross. Even the country where Christ walked without being seen had very many sick and otherwise troubled people. Our comforting words and prayers for help will benefit them greatly. Although they are now sick and are undergoing all sorts of trials, all people of the last transport are eagerly waiting for permission to settle in Ebenezer.

The 18th of June. As it should be, the Lord's day is always an important and blessed day. We spend it peacefully with singing, praying and discussing God's word. No worldly and sinful behavior can be seen or heard here, and that, in many respects, contributes to our edification. Whenever something annoying and offensive comes up, we squash it immediately. In this, we are much more fortunate than other communities where they experience many nuisances on Sundays, much to the chagrin of Christ's true servants. Yet we have much other misery here, since our wondrous God tends to grant His favors by imposing one suffering on one person, and some other misery on another person. Everybody gets something, as He in His wisdom believes it will benefit us. For that reason everybody needs the compassion, intercession and assistance of the other person.

This is how our wise God provides His children with an opportunity to prove their love among themselves and for one another, as we have noticed many times when we were in distress. Thinking about it moves our hearts and we praise our Lord. Yes, we are ashamed that we have enjoyed so much love from many Christian believers, while we have done so little, although we know very well that our dearest patrons and benefactors do not expect any repayment in kind. We can little afford such repayment and will probably continue to need their help for quite some time to support our congregation here.

To come to the point which I want to bring up: with God's help, the time had come yesterday, the day of the Holy Trinity, for Mr. Boltzius to bid farewell to the entire congregation on behalf of both Capt. Krause, who had spent the entire winter here and now intends to return to Europe, and his one and only beloved son, who, accompanied by dear Mr. Krause, is being sent by his highly respected parents to our dearest Father, Court Chaplain Ziegenhagen, in London. From there he will be taken to the blessed institutions of the orphanage in Halle. At the same time, the travelers were commended to the faithful intercession of the entire congregation. This could not be done without much emotion, and we hope that some people, especially believers, will support these departing dear friends, among them the merchant helper Guenther, who came here with the late Mr. Kraft a year and a half ago, with their sincere prayers during the long journey, as they had requested. In memory of this occasion, these words were called out to us: "In Jesus Christ, neither circumcision availeth anything or uncircumcision, but faith that worketh by love."[14] They preface the third chapter of Johann Arndt's first book on true Christianity, which is recommended for careful reading, and they are in line with the presented material dealing with the important change that is the only way for us to enter God's kingdom. Oh, may neither the departing travelers nor those who are staying behind forget or ignore them!

This morning our dear friends said a particularly moving goodbye in our homes and, in God's name, started their journey at 8 o'clock. Mr. Boltzius accompanied them to Savannah, from where they will continue their trip to Charleston in our boat and with our people, unless they find some other opportunity. May the Lord hear our sighs and prayers for them for Christ's sake. We hope that He will do so in His kindness!

The 19th of June. Our pious Mrs. Kalcher suffered another serious attack yesterday afternoon, which made her very weak. She called one of us to her house at a late hour because she did not know God's plans for her. She was found in bed, completely still, and unable to say much. She was told the story of the Easter lamb, which we had read earlier on another occasion, and applied it to its counterpiece, the Easter lamb in the New Testament, about which we usually sing: "Its blood designates the door, faith guards it from death, the murderer can not touch us."[15]

She complained about her lack of faith and did so again this morning, wishing she could believe without feelings and be assured of the forgiveness of her sins and of God's grace, but she saw nothing but sin and sinful misery. In response she was told of the signs of true repentance and faith as well as of the wonderful promises God had made to those willing to atone and believe (see Ezekiel 33:14-16, Luke 24:47), and the conclusion was: "Where there are signs of faith in God's word, there is also faith, and where there is faith, there is also the forgiveness of sins through God's promises," and she no longer had any doubts.

Of course, it is true that nowhere in the Bible is there any reference to the feeling of forgiveness of sins; however, we often experience that, if some souls are uncertain about this, the fault is theirs. They are not constant in their awakening and praying, do not allow God's word to feed their souls each day, do not take themselves and other people they deal with very seriously, can hide much in their conscience that is not right, deal with a certain sin, which they do fight, but do it in the wrong way until they have overcome it. Thus, no wonder they cannot be sure that their sins will be forgiven and they worry in addition a great deal in their conscience. In some people, one of the reasons for their spiritual uncertainty is the fact that they do not have a clear and adequate understanding of their spiritual condition and the order of salvation. However, a distinction must be made between them and the doubters.[16]

On the other hand, there are people, and we also have seen examples of them here, who are very serious about their Christianity, who break through[17] in their own souls and the souls of others, who want to find them in it,[18] and who attest to the truth.

Although such people are not always sure of their condition of grace, they do taste God's peace, have an easy conscience, cling all the more to God's word, which is more certain than the strongest feelings, and hence are very certain of their present state of grace and the salvation they hope for in the future. What a shame it would be if a true Christian, with God's gracious help, could not even hope with certainty that God will welcome him in His heavenly kingdom once he must leave this world! The late Kalcher, in particular, was an example of the latter kind which remains fresh and blessed in our memory.

Today we had the opportunity in both the Jerusalem and the Zion Church to announce something from some edifying written reports. In the Zion Church we impressed upon our listeners the words in Hebrews 3:12-14, and in the Jerusalem Church those in Psalm 51:6. They seemed to be very moved, and our words may have penetrated their souls. May God grant that this be permanent, at least in some of them! The reports have proven to be of great benefit to us ministers; this is why we thought it proper to try them out on our listeners as well.

The 21st of June. Although we preach the Order of Salvation clearly, emphatically, and diligently, there are always some people who believe that justice has already been done. Sometimes this is now shown in people who do not believe, when they are sick, that they need their ministers' comforting words. If we visit them nevertheless and talk to them about the way they should live and if we like to show them the way from beginning to end, they find it very strange; also they refer to the quotations they have learned, verses from specific songs, good works, etc., which they recite and thus act very pious. If they are told that none of this is enough, but that they must change in their heart and that it must be united with Christ through faith, they cannot understand that they are not and cannot be considered good Christians.

The 23rd of June. We know from several experiments we have done that there is nothing we can do with know-it-all servants: either they do not want to do well or they demand extremely high wages, apart from the fact that they are rarely available and that some become sick soon. We do not have enough money for Negroes. Thus this matter continues to be among to Ebenezer's

desiderata, and it is among the most urgent ones, which God undoubtedly will take care of, if it serves to glorify His great name.
Unless this happens, the congregation will very likely be unable
to sustain itself. This is one of the reasons mentioned in the reports from Pennsylvania where our dear co-religionists are in
some respects similar to us. They have to work hard just like us,
probably harder than in Germany; and their work is poorly
paid. In addition, the weather is already quite warm, and the
most urgent, though not heaviest, work that can least be
postponed must be done in the hot period. Therefore people
must spend their strength and health if they want to feed themselves honestly and have no help.

But there is much that has already been written about this,
and the little we report can only serve as a confirmation. We are
looking to God, the ruler of heaven and earth, in whose hands
everything rests, to see what He does. He has His wise reasons
and we should and can be satisfied. Yet it is only fair and helps us
greatly, and our dearest Fathers will not hold it against us, that
we write to you about our troubles and also look, next to God, to
you for advice and comfort.

In the meantime we take heart from knowing that everything
must turn out for the best of God's children, that, as a loyal God,
He will not test them beyond their endurance. "He who hopes
for God and trusts in Him will never be in disgrace, . . . " etc.,
etc. He helps those who believe in Him. All of them."

The 25th of June. Today I visited some families in town and
on the plantations, including a woman from Salzburg, with
whom I spent about an hour that was edifying. They were very
grateful and called it an invaluable blessing to have such an
abundance of means of salvation. They said they are satisfied,
regardless of how hard their life is, if only our dear God fulfills
in them His reason for bringing them to His word and sacraments and they do not incur any debts or become a burden on
other people. They were well aware that they could not handle
good days, and if they had the latter, they prayed that leaving
their fatherland for religious reasons might be more damaging
than beneficial to them. In the remaining families there were
some patients with whom one could talk only as circumstances
required it, just as with healthy people.

The 27th of June. Today I had to hold the edification hour on the Blue Bluff, where we discussed the impressive words in Deuteronomy 11:26-28. They had also been examined in the Zion Church last Sunday, the first Sunday after Trinity; and, as I heard at the time of our visit, not without blessing. I hope they have also made an impression on some people in that place. Indeed all our listeners could be happy if people would let us advise and warn them and if they would meet the conditions under which God will give us His blessings. By God's grace we have shown them in a simple, but clear and evangelical manner what they must do to fulfill these conditions and how they would have to start their obedience and follow Christ's demand in Mark 1:15, etc., with which the wondrous promise in Ezekiel 36:26-27 has been compared.

Because we had to take down the names of those who wanted to take communion next Sunday, a good number of listeners had come. Usually the long way to the assembly house keeps quite a few people away.

On the way there I had a useful conversation with the man who came to pick me up about religious services in the home. He told me that he and his family practice God's word each day, and while he used to pray from a book, he now is occasionally praying on his knees in the morning and evening. However, after he started with this practice, his wife said that, unless she was reading the morning and evening blessing from a book, it was not right. Eventually she followed him and is now doing it the way he does, that is, she not only prays from the book, but in her own words. To do this, God had blessed on them the sermon of our first dear colleague, who told them that the printed prayers do not always fit their special circumstances and that they should therefore learn to talk to our dear Lord about their troubles in their own words, etc. It gives us reason for good hope if people start by themselves to bend their knees before God in their prayers and secrets. It takes some people a long time before they reach that stage. Still, God is pleased by a prayer from the book, if it is done with comprehension and faith.

At the end of last month and at the beginning of this month we again had very much reason to praise our dear God for the kindness He has bestowed upon us. We received another written re-

port from Halle; and it pleases me particularly and encourages
me to follow the author's example of describing in detail and in
very Christian words the many good deeds that God showed his
church, his servants, and his work last year and awakened him
and the readers for praising our Lord. We find this special report on God's kindness under and after manifold tribulations so
welcome and edifying.

I trust that our Fathers and friends will not consider it unpleasant and superfluous for me to describe again at the start of
this month (as I have always done) some spiritual and physical
benefactions (including God's trials and help) to the glory and
praise of our almighty and kind giver. I saw it again in the esteemed Pastor Mueller's blessed letter from Constappel[19] to me
that Christian friends who are reading our news participate in
our good Ebenezer, rejoice with us in God's kindness, praise with
us the Lord's name, and pray for us. May He bless them!

First, our good Lord has given us in these two chests from
Halle such a great blessing of very useful books for our ministers
and our listeners that, while unpacking them, we could neither
wonder, rejoice nor humble ourselves enough in light of our un-
worthiness and the ingratitude of some listeners. Much of it was
gifts, and other things were debited to my account because I had
specifically asked for them.

An unknown, pious and noble benefactress sent me through
Pastor Mueller the precious book of the wise and pious Goodwin, and for our congregation some volumes of *True Christianity*
printed in Halle as a new edition of six books. In addition we
received some selected verses of encouragement, from which I
and my dear listeners are planning to benefit at the first assembly. Doctor Baumgarten,[20] my former upright and blessed benefactor, gave me the valued and very useful gift of the first part of
his explanation of the Evangelical texts; maybe he will also think
of me with regard to the second part.

The blessed institutions of the orphanage in Halle sent us
many Bibles in twelvemo and octavo copies, many excerpts from
Freylinghausen's songbook in twelmo and octavo copies, many
new treasures, news about the dear missionaries in East India
and God's work in Pennsylvania. Not to speak of other books.
God's omnipotence and kindness were so strong that not a single

book was damaged, although one box was forcibly broken into (presumably in the customs house in London). If one could add up the total cost of the many books the bookstore of the Halle orphanage has sent us, it would come to a very large sum of money. Our gracious God, in His providence, has always seen to it that we did not have to worry about paying for them. For this very great kindness we praise Him wholeheartedly; by doing so, He is building and expanding His Kingdom among us! The fact that we have the same books in our churches and schools stimulates edification greatly.

Secondly, in addition to this gift of books there was the large supply of selected well-prepared simples and medications for Mr. Thilo, Mr. Mayer, and our homes that cost a great deal of money. Many of them are gifts, and our doctor will take care that the rest will be paid for. May He give us the wisdom to arrange it in such a way that they benefit the poor members of our congregation! At that occasion, we also heard that dear Doctor and Professor Junker, Inspector Grischow, and Mr. Schulenburg, whom we greatly appreciate as friends of Ebenezer, are still alive. May He keep them for some more years for the benefit of His work!

Thirdly, God has strengthened us three ministers sufficiently so that we were able to receive the books and medicines and dispose of them this morning, as necessary. Mr. Rabenhorst had to get used to this country and its climate through a somewhat lingering fever, and God has started to help him get back on his feet. His wife has expressed the same hope. My dear colleague Lemke was also sick last week and a fever overcame me yesterday afternoon in church; and our dear Lord, who holds everything in His hands, has helped us both. Although my wife is still in poor health and, especially at night, has often very severe symptoms, our dear God has provided advice and means to relieve, if not cure, her illness through dear Doctor and Professor Junker and the arrival of strong medicines.

Fourthly, because our corn, beans and rice did not turn out too well last year, many poor people in other places suffered from a lack of food. To our people, our dear God has always, and sometimes miraculously, given their small piece of bread; and last month he let them see the beginning of their crop of

European farm products, such as wheat, rye and barley. The
barley and rye showed very good results, but wheat was once
again damaged by rust, and that made the grains in most plantations smaller than rye grains. We know from long experience
that this climate is not for wheat and spelt.

Fifthly, our mills are in good working condition, and the fact
that the sawmill has had enough water for cutting wood has
been a big help in repaying some of the debts we incurred when
we had to construct new, very useful gear, which can be raised
and lowered, and to repair our rotting dam, and in paying interest on the borrowed money. These mills are a very great benefit
to our community, without which it would look bad for us. It is
also a great benefaction that God has protected our best carpenter and sawmiller from an accident that was more serious than
the one he actually had. While loading a pistol, the gun went off
and hit his face, injuring his entire face and both eyes in such a
way that we thought he would lose at least one eye, if not both.
However, he is beginning to again use them both. His skills have
made him almost indispensable to us.

Sixthly, most of our dear listeners remain honest lovers of
God's word and the Holy Sacrament and entrust themselves to
the gracious effects of the Holy Ghost. Nevertheless, our faithful
God applies many other means and disciplinary measures to
lead them increasingly away from the external and internal con-
formity to the world and to the order of salvation and to Christ.
So far the members of our congregation have been in good
health, but now the fevers are setting in, and I think it is remarkable that our wondrous God, who makes everything well, has bestowed on us at this very time such a large supply of the best and
safest medicines to be used by Mr. Thilo, Mr. Mayer and our
homes. The requested medicines Mr. Thilo and Mr. Mayer have
received cost a total of more than 165 Reichsthaler. Oh, that God
see to it that, in His time, this large sum will be paid by Christian
patrons! We think it is fair that, in accordance with Dr. Francke's
proposals, this medicine will be dispensed in a way that the people in the congregation who are able to pay for them and those
who help to upset the good order made by the doctor and the
surgeon will pay not only for medical services but also for
medicines, while the poor, and among them particularly the

Salzburgers, will get part of the medication either for free or at half-price. This would allow us to order more medicine against payment, since we can no longer expect it to be sent to us at the expense of the Halle orphanage or be debited to our dear benefactors in that area. I am afraid we owe Dr. Francke a lot of money.

Seventh, it is a really great blessing that we three colleagues are linked by the bond of true brotherly love and seek to ease each other's work. May God keep us in His grace, and may He let us grow in it, so that this bond of love will grow ever stronger!

Eighth. The letters we received last month from dear Senior Urlsperger revealed to our pleasure that our loving God has started to provide for the support of our esteemed colleague Mr. Rabenhorst. To this end, a nice sum of money was received by our dearest Samuel, who never tires of interceding, and looking out, for Ebenezer in many other ways. Dear Lord, we do not deserve the mercy and faithfulness You have been showing for over 19 years towards Your servants and their listeners!

Ninth. From the letter I received from dear Court Chaplain Albinus last month and from the letter that just now arrived from Pastor Mueller at Constappel, I have seen with great joy new signs of God's providence for our congregation in that He continues to awaken Christian and kind hearts to take care of the physical misery which still prevails among us. Those who know our circumstances the way we do, who know how difficult it has been for us and which trials our dear Salzburgers had to endure, will not be surprised to hear that the congregation members and their ministers continue to need the help of European benefactors.

It is amazing that the Germans in famous, healthy and fertile Pennsylvania, where everything is said to be, and is indeed, much cheaper than here (because many things such as flour, beer, butter, cheese, apple cider, onions, etc., are exported for sale in Carolina and Georgia), continue to need so much assistance in terms of money and goods from Europe, and we are glad to read in the printed news from Pennsylvania that God has abundantly blessed the efforts of His true servants in London and Halle to remedy those needs, to establish the congregation and to provide for its ministers during the journey and in the country, as we now read in the very noteworthy reports in the fourth continuation of the printed reports from Pennsylvania[21] Just as they were unable to do much without help from Europe to establish and support God's kingdom, I must say the same, if not more, about us for well known reasons.

Although the suffering of the dear Salzburgers, which has been sufficiently reported elsewhere, affects me again now, I am refreshed and strengthened by thinking of their lamblike acceptance of all the misery and tribulations they encountered; and that has greatly impressed and edified me time after time. There were very honest souls among them, in whom one could clearly see Christ's true evangelical thinking. Most of them died with joy, according to God's wondrous counsel, like steadfast carriers of the cross, in the prime of life and with the strength of a man. Some are left behind with a sick body; also, most Salzburger orphans are now married and have started their own families: however, most of their children have preceded or followed them to eternal peace.

For good and well-founded reasons, the Lord Trustees passed a law in the King's name that in this frontier colony, close to the dangerous Spaniards, no Negroes may be imported into the country, especially since an almost unbelievably large number of such slaves are already living in South and North Carolina and also Virginia. This colony, they stated, was to be a free city for only poor Protestants, who wanted to eat their bread in the sweat of their brows, hence to work without the help of Negroes. The Salzburgers not only accepted this measure wholeheartedly because the country's safety was involved but also because they considered themselves bound by their conscience to obey the authorities and the human order for the Lord's sake. For a long time they could not get any white servants and, since they have been able to get some for the past four years (almost all were wild and irresponsible journeymen), they have suffered more grief and harm through them than help and relief, except for a very few who gradually came to assist their landladies and adapted to Christian order. Although these upright and industrious people had spent their strength in Old Ebenezer on infertile land, by working with their clumsy boat and sledges on dry and uneven soil, just as most of those in Ebenezer who had become exhausted from the mentioned boat and their work on unfamiliar, uncharted land and who, after getting their own plantations in about the fifth year, had used all of their remaining small fortune to build homes and stables and to till the land. To achieve this, they did not yet have plows, but only axes and hoes because the plantations were full of trees, bushes, trunks, and roots. They also lacked horses and plows, which they did not get until some years later. They would very much have liked to follow the Lord Trustees' good intention to settle this frontier colony with white people only, without Negroes, and to prove, through their example, that such a measure could ensure the safety and welfare of the land. Hence, they used all their strength to equip their plantations well, so that they might be able, through God's grace, to serve other newcomers with food, beef, and pork, just as the Lord Trustees had helped them.

The country is very hot, and the crops must be planted during the hottest period. Since they had no man-servants or maid-servants, or else the servants either fell sick or ran away at a time when they were most needed, all men, women and children had to use the little strength they had to cultivate the fields. If they turn out well, the field crops here are cheap, owing to the many Negroes in neighboring Carolina; on the other hand, goods brought here from England, the West Indies, and the northern colonies are very expensive. Thus our workers could not live on farming alone, but from the very beginning, we ministers gave them the opportunity to earn some money for their clothing and other necessities in Ebenezer so that they could augment their income from farming and cattle raising.

Our almighty and merciful God has given us through the kind hearts and hands of our dearest known and unknown European benefactors many alms, which we have used to build and maintain the three flour mills, the two sawmills and the rice, stamping, and peeling mill; and they recently made it possible for us to repair them. Also, such European benefactions were used to build our parsonages and what belongs to them, the two churches and the school, the former orphanage with all its equipment, the spacious house where Mr. Mayer now lives and where his store is, and many other things. This has provided our

listeners with an opportunity to earn some money without forcing them to neglect the church and their households.

With regard to food, they are also greatly hampered by the
fact that they have not found much good land in New Ebenezer
either. Therefore they had to improve the remaining land by
fertilization, which requires much work and produces little benefit on this kind of land, especially since wheat does not grow
well there. Because they left their fatherland for God's word,
they were satisfied with the little good land in our Ebenezer area
and with being close to church and school, rather than being
scattered for the sake of their stomachs.

I can say in all honesty that Christ's admonition, "Seek ye first
the kingdom of God, and His righteousness,"[22] has been their
maxim and rule of life. Hence I have no doubt that He will also
fulfill His promise to these worn-out Salzburgers who live on
bad land: "and all things," namely food and clothing, "will be
added unto you." Although there is good fertile and well-
situated land on the island on the Mill River, it is sometimes
flooded at a crucial time and would require much work during
the day and much watching at night because of the many bears,
wild cats,[23] squirrels and other pests that damage field crops,
and they have no strength to do that without Negroes.

I could list many more reasons why our dear inhabitants had
to live in such bad physical conditions, but I am concerned that I
might cause our readers to worry. However, this may be enough
to convince our benefactors and friends not only that the alms
they have sent us in the past have been put to good use, but also
that they still have an opportunity now to give benefactions and
to show compassion to our congregation. If God made it possible
for us to help the weakest among the Salzburgers to get Negroes,
God's blessing would soon help them. However, without assistance from Europe our congregation will be less able to exist
than a community in Pennsylvania. Therefore all past benefactions would have been in vain.

On Monday after Holy Trinity (June 18th), Captain Krauss
traveled in God's name from Ebenezer to Savannah. He was
planning to take our big boat to Charleston, and from there go
directly to London or, if there was no opportunity, via Pennsyl-

vania. He stayed at my house as our esteemed and dear friend and enjoyed our bad hospitality. He has grown fond of our only young son Gotthilf Israel; and, since he knew that we were planning to send him to the Latin school of the orphanage in Halle, he graciously offered to take him along to London and to introduce him, with God's help, to dear Court Chaplain Ziegenhagen. We viewed this offer as a sign of God's caring; and, after thinking some more about God's good and merciful will, we decided to entrust the boy, who is very anxious to study and to go to Halle, to the care and guidance of this experienced and prudent friend as far as London.

We prayed for him and prepared him with many thousands of good wishes and prayers by parents, ministers and inhabitants for the long and dangerous voyage, in fact for his entire future life. On the 19th, at night—the moon was shining and the weather was pleasant, the captain left with him with my farewell prayer and best wishes. Since then, my heart feels very light and content because this boy, who is devoted to God and His church, is in God's hands and in good company, including such dear men as my esteemed Fathers and proven friends, and he will be in such good institutions that, with God's grace, he will be well taken care of and find ample opportunity to achieve the purpose of why he was sent there. He is carrying with him some letters from me to our most reverend Fathers and my esteemed benefactors and old friends, in which I have taken the liberty of commending this young and somewhat naive boy to their love, favorable attention, and prayers, which will not be without benefit. The captain has the benefit of not being forgotten in our public and private prayers since he is responsible for, and guides, this boy who is very dear to us all. On the evening of the 21st I came home feeling somewhat ill. But soon God gave me new strength. May He continue to help us through Jesus Christ, Amen!

Our wondrous God has visited the usual fever on many of our old and new inhabitants at this time of the year.[24] We are making every effort to emphasize to our dear listeners God's fatherly intention which we do not understand by ourselves or not only from reason, but primarily on the basis of testimonies and examples cited in the Holy Scripture, such as the 73rd Psalm. We visit them frequently, talk with them diligently about God's word and pray with them, which our merciful God rewards with much blessing. It would go too far to talk here about the pious talks of our Christian and God-loving patients, since we have sometimes done in diaries in past years.

My two esteemed colleagues will also write something for our Reverend Fathers about their official duties, so that it no longer looks as if I am the only one who takes care of the congregation. I then can be so much briefer in my diaries and comment on many other things that are part of this century's history and of the kingdom of nature. Perhaps God will also give me the time and opportunity to collect some natural and other things in this country our European friends may want to hear about and to add my written comments, as I have been asked to do several times.

In Savannah I found a letter from a dear friend in Charleston, and it was only three days old. He had heard that wine was not only very expensive, but also almost unavailable in our colony. So he sent a barrel of good Madeira wine for sale in the community, and it and the letter got here very fast and without difficulties. Like our agricultural crops, the grape harvest in Madeira was a failure last fall, and that made the wine expensive and rare. The pipe costs 20 pounds Sterling and holds 100 gallons, or 400 English quarts, and that is an acceptable price at the present time. Transporting such a barrel of wine from Charleston to Savannah, just like transporting a barrel of rum and syrup of the same size, costs 10 shillings Sterling. My friend reported that some hostile Indians in Carolina had started new unrest, but that it had soon been squelched.

An acquaintance of mine in Savannah gave me a West Indian cashew nut that grows on a medium-sized tree, looks like a small kidney or large thick horse-bean and has a sweet healthy pit, but a poisonous juice between the pit and the thin little membrane underneath the thick skin. Some people who want new and smooth skin rub the skin of the cashew nut over their face and hands and then their skin peels off.

A woman showed me in her garden some local saffron, which does here very well and grows in abundance. She cut off a large quantity of it and boiled some of it. She then used the water to pour at frequent intervals on the remaining pressed saffron, hoping to get good saffron, since she was worried that she did not quite know the right way of preparing it. It still had a faint smell, although it had the beautiful color of European saffron. It may be possible that good saffron grows both here and in Austria, provided the proper seeds are planted. The seeds here look almost like small sunflower seeds.

Captain Kraus went ashore on President Dr. Graham's[25] land to learn about indigo plants. He had told his Negroes to plant the seed on a four-acre field and now the dark-green indigo plants are growing beautifully. He said that they are so high that they are close to blooming, and this is exactly the time when they must be cut and put into vats especially built for that purpose so that the indigo can develop. Mr. Krauss showed a drawing of the vats, which any carpenter can easily put together from heavy boards. All that is needed for the production of indigo are two vats, two sticks for stirring and a bag; and that will create easy and yet profitable work for the poor.

Planting indigo plants does not require any more work than planting Indian corn, but is more profitable. No barn or house is needed for storing the indigo, and it does not cost much to bring it to market because one barrel takes several hundredweights and one man can transport eight hundredweights in one of the local small boats. This spring I did not only buy, but also planted very good indigo seeds in order to get sufficient seeds from them for next year. However, I am surprised that they do not want to germinate, whereas Doctor Graham's indigo plants from the same seeds did so well. I am worried that we made a mistake when we planted them.

It will be hard to get our inhabitants to plant indigo, unless somebody from our community sets an example and shows them all the benefits, the same way we did with our silk production. Also, most inhabitants do not have good land and the island in the mill river is not a good place either for planting indigo. It lacks high, good corn land. In the middle of this month Doctor Graham planted local wild indigo as an experiment, hoping that sufficient time was left for it to ripen. The wild kind has the advantage of growing for three or more consecutive years from the same root, i.e., unlike the cultivated indigo there is no need for annual sowing. Its color is even better than that of the cultivated kind, but not much. The seeds are often gathered from the wild indigo plants which, in good pine woods, grow two feet tall and one-and-a-half feet wide at the top and look quite nice like small trees. I have again sent some samples of the wild and cultivated indigo seeds to Europe and added for some benefactors some other seeds that are locally common here, but unknown in Europe.

The 25th of June. We heard from Augusta and Savannah Town that their wheat crop was just as bad as ours here. The inhabitants set fire to their wheat fields, burning them down in order to plant Indian corn. The most recent good wheat crop last fall encouraged the inhabitants to plant wheat on very large fields, and that was a very big mistake on their part, as it was for us and the inhabitants of Purysburg. We will probably no longer grow this type of grain because planting it in this climate here is so uncertain. The prospects for rye are better, and rye bears rich yields.

It has been reported that the Indians up there are once again very restive, and the governor of Carolina has dispatched troops to deal with them. They like to start fights and trouble about the time the fruits on the trees, Indian corn, and melons are ripening. May our merciful God keep our peace! The Indians have retained certain areas of land for themselves, and General Oglethorpe and the Lord Trustees have protected these areas as Indian property so that they do not need to go to war. A short time ago the Indian land was surveyed, in large areas, for the country's most distinguished people.

The 26th of June. Because our dear colleague, Mr. Rabenhorst, is well again, thank God, I told him and Mr. Lemke what I had heard from the President and another knowledgeable member of the Council about the plantation that is to be established to support the third minister. 1) In this country there is no better and more advantageous way of investing capital in a safe and beneficial way than buying a number of Negroes and setting up a plantation under the supervision and management of an experienced and reliable man. 2) I should not give my glebe land to such a plantation because of my successors, because the Society would then stop paying the salary (as it happened in other old English colonies, including recently in South Carolina).

To my knowledge, all English ministers in the American colonies do not only get their 300-acre glebe plantations and are exempt from any levies, but also have large, well-equipped plantations for their own families and hence can easily do without salaries and other help from England. 3) I should be permitted to give my present glebe land in Goshen to the plantation planned for the third preacher and to have an additional 200 acres added to it, but I would have to accept for myself as a regular minister and for my successors 300 acres as glebe land in another place I like.

I like this proposal very well, and we are now looking for good land up the Savannah River either for use as glebe land or possibly for the plantation to support the third Ebenezer minister. Then the glebe land in Goshen would remain as it now is. But I believe that the Goshen glebe land and the adjoining district would be the best choice for a profitable plantation for the third minister, especially since about 14 acres there are ready to be plowed; they are well fenced in and already have some dwellings on them. Although it is not situated directly on the river, but about 2 English miles from Abercorn, a straight path leads to the Savannah River; and the land is very fertile and suitable for cattle raising.

If the highly praiseworthy Society were indeed to discontinue paying all our salaries[26] (About 18 years ago in Old Ebenezer I saw something printed to the effect that the Society would only pay the salaries until the Salzburgers were able to support their own ministers), the intended establishment of the plantation would be very necessary as an easy way of supporting not only one, but gradually more and more ministers without burdening the congregation, especially since it has been growing with God's blessing. We already know a reliable, hard-working and experienced Salzburger, Christian Riedelsperger, who could supervise and manage the plantation; and, if he should leave in the future, our dear Lord would give us another one like him. However, the third minister would have to have overall supervision over the plantation and, in a sense, be its manager, whom we two other ministers would support in whatever way we can.

It now is up to us to give this important matter some more thought and wholeheartedly pray to God that He advise us as it pleases Him and that His good spirit lead us on an even path! As it was my duty I have reported to the best of my knowledge in my earlier special diary on related matters and on how much money would be needed to set up such a plantation and what the annual income could be.

The 27th of June. Today Mr. Lemke conducted the weekly sermon on the Blue Bluff for Mr. Rabenhorst, who is still weak. Afterwards he had the opportunity to look at the land around the outer plantations of the Blue Bluff on the Savannah river. I then talked to Peter Schubdrein, who, together with his brothers and brothers-in-law, selected adjoining plantations in the upper part of the so-called Blue Bluff. In one district we got such a favorable report on a large plantation that I am quite inclined to take the glebe land there and exchange the one in Goshen for it to be used for the plantation planned for the third Ebenezer preacher's plantation.

If these areas were settled with some Negroes for the benefit of the Ebenezer minister and his congregation and if they were planted with rice and indigo, we soon would have, with God's blessing, the long-sought trade and hence better support, especially if our highly respected benefactor would move to settle on his plantation. We would be pleased if our dearest Senior Urlsperger's collection for the support of the third Ebenezer minister would also improve food conditions in the congregation!

This afternoon I christened with joy and edification a newborn Negro girl, parented by the late Mr. Kraft's Negro man and Mr. Leimberger's Negro woman. The black parents are still heathens but wish their child to be baptized and brought up as a Christian. The Negro father came to church, neatly clothed, knelt with us in prayer, and eagerly followed the baptism of his child. At the master's request she was named Catharina. I reported earlier that the master and his wife who own the mother of a new-born Negro child act as godparents and publicly promise at the ceremony before God and on their conscience to make all possible efforts to educate such a baptized heathen child in accepting Christ and to practice true piety, just as if it were their own child.

If the almighty, all-knowing and ever-gracious God saw to it that a plantation for the support of the third Ebenezer minister were established and that the glebe land were occupied to improve the living conditions of my dear and true colleague, Mr. Lemke, then we could concentrate on spreading Christ's kingdom among the adults; and, failing to do so, among the children born here.[27] We want them to have the pleasure of getting married because this will keep them from running off and prevent annoying excesses.

Women must work in the fields as much as men. As for their reproduction, the Negro situation is like that of white people: some have many, some have few and some have no children. Some Negro women, to spite their masters, know how to prevent a pregnancy, and they know other harmful tricks which the prince of evil taught them through his wretched tools, possibly even through dastardly and unscrupulous Christians.

The 28th of June. In my private Bible reading today I was particularly impressed and I derived special comfort from the words of Jesus Christ in Saint Matthew 10: "The very hairs of your head are all numbered," likewise that the sparrows are also under God's providence and His protective and beneficial kindness, with the comforting phrase: "Ye are of more value than many sparrows."[28] I am using this and other edifying verses with our patients, of whom we now have very many; and one has to keep reminding them to look at their illnesses as befits a Christian who believes in God's providence and considers the Holy Scripture to be God's word, which serves us as model and example of how our wisest, best, almighty, and fairest God will rule in His church to the end of the world. This brought me back to the careful and edifying words of an anonymous author in Memmingen that had been printed on two sheets of paper, *Contemplation of God's Providence for Mankind*," that deserve frequent reading by all Christians.[29] God be praised because, although He punishes us, He also comforts us abundantly through Christ, so that we can say: "We know that for those who love God all things will be for the best."[30]

JULY

Yesterday our dear God visited me with a fever which kept me from delivering the morning sermon. But through God's kindness I regained enough of my strength to enable me to help Mr. Lemke administer Holy Communion and also to communicate with the congregation. This time there were only 70 people at the Lord's table; the rest could not come because of the fevers currently afflicting our congregation. Hearty praise be to God for the mercy He has shown us in many ways on this first day of the week and of this new month. We could tell one another: "It is due to the Lord's goodness that we are not down; His mercy knows no limits; it is new every morning, and thy faithfulness is great." To comfort ourselves and reinforce our faith during the present tribulations, we read in our very popular *Little Treasure Chest*[1] under today's date: "He who has pity on you, will guide you," which was my and my late colleague's /Gronau's/ verse of comfort during our voyage from Halle to Rotterdam and from there to Ebenezer. Hence it could be called Ebenezer: This is where our merciful God led us,[2] although under the cross and through much misery, like all our fathers and brothers.

I recently heard to my very great surprise what my dear colleague Lemke said about one of our misbehaving listeners, as if he resented the ministers' love for their congregation when they make every effort to ease the life of the poor members of their congregation by setting up good external rules and by giving material and providing many other kindnesses. Not a single person who knows us can honestly accuse us of neglecting even the tiniest part of our responsibilities towards our listeners; and we all know that in our sermons and prayer meetings we have cordially offered time and again to help them and their children even more with our work as ministers than in the past, if only they give us an opportunity to do so. Every Sunday and holiday we preach two sermons and one repetition or prayer hour in town. Every two weeks, and sometimes even more often, they also hear two sermons on Sundays on the plantations. In town we hold prayer sessions every evening after work and dinner, and on the plantations we conduct weekly sermons twice a week. And that is a time most inconvenient to us ministers, but most convenient to our listeners because it does not keep them away from their work for a long time.

School is held every day not only in town, but also on the plantations in the schoolhouse that was built for that purpose and to which nobody contributed anything, and we have to pay the schoolmaster's salary. The children pay very little money for their education. Each child is expected to pay 6 pence a quarter; but, if they do not, the parents are not admonished. Children of poor parents even get their books free; not to speak of those children who do well in school and are awarded some kind of gift once in a while. We baptize their children, and we marry engaged couples in both churches, wherever is most convenient for them and their relatives and friends.

We do the same in the case of burials. At each funeral we deliver an edifying sermon, and we tell them from God's word how to lead a Christian life and die in peace. They ought to pay some money for baptism and marriage ceremonies to support the church and school, but not everybody does so. In the case of funerals it is entirely up to them, and so we do not get anything for them. Whenever some contribution is made for baptizing children and for marriages, it almost always is less than a shilling, which is very little money in this country.

Some time ago the ministers and leaders of the congregation thought it might be a good idea to put out the collection plates at both church doors during Holy Communion. Then those who want to, can deposit something *ad pias causas*.[3] Apart from that, I do not know what the members of the congregation are required to contribute to support their churches and schools and cover the many expenses the congregation incurs each year. The only other thing they are required to do is for every father of a family to cut some trees in the woods for his ministers one day a year, which we ourselves must then cart away. Otherwise, whenever they do any work for us, we pay them in cash, and we do so willingly.

Not too long ago some well-disposed people cleared trees and bushes from a piece of land for Mr. Rabenhorst, and I paid for the additional cost of burning them and for planting. However, since I relied on the people and did not check personally whether they had done the planting in the right way, whether all corn had germinated or whether the ravens had picked out the seeds, nothing came of it; and it would have been better had the forest been left there. Mills, churches, schools, bridges, and many other things would go to ruin unless we ministers tried in every way possible to prevent such evil. Many a person is much too uninterested in those things and indifferent, depending on their temperaments, and other superiors are not taken seriously so that we ourselves have to find ways to prevent damage and support a good endeavor.

For some time we have had in our employ the honest, experienced, and hard-working Hans Flerl, who takes care of the milling business and related management matters; and he saves us a lot of worries about the mills and other related things. Therefore, many people are envious of him; and we are also coming under attack. Flerl has sole responsibility for the boards, while Mr. Lemke does his bookkeeping and puts it into English. Once in a while we have to make a trip to Savannah at the request of the President and the Council and, without being asked to do so, to write many letters to addressees nearby or far away; and we have to put up with strangers asking favors of us. These are probably all the things we do out of love for our congregation. However, they do not keep us from meeting our proper responsibilities.

We also pay frequent visits to the members of our congregation; we bless their homes with God's word and prayer, prepare them for Holy Communion, and often invite them to our homes to talk to them from God's word about their spiritual state. We have offered to resume the former blessed singing hours and private catechism exercises with young people who have missed them, if only they would take a little time from their physical work and take care of their souls, Christianity, and salvation.

Shortly before my current fever I quizzed the children and some other young people in my weekly sermon about some

Christian teachings from God's word, and then I told the entire community that they would now have a chance to hear them again because their children and young people and even many of the older population were in great need of instruction from God's word and the catechism. At the same time I again offered to join them on their plantations and to devote my last years in office to the school and private instruction, provided God gives me the means to build a small house on the mill land. I said that, in view of their unwillingness and inability to come to town for instruction, I would be glad to make it easier for them by my moving there.

It is my greatest joy to carry out my responsibilities faithfully, and my two loyal and hard-working colleagues support me in this. This is where the office affairs in our Ebenezer congregation currently stand. However, when we are wrongfully accused, we pray: "Father, forgive them for they know not what they do."[4] Nevertheless, despite all of this, we are convinced that there are, thank God, very few nasty people in our community who pass judgment on us and whose judgment tends to be very different from ours, especially since those who have come to recognize the truth through our gospel teachings know and also acknowledge that it would be difficult for the congregation to exist unless their ministers also took care of the worldly things that affect their continued existence and the improvement of their material well-being as well as the good order of our community. How we were overrun in the aftermath of the most recent crop failure with requests to permit the purchase of a sufficient quantity of corn, as we did!

So far we have discussed with knowledgeable members of the community and experienced men from out-of-town what would be the best and most advantageous way of investing some capital in order to ensure the support of the third minister. Because everybody believed that the best way would be to build a plantation with Negroes on a fertile and well-situated piece of land, they are now trying to find such land and we are making all possible efforts to find it; for this purpose, we will have to employ experienced people.

Should it please our dearest Fathers and benefactors to use all

offerings for the intended purpose here, then this very important matter, which affects not only the current ministers and
their listeners but also our future, could not be entrusted to the
supervisor and manager of such a plantation. Instead, one of the
ministers would have to have the overall responsibility, similarly
to the many righteous preachers in Germany who make their
living from the fruits of their field and garden plants and must
keep a watchful eye on the servants, even entire households.

I almost wish one of us ministers would be asked to preach
only on Sundays, if he could do so easily and, if necessary, help
with the necessary official matters, e.g., if the other two colleagues are sick or die an untimely death. However, ordinarily
he should be free of them so that he could take care of the physical well-being of his congregation here and elsewhere and supervise the planned plantation. While he would have to travel
occasionally, he could serve people elsewhere by preaching to
them and in other ways and be something of *una fidelia duos deal-
bare parietes*.[5] He would hire himself a skilful and faithful worker
or servant who would make everything very easy for him.

The people who started to settle on the Blue Bluff after their
arrival with the two first Swabian transports would very much
like us to build them a bridge across the Ebenezer river and a
mill on the land set aside for that purpose and to help them otherwise with money and food. However, in view of the fact that we
already advanced them a sizeable sum of money for a variety of
foodstuffs and cattle (much to the frustration and displeasure of
the old inhabitants), most of which we are going to lose, we can
not agree to their demands for the construction of a bridge or
mill or for any other material things. They do not understand
how to farm and manage and are not interested in working with
timber, so that they are becoming poor.

We have offered some money for the construction of the
bridge (we made a good start at the year end), provided they all
would work on it until it was completed. But most of them do not
like such a requirement. Because there is no bridge, we cannot
serve these people with our office as much as we would like to.
Every Wednesday we deliver a sermon for them on the Blue
Bluff. For that occasion they send a small boat, rowed by only

one man, to get one of us up there. Part of the transportation fee
we have to pay ourselves. Such boats have a tendency to turn
over.

We had very heavy rainfalls five days in a row, and the Savannah River and other[6] small rivers have risen very high. Yesterday
for the first time, we again had dry weather and sunshine, and
we praise God for it. A year ago God visited the land with a
damaging drought; and, if He would do it again this time by way
of damaging wet weather, we would have to say: "Lord, thou art
righteous, and thy judgments are righteous." This is what it says
in Psalm 103: "He hath not dealt with us after our sins; nor rewarded us according to our iniquities."[7] May He mercifully see
to it that the current hard trials pass soon: there is hardly a house
in which not one or several people are ill with fever. Not only the
new, but also the old colonists are suffering from fever. Although many of them are very poor, we do not have anything to
help them with because we ourselves do not have it. May God
have mercy on our misery!

A Swiss man from Augusta, who trades with the Indians as far
west as to the borders of Mississippi, visited me and wanted my
advice in a legal matter he has to deal with in Savannah this
weekend, but I politely declined. He described the Mississippi
River and the land bordering on it a few hundred miles from the
ocean in such exuberant terms as if there is nothing like it in the
world. Towards the sea, it is supposed to be poor and bad as in
other English colonies. However, that area is being settled first
for security reasons, as it also happened in Georgia and Carolina. The river and the region, which is considered very fertile,
is about 900 English miles, or 300 hours, west of Augusta; and it
is inhabited by the strong nation of the Choctaws, who side with
the French because the English are too far away from them.
They plant Indian corn and all kinds of beans and have no meat
except buffalo and deer, of which the woods are full, so that
there is no need for them to raise cows or pigs. These French
Indians are constantly engaged in bloody wars with the English.

In addition there are the Nottowegs who, though they live in
the direction of Canada, have the gall to come down as far as
Carolina and Georgia in their thirst for murder and robbery.
Not too long ago one of the Nottowegs was shot near Augusta,

and the other was cruelly tortured to death. Sixteen families from Virginia, who had settled in the northern part of Mississippi, were recently killed by the French Indians, but the governor of Virginia will now seek revenge for these murders. The Indian land some 100 miles from Augusta is not only reported to be much more fertile, but also much healthier than ours down here, and many Indians reach the age of 100. It is not supposed to be so hot there, and the water is very healthy.

A prominent benefactor recently sent us an excerpt from a Hamburg magazine in which a Mississippi colonist claims that their wheat grows as well as in France. The only thing is that one has to try to prevent the harmful rust, which tends to dry up the stalk before the wheat is ripe, by sowing the seeds on not-too-fertile land between the rye. Here, no wheat grows on fertile, even less on poor soil unless it is well fertilized by the river or our cattle. It does not grow well underneath rye because rye, if sown together with wheat, usually overgrows the wheat, suffocating it in the process. Also, rye matures earlier than wheat. I will pass this on to our farmers.

A dear friend from Savannah wrote me on the 21st of this month that never in his 16 years in this country has he seen more sick people in his area than this summer. They are suffering from fever and dysentery. On us, God is visiting fever. Our dear brethren in Pennsylvania, including Messrs. Muehlenberg, Brunnholz, Handschuh,[8] and others, are carrying a heavy cross.

The 8th of July[9] On this third Sunday after Holy Trinity our dear Mr. Rabenhorst substituted for me in the Jerusalem Church and preached my sermon, while conducting his own catechism session as well. Mr. Lemke did both at the Zion Church. Mr. Rabenhorst has just recovered at the right time from his long illness, since our dear Lord has not yet made me well enough to take care of my official duties. May He be praised for His kindness in making me feel well again! It has been a long time since we held our popular and useful hymn-singing sessions; and that shows its adverse effects in our public meeting, as I noticed again today. We discontinued the sessions partly because of too much work at home and physical weakness among our women, and partly because of my troubles (especially some weakness in my chest).

I recently heard that several of our wealthy inhabitants have collected some money which they want to give to Captain Krauss to take along and purchase a small organ for the Jerusalem Church. However, he reportedly promised to get one without their contributions. We were supposed to get one here several years ago, and I am glad this did not materialize. Not only does such an instrument need an organist who knows how to play the new songs in Freylinghausen's songbook in an uplifting way, but it will also require constant repair. We have neither. Even if we found such a skilled man, we would have to pay him for his services, and we have no money for this. I wish and pray in my humble prayer that our gracious God will give us enough money to pay the schoolmaster on the plantations a salary and help our widows, orphans, sick and other poor people.

The 4th of July. Because my dear colleague, Pastor Boltzius, is well again, I have decided to keep a diary of my own and to enter in it the major aspects of my official duties and anything else I consider noteworthy. May God guide and lead me through His Holy Spirit so that my undertaking and weak attempts will glorify His name!

The 7th of July. Today I visited some sick people in town and enjoyed it greatly because I heard from them that their illness has not remained without blessing. A certain person, in particular, seemed to be greatly moved. She could not understand why God has been treating her and her husband so well: He only imposed slight punishment on them, although He made them both sick at the same time, and He directed good people to them during their illness, who took good care of them so that they did not want for anything.

The 8th of July. This Sunday our gracious God edified us in the Zion Church with the unique verse in 1 Timothy 1:15: "This is a faithful saying; and worthy of all acceptation, etc."[10] These words were a real balm to me, which reinvigorated my heart; and I hope they did the same for other people. A rather large number of listeners came in the morning and afternoon, and that encouraged and pleased me because I wanted to tell them with all my heart all the good things in this gospel. In the afternoon, we catechized on the prescribed Sunday gospel Luke 15:1.

The 10th of July. Since yesterday I have been too weak to accomplish much, and I am particularly saddened that I was unable to visit our present patients, because they not only like our comforting words but had specifically asked for them. I visited some of them yesterday morning, but I returned home feeling sick. Hence I praise God's kindness in letting Mr. Rabenhorst be strong enough again to perform the necessary official duties. This morning he conducted the weekly sermon on the plantations, and in the afternoon he delivered a funeral speech in town. I hope God will see to it that he does not suffer any harm, because it is so hot now and he is still recovering.

At this time, not only here but also in other places, many of those who arrived last as well as the old inhabitants have come down with fever; and this may be partly due to the exceptionally rapid and frequent changes from rain to sunshine and from cool to warm air. When it does not actually rain, the sky is clouded, and then the sun breaks through—and they alternate all day long, causing a beastly heat. In between, the dark clouds bring cool air with them, which may either slow down any earlier perspiration or make it disappear completely. Under these circumstances one should dress with caution. Those who continue to perspire by moderately moving around, but then change their clothing and cover themselves with several pieces of clothing, fare best. No attention should be paid to the discomfort these clothes cause. It is also good to stay out of the sun as much as possible during the noon hours and to avoid fruit, including melons, which, as a result of the heavy rains, contain a lot of water and start going bad before they are fully ripe.

The 13th of July. After staying home for several days because I did not feel well, my health has—through God's goodness—improved so much that I could conduct the weekly sermon at the Zion Church. Last week some children had been unruly in school and hence got some scolding. I chose those admonitions not only because I believe the children would understand them but also because they would make them think and move them. Since the schoolmaster has not yet arrived, I met with them today. They not only behaved well but also delighted me by singing the song: *Seelenbraeutigam* . . . etc., which, to my great surprise, they started to sing on their own.

Our dear Pastor Boltzius has now been sick for three weeks and there is still no sign that he is feeling better, as I very much want him to, and we ask God in our public and private prayers to restore his strength soon.

The 15th of July. This Sunday our colleague Boltzius was still unable to preach, so the congregation heard God's word from Mr. Rabenhorst and myself. And we have to be grateful for God's help in this, because we both continue to be physically weak.

The 16th of July. A man I visited today in his home told me that he felt it was a blessing that God made him sick. He interpreted it as a sign from God that he needed such punishment. In good health, he had often neglected to think of God, but now He is awakening him; and that is the reason why he thanks Him for his illness. He is now beginning to get better.

The 17th of July. Our N.N. has many good intentions, but it seems that this is about all there is. He has also had the fever and is still weak from it. Apart from that he is poor, so that he has much trouble managing his household affairs. We have to feel much sorrier for this kind of people than for others: they are badly off in this world and, unless they go beyond the awakenings, they will find nothing better in eternity. Although we wish this man a better lot, he must be much more serious if he should end well.

Our hard-working and useful carpenter, J. Schubdrein, also fell sick suddenly last week. It looked pretty bad with him last night. He sent me several requests lest I forget to come and visit him. Hence, immediately after catechism hour, I went to him and found him in bed with high fever, but fully conscious, although that had been different during the night. He received me with great emotion, saying that God had good reason to punish him like this. So far he had not behaved the way he should have, and there were many things inside him which should be resolved, he added. I could only confirm what he said, and I added my view that he could be helped and that it was not God's wish to lose him. I explained to him that this is the reason why He made him aware of his sinful behavior and was eager to lay the foundation for him to lead an upright Christian life so that he would be even more useful in the future than he had been in the past. After talking about this and other matters, I concluded my conversation by praying in the presence of several members of his family.

Jos. Schubdrein fell sick while repairing our house. The wooden two-story house had only two rooms. The lower story was largely rotting and the whole house was about to collapse. But, because the upper part was still good, the lower section was torn down and the upper was lowered. Such houses may be all right in cold countries, but here they are very susceptible to rotting, and they shelter numerous insects, which the people consider a tremendous nuisance. Therefore building a new story underneath was inadvisable. About three years ago, when we needed more space, a living room and kitchen were added, but they had been infected so badly by the old structure that they collapsed while the change was being made. So we had to build a new small house, about the size of the former addition, at some distance from the old one so that both would have enough air and neither could harm the other. This structure, small and modest as it started out, was very expensive to build in this country because of our high wages. Although our dear Mr. Boltzius has seen to it that there is enough money to pay the workers, we now have to do without that money somewhere else, where it is equally badly needed. And because we did not have enough money, we had to incur several pounds of debt. "Cast thy burden upon the Lord, and he shall sustain thee."[11]

The 19th of July. Paul Mueller was very close to death, but God had pity on him and his family and made him recover. He very much wanted to see a minister, but circumstances here did not allow anybody to visit him. However, I saw him early in his illness. Today he told me what had happened to him and how God had so obviously helped him. He praised it as a great blessing that his wife, despite the many troubles she had by day and by night, had not fallen ill. I gave him some necessary admonitions, and then we awakened each other by praising God for His gracious help. Our carpenter, J. Schubdrein, is also feeling better; and one by one our patients are beginning to get well again. Praise be to God!

The 30th of July. Our kind God visited some new fever on me about a week ago, i.e., the 21st, on the eve of the fifth Sunday

after Trinity. Although I conducted the service in the Jerusalem
Church, it was difficult for me. At the beginning we heard the
beautiful verse from Psalm 37:4,5: "Delight thyself also in the
Lord, and He shall . . . " etc., which I liked so much that I almost
forgot the fever that had befallen me and continued preaching
for a while. When I came home, I immediately lay down, and
from then on I had a fever every day, which gave me the time
and opportunity to think about my own inner state and examine
it carefully. While I was doing that, I eventually came across
David's words: "But it is good for me to draw near God: I have
put my trust, etc."[12], which impressed me deeply in view of the
devotion of the holy scribe and other servants and children of
God, for whom he speaks; and that made me bow before God.
Although I have now been without fever for several days, I still
find myself weak and unable to work; and I will take it easy for
some more days until my health has improved.

Among the Swabian transport there was a man we considered
to be sensible—at least in the beginning. He thought that he was
also a good Christian. But this man has now demonstrated how
very blind he is. He claims that going hunting on Sunday is not a
sin and lists examples he saw in Germany. Moreover, he says, no
human being can live the way the Bible says; we must be saved
through grace. This is a concept of Christianity that is obscure
and confusing enough. And this is what poor people think who
know everything by themselves. Those who desecrate the Lord's
day by hunting, and hence annoy others, are behaving in such a
way that the threat will come true on them: "Woe unto the world
because of offenses."[13] How painful the wilful waste of precious
hours on Sundays will be for them! How unbearable for them
will be God's burning anger in the future, which He, as our supreme judge, has threatened to unleash on those who violate His
commandments! Once in a while somebody here tries to waste
his Sundays in this way, but as soon as it becomes known, he gets
his reward.

Whoever believes that nobody can live the way it says in the
Bible either does not understand or does not want to understand the Bible; he has never tried, not even made the slightest
beginning to live according to the Bible, and hence judges some-

thing he neither understands nor has ever experienced. May God open the eyes of all spiritually blind people!

Several setbacks have kept me from continuing this diary. But now our gracious God has helped me so much with my illness that I could travel to Goshen, preach God's words to the people there and administer Holy Communion. Before confession, I first delivered a short sermon to them about Psalms 32:1-2. That sermon awakened one man's conscience so much that, after I finished it and was about to begin confessions, he got up in public, asking me to permit him to make peace with another man and ask his forgiveness for having wronged him. He then asked whether he could now take Holy Communion. I was very happy to accommodate him. This was a sensitive man, but wrongdoings he had experienced had led him to say a few cursing words to a man he believed had slandered him, which he now realized was unjustified and which he wanted dismissed. I must say that, overall, I found the people somewhat confused this time, but with God's help I was able to straighten out many things. They very much needed the words in 1 John 4:20, which I had covered in my morning sermon: "If a man say (and oh, how many speak like that) I love God, and hateth his brother, he is a liar: for he that loveth not his brother whom he hath seen, how can he love God whom he hath not seen?"

AUGUST

The 13th of August.[1] Because of my physical weakness, I could not visit my congregation and therefore have very little to report here. My two dear colleagues also feel sick, but they attend to the most pressing official duties as best as they can. This is very comforting to me in view of my own present great inability, and the congregation should rightly recognize the great blessing the Lord has given them by sending them three ministers.

Among the latest Swabian transport there were a 70-year-old woman, Juliana Hagemayr, and her 32-year-old daughter, a spinster named Eyphrosine, who came to our community from Blaubaeuern. We took care of them to the best of our ability and they are acknowledging this humbly and gratefully. They have given us much joy because of their love for God's word, the ministers, and all Christian rules. The old mother started to help some people as a midwife. The daughter tried to earn a living by sewing, in which she was very adept, and the old upright mother helped her as much as she could. We found for these two dear people a place to live in the building where school is held, which they considered a dear blessing because, in their small room, they could listen to the catechist teachings of the children. During the trip over, they eagerly and beneficially used the office of our dearest colleague Mr. Rabenhorst and he recommended them to me greatly. They were very attached to each other and reminded me with their behavior of the edifying story of the old Naomi and Ruth. The mother had an important reason for coming to Ebenezer, and they then said about this virtuous and Christ-loving daughter: "Intreat me not to leave thee, or to return from following after thee: for whither thou goest, I will go; and where thou lodgest, I will lodge: thy people shall be my people, and thy God my God: Where thou diest, I will die, and there will I be buried, too."[2] And this is how it was with these two people who were so closely bound to each other in love. The daughter suffered from a long tubercular illness with very high fever and diarrhea, and the mother faithfully cared for her day and night. On July 9th, she was so emaciated that she took leave of this world in a blessed death. A few days earlier the mother had become sick, suddenly and seriously, had high fever and some kind of somnolence and died two days later in peace. Mr. Rabenhorst delivered the funeral sermon for both the daughter and the mother. I was very sorry that I could not visit them in their last hours because of my own illness. Otherwise I could have reported many uplifting things. Whenever I visited them in their solitude, I was greatly impressed by their great love of God's word, religious songs and devoted praying.

In a calendar Franklin had printed in Philadelphia there is an elaborate description of an infallible cure of the real, in this country so common, "stitches"[3] by way of a recently discovered Seneca rattlesnake root which is said to have helped Dr. John Tennent, the developer of this method, achieve many successful cures in Virginia. The plant often grows in the woods of Virginia, Maryland and Pennsylvania (without doubt also in Carolina and Georgia). The root has a light-yellow color and its texture and form look like the Ipecacuana, except that it is broader. Its leaves resemble green tea, and its stem is usually 6–12 feet high; it has white blossoms on top which, as long as they are in the bud, look similar to the rattles of a rattlesnake. This flower is one of the first flowers in the field. The stalks are branchless, but several stalks grow out of one root; yet sometimes there is one stalk per root. This root is now being sold in Charleston and we will send it to our friends.

The 16th of July.[4] We learned that in one of the Swabian transports there was a very disorderly family who caused much trouble. Several people came with these transports to our congregation and their behavior does not at all agree with the recommendations they brought along. Some, in my view, came to their judgment in America through their own fault or from the old to the so-called new world. There they were people who had not been converted, and they added to their sins during the trip to America on water and land. Contrary to what they claimed, their move to America had nothing to do with God's kingdom and serious preparation for their salvation in solitude, but to achieve with little work, if not a wealthy, then a more leisurely life. If God makes them succeed with this kind of thinking and such plans—and some of them are successful in acquiring material wealth—they tend to develop at this frightening time into usually very frightening people who abuse the freedom of this country to cause much trouble and harm for their children, giving the Germans an ever more stinking reputation. However, when they do poorly, they feel betrayed in their plan to make their fortune here, when they have eaten up their little money during the long journey or even arrive here in debt, they start selling the things they brought with them, have to work very hard on their new, completely overgrown land, must eat simple food without beer or wine, lie in poor huts, sometimes perform unnecessary work because they do not know any better or are stubborn, have neither milk nor lard and other things they must pay for with money, since they have no cattle during the first year because of their many other expenses—and one or two heads of cattle on uncultivated plantations do not yield much milk and lard. When they have to live this way or under other difficult conditions (which may be considered bearable compared with what the first Salzburgers had to endure), they usually show themselves for what they really are in their hearts. Instead of acknowledging and being prepared to pay in their present troubles or plagues for their sins, and changing their true thinking and lives through much preaching of God's word, they become hardened, have little regard for the ministry and the good opportunities for edification, use bad practices and injustices and become increasingly the subject of God's anger. Oh, how sorry we are for them!

The 16th of August. It has now been seven weeks since our wondrous God has visited such an illness on me, and I can neither preach nor perform some of my other official duties. I now seem to be gaining some more strength through the kindness of God, although I am not yet entirely over my illness. God be praised for this punishment, which gave my soul many good things that, through the mercy of the Holy Ghost, will also benefit the congregation in my remaining short life and office affairs. My two dear colleagues also have been sick with fever for several weeks, and therefore, on one Sunday, we had no public church service at all, and, on two Sundays, only in the morning, and that was the first time in these nineteen years our congregation had to go through such a test. Neither were we able to hold prayer sessions in town, the weekly sermon on the plantations nor the catechistic sessions in the town's school. School on the plantations had to be interrupted as well for lack of a good schoolmaster and for other reasons. This is how God can keep our congregation on a short leash and make His word dearer and rarer, regardless of whether we have three preachers and two schoolmasters. Oh, may we recognize in good time, and with a willingness to repent, what helps us attain peace! Many other members of our community have endured long and painful illnesses, but few have died of them. The whole country was punished this summer with fevers, red dysentery, and painful limbs; and now God imposes on us a new cattle and horse plague in both Carolina and Georgia. As a result of the excessive rain some months ago, the Savannah River has overflowed its banks and will cause much damage to our agricultural crops and cattle and horses in the wetlands on both sides of the river. It keeps raining almost every day. In our community, the agricultural crops continue to grow beautifully, and the flood will probably not do much damage, unless it lasts too long.

A pious widow suffered from a serious illness at her neck, but was encouraged by Christ's words—all things are possible for those who have faith—and used them to strengthen her faith in Him, which then was blessed to her early, quite remarkable recovery. Afterwards she experienced that it is true: we know that for those who love God all things serve for the best.

The 17th of August. If our good Lord begins to make our dearest colleague, Mr. Rabenhorst stronger, as He graciously has begun to do, we will administer this Ninth Sunday after Trinity the Holy Communion, which we had to postpone for several weeks. This morning he had to ride on horseback to Joseph Town behind Goshen in order to baptize a small child. The people in that area have asked us urgently to preach and administer Holy Communion to them. May God awaken in them a true hunger for the word!

The 19th of August. Although Mr. Rabenhorst suffered a relapse following his trip to Joseph Town, God graciously made him well enough to hold confession yesterday and to administer Holy Communion today to some of his listeners, including some from Goshen, in which our weak brother Lemke assisted him beyond his physical capability. In the afternoon, we held neither catechization nor the usual Sunday prayer hour. May God have mercy on us and give us ministers—including me who is unworthy—all our strength back! That is our sincere wish for the benefit of our work. While I was unable to attend our public church service because of my continuing physical weakness, our kind God saw to it that I could edify myself by praying with a small group of honest souls in my room in the early evening hours. Among them was Kegler's[6] eldest daughter, who was seriously sick for nine months and whose health God restored against all human expectations and to the great joy of her parents and other friends. The verse, "Blessed be the Lord, who daily loadeth us with benefits . . . " etc., applied to them and all of us. Although I noticed today that my new strength is coming back, it was a day of much sadness which affected my poor worn-out body. Oh, Lord, I deserved it. Have mercy on me!

Today I was able to ride to a pious family on the plantations, since I have not had a chance in recent days to visit that neighborhood. As I was riding down the road with a sad heart, a Salzburger called the little verse to me: "Entrust your ways to the Lord and trust Him, He will make it well."[7] And our merciful God then blessed it abundantly through the Holy Spirit on me and other people I visited, including the very ill Mr. Thilo. Under the cross, our hearts can well flow together, and I believe much spiritual benefit will come from this sickness.

The 24th of August. Throughout the so-called dogdays and earlier, we had rain and thunder, and at times the cloud bursts were so heavy and violent that they flooded rivers and low areas. God has restored my strength so much that, for the first time, I could ride to the mill on horseback, which is a round trip of eight English miles from my house. I had no idea that a wedding was celebrated in a fashion in our Christian inn near the mill. And my joy and that of the dear wedding party was all the greater since our meeting was such a surprise. We were happy in the Lord and praised His name with the beautiful words: "He doeth . us every kindness."[8] On my way back I was told that one of our pious school-children, who had given me much pleasure in the plantation school, had departed from this world, full of faith and willingly.

In the mill we have a fine, orderly servant of the kind we would like to have more than one of in this community. On him, God visited a very strange illness. After he had suffered from cold fever for a while, the fever went down, but then it developed into melancholy so that he was not in control of his senses and the healthy use of his mind. The hot and cold fevers this summer usually leave dangerous symptoms behind or are accompanied by them, as I and Mr. Lemke know. But, thank God, almost nobody has died of them!

Because we do not have enough loyal servants, our income from the mills is small, although they remain an indispensable blessing to the community. May God help us in His wisdom, kindness, and almightiness to get out of the debts we took on some time ago when we had to do major repairs at the mill and for other reasons!

The 3lst of August. This morning we joyfully dedicated our dear Rabenhorst's new house with the word of God, and with songs and prayers, for which he used the 117th Psalm. At the same time, we celebrated with joy and by giving praise to God the birthday of our dearest Samuel and father, Senior Urlsperger, who loves the entire Evangelical church and especially our Ebenezer, as he enters his 69th year on this last day of August. May our Triune God protect him and all our dear Fathers with His grace and truth in eternity: Hallelujah, Amen!

SEPTEMBER 1753

The 2nd of September. On this Eleventh Sunday after Trinity, our merciful Lord gave me, an unworthy man, sufficient strength to deliver to the entire congregation at the Jerusalem Church this morning the first public sermon after my serious nine-month illness. And I experienced once again what it says in Isaiah 40:29: "He giveth power to the faint, and to them that have no might He increaseth strength." And: "They that wait upon the Lord shall renew their strength." My dear colleagues and listeners faithfully prayed for me, an unworthy man, and they continued to do so, and that helped me: "He will fulfil the desire of them that fear him: he also will hear their cry, and will serve them."[1]

The 8th of September. I had a very good opportunity for a trip to Savannah, and I took it at the advice of Christian friends and the doctor. My hope was that the change of air, the rest, and contact with old Christian friends would make me stronger; and I stayed there from Monday through Friday. To my considerable relief, I was able to settle an important money matter, which I had considered taking care of while I was still sick. In doing so, I felt God's fatherly love on me to an extraordinary extent. On the other hand, as for my health, it was more damaging than strengthening; and for that reason I truly longed to be back home in my routine.

In Savannah I received such a nice letter from the highly praiseworthy Society *de promovenda cognitione Christi*,[2] which could not have been any nicer. It comforted me quite a bit and lifted my heart in the sadness and worries I felt when I received, in the same hour, news of an accident in Ebenezer. I also received an impressive gift that will enable me to pay for certain necessary expenditures in the congregation. Our sincere and humble praise goes to God for these and innumerable other signs of His love and caring. May He keep and bless all our dear benefactors and the most distinguished members of the praiseworthy Society, and may He let His grace and truth be with them in eternity!

The 11th of September. In Savannah I got the sad news that, due to the carter's carelessness, a falling tree had suddenly killed two of the sawmill's work horses in front of the wagon. This is another big test for us since we still have not paid up the costs of the most recent major construction work on the dam and millstones. Maintaining the wide-flung grinding mechanism, without which the community cannot get along, costs a great deal of money because the work of white people is very expensive and the timber we have to use for the construction rots very fast because we do not have any stones. It is typical of the Savannah River that it is sometimes high and sometimes low; and hence the dam and other things that are part of the mills sometimes stick a great deal out of the water and sometimes just a little, and so they are subject to easy rotting.

At the same hour when I got the above sad news, I was handed the friendly letter of dear Secretary Broughton,[3] which contained two pleasant news items in this difficult time of tribulations in that it brought new testimony of God's fatherly caring for us ministers and our listeners that: 1. As a result of falling interests rates, our salary had been cut to 12 pounds 10 shilling Sterling, but that the dear members of our highly praised Society had found ways to continue to pay us the entire salary. 2. The Society had received a 50 pound Sterling legacy for our congregation, and they asked me to only let them know how I was planning to use it for the best of the Salzburgers. At the same time, I was asked to answer some questions concerning our living conditions.

Because of my current weakness it took me today and yesterday to prepare the reply. In my answer to this important and detailed letter, I could feel God's marked assistance in response to our heartfelt prayers; and I have no doubt that God will see to it that the mouths of our slanderers in England will be shut and that the highly esteemed Society will learn the true reason of why our congregation of Salzburgers continues to need the help of our dear European benefactors. The Society also wants me to tell them the names and age of the men, women, children, and all members in the congregation: They did not indicate why they wanted this information.[4]

The 13th of September. One of the difficult tasks of my office is to reconcile squabbling married couples or neighbors. This work has taken much out of my weak energy, but I hope it was not in vain.

We keep having the most torrential cloudbursts, and others tell me that we have never had such a wet summer. All summer the river has been extremely high, and it will rise even higher this fall so that it has also stopped our mills. Corn, beans, pumpkins, and potatoes will suffer much damage in the low-lying, naturally wet areas, although field crops tend to grow best and most abundantly in such soil.

The 16th of September. My most recent trip to Savannah did not benefit, but rather harmed, my health, as I found out afterwards. My last illness, which was accompanied by much pain in the abdomen and chest and tiredness in all limbs, has returned, and that has forced me to spend the 13th Sunday after Trinity in bed and at home and to leave it to my two dear colleagues to administer Holy Communion. Thank God that at that very time God's kindness released my very hard-working and faithful *parastata*[5] Mr. Lemke from his fever and other worrisome conditions so that he could assist dear Mr. Rabenhorst in holding Holy Communion, in which 108 guests participated. He also baptized, in the early evening, our schoolmaster's small daughter who was born today. Mr. Thilo is also beginning to feel better and helps me in all possible ways. God has also shown mercy to his soul in this illness.

The 17th of September. Although I cannot write much because I lack the strength for it, I must not neglect to mention today's unexpected, enjoyable visit and encouragement by our pious miller Zimmerebner. Some years ago our dear God had already blessed on him my work overall, and particularly the private encouragement I had given him in connection with his thorough conversion. This is the reason for the very tender love and closeness between us. This time it was as if God had sent an angel to me and given me significant strength by talking to, and praying with, me. He has an Abrahamitic faith and leads a patriarchal life, but he also has a patriarch's worries, which have made his faith very pure and wonderful.

The 19th of September. The dear Lord has abundantly blessed the evening prayer my dear colleague Mr. Lemke delivered yesterday about the dear words of our most beloved Savior on a person very close to me. It was Mr. Lemke's first prayer session following his long-lasting fever illness. To her, these words were a refreshing drink from God's cup of comfort in her mortal agony caused by a very violent fever and other old perilous conditions. During the sermon she remembered the beautiful words: "This life will begin here in you; and, if you maintain it in time with constancy, then you will exult in it forever."[6] After our gracious God had somewhat strengthened her, she opened the book by herself to the superb song *Du meiner Augen Licht, . . .* etc., from which came the very instructive verse quoted above. She read part of it herself and had part of it read to her, to my and her very heavenly edification. I compared to it the dear verse in 1 John 3:1, etc.: "Behold, what manner of love the Father hath bestowed upon us." Also, "It doth not yet appear what we shall be." Oh God, be praised thousands and thousands of times for ever for leading us to Him and His son through the Holy Spirit and the Holy Gospel. May He have mercy on all spiritually blind people!

The 21st of September. We have every reason to praise our merciful and almighty God for the current dry and warm weather that started a few days ago. The many and long-lasting rains have damaged some fields, in terms of harvest and hay. On the island near the mill river, the inhabitants could already have made hay since May but the river flooding, which also closed down our mills about this time for several days, prevented that and completely flooded their beautiful rice. The Lord does this, too: He is aware of our misery and sighs; He will hear them and be merciful, and He will neither abandon nor forsake us. I must mention these external matters and tribulations in this special diary so that our Reverend Fathers, benefactors, and intercessors hear from time to time about how we are doing.

I have to conclude from the recent letters I received from the highly praiseworthy Society and from the questions addressed to me that in England (and the same is probably true in our German fatherland) they cannot accept that the majority of our Salzburger congregation continue to live in modest conditions, have little contact and dealings with other places in this colony and its neighbors with regard to field crops, timberwork, meat, butter, etc., and are still unable to support their ministers, but need continued assistance from Europe to maintain and carry on with their public buildings and institutions.

I have responded to the charitable Society in simple and clear words that, although quite a few Salzburgers and other colonists who came with them are well established and are making a good living and have some contact and business dealings among themselves and with Savannah and other places, some landholders find it hard to feed their families and they remain needy. That is mostly due to the bad land they must cultivate and their extremely physical condition caused by overwork, in both Old Ebenezer and this village. They are without servants, and if they had any in the past, they were more of a burden than help to them.

They left the papacy for God's kingdom, and for the same reason they settled close together near the town and at the mill river in order to benefit from our public church sermons and schools, in the hope that they, on their meager land, might be able to work the large island between the mill river, Purysburg, and Abercorn. However, since they could not do so as a result of repeated, often inconvenient floodings, losing their rice and hay crops in the process, they are now materially worse off than other colonists, including Germans, in this country, who only looked for good land and were not interested in whether or not they were also close to religious relatives, church and school.

That it is slander on the part of our false friends, ill-willed enemies, and envious persons if they blame carelessness on the part of the Salzburgers for the lack of flourishing material conditions and extensive commerce, I could ostensibly prove by the many public buildings, works, and institutions we have, a few of them in Old Ebenezer and several in this place, the likes of which are found nowhere else in this colony. True, the Lord Trustees and other dear benefactors in Europe have contributed much through gifts (for which may our gracious Lord reward them and their dear descendants in time and eternity!); yet had the Salzburgers not worked without pay to establish and maintain such efforts, they would have suffered the same fate as the mills in this country, some of which perished even before they were completed, and in the case of others, soon afterwards.

Every public building in this country was built at the expense of the Trustees, and very little is still in existence. We for our part have also made many mistakes, simply because we did not know any better, but it will serve or help those for the best who love God. In our home today our little *Golden Treasure Chest*[7] called to us "Why are you, my soul, so sad and so restless in me? Trust in the Lord . . . ," etc. The comments underneath that are to explain and apply these words are very instructive and comforting and fit our circumstances very well: "My Jesus, the Beginning and End of our faith, give us persevering faith amidst all the trials which we do not understand at all, but which are necessary and salutary, and we will see Thy glory, and we will also say with certainty: *Per aspera ad astra*.[8] Although we are very miserable people in the eyes of the world (including the respectable and half-converted world), we are content to enjoy Thy word, Thy grace, Thy caring and the kindness and intercession of Thy chosen servants and children. Keep and preserve these jewels for us at Thy cross, for our future descendants. Amen! Book of Wisdom.[9]

The 25th of September. To my delight and God's praise, a Salzburger living at the mill river told me that, despite the heavy flooding caused by the river, our almighty and merciful God has spared the rice crop on the island so that it suffered no damage whatsoever, except for two plantations adjacent to the Savannah river, at a place where that river flows into the mill river. Praised be God for His caring and for lifting my downcast spirit with this news. It would have been a hard test, and our enemies and those who envy us, including some among the poor Germans, would have gloated if others throughout the country had harvested rice while our poor and hardworking people had gone empty-handed. The entire field crops, including corn, beans, rice, potatoes, turned out exceedingly well everywhere, so that we hope for a year with very low prices instead of the very high prices last year. May God also give us the desired hay and good harvest weather!

Ursula Ekert, who is married to the industrious and upright Salzburger Landfelder here, fell seriously ill recently; and, at her sincere request, my dear colleague Mr. Lemke gave her private Communion yesterday because she suspected that she might die. However, the Lord, who heard her prayers and is eager to help, has also started to help her physically and she now seems to be out of danger. We joyfully praised God and the father of our Jesus Christ not only for this, but also for the invaluable gift of Holy Communion yesterday (oh, what a great benefit it is and yet how very often it is abused and looked down upon) and for all the other deeds God has done to her and my soul at other occasions and in this illness, and we awakened ourselves that we might win Jesus in our remaining short lives and be found in Him.

She heartily praises God for His great kindness of bringing her here to this solitude and pitied a certain unmarried person who came here with the latest Swabian transport and found good employment but has now moved somewhere else where she probably will pass judgment on Ebenezer. The reason is that people like her have to justify why they did not stay here. From the very beginning we ministers, and particularly I, an unworthy person, and our dear Salzburgers and other honest listeners have not only been attacked, unkindly judged, and slandered by people all over the world, but also by half-converted persons and hypocrites; and they are still doing it as I sometimes happen to hear. But be comforted: God always helps us, blesses us in Christ, and gives us much comfort and edification for many listeners, including those whom blind and inexperienced people do not take seriously.

The 29th of September. I visited today some Salzburger families near Zion Church in matters concerning the schoolmaster who will be hired for the plantations, and that caused much sincere joy among the parents and children and also in myself about our unexpected reunion and get-together. What I discussed with one of the mothers and her two well-behaved children made such a strong impression that they all showed frequent tears of love, joy, and praise during the conversation and our prayers. Overall, the children in our community, and particularly those on the plantations, have so far given me and my dear colleagues much joy and hope that they will grow and become good people. Therefore I would consider it a special pleasure to live the last years of my life and office among the old dear Salzburgers and their children on the plantations, to visit them diligently, and to instruct their children. However, the only thing that keeps me from doing so is my inability to build a small house for myself and my family, and also to build a kitchen and to plant a small kitchen garden. If this is God's will, He can easily make it possible for me.

The 30th of September. Some days ago our dear colleague Rabenhorst had planned with God's grace to take a health trip with his dear, frequently-ill wife to a place near Tybee in order to breathe the fresh sea breeze and to preach today, the 15th Sunday after Trinity, in Savannah. However, all of a sudden he was struck by a quotidian fever accompanied by vomiting. So he could neither do what he had planned, nor preach here. Hence for the first time since my recent illness, I held the morning service; and I must praise my God for proving in me what the Ephesians 2:20 say of Him in very strong words: "He is able to do exceedingly abundantly above all that we ask or think."[10] At the same time He is a wonderful God who, in the past, has visited long physical weaknesses, almost always at the same time, on us three ministers in Ebenezer who are so devoted to Him.

Our dear brother Lemke continues to be sick and often works beyond his ability, and his sole reason is that the children and adults should not be without spiritual nourishment and care. During this month which just ended I have suffered from much internal and external pain, which may have delayed my recovery somewhat. Nevertheless I can say with a joyful heart and mouth: "It is of the Lord's mercies that we are not consumed, his compassions fail not. They are new every morning, great is thy faithfulness."[11]

OCTOBER 1753

The 1st of October. In the name of my Savior Jesus Christ I am taking the pen at the beginning of this month to write down for our dearest Fathers and benefactors a few words about what is happening in the realm of nature and grace. Although I feel that I lack the mental and physical ability for it, I believe that it is my duty to do so. When our dearest Father in heaven makes my two dear colleagues strong and healthy again (my very dear colleague Mr. Lemke has suffered another fever attack during yesterday's afternoon sermon), I have no doubt that they will relieve me of the task of writing this official diary so that, in the little time and with the strength I have, I can report in a special diary on natural, economic, historical, and civic matters (however, *spiritualia* and *ecclesiastica*[1] will not be entirely excluded), and send it, together with the general official diary written by my two dear colleagues, to the Reverend Fathers. May God give us the necessary strength and ability!

As this month starts, I am faced with all kinds of misery, but—thank God—I am comforted and uplifted by the beautiful words in the Bible, which are also for my benefit: "Weep not: behold, the Lion of the tribe of Judah, the root of David." Or as the Lord himself expressed it in somewhat different words: "In the world ye shall have tribulation: but be of good cheer, I have overcome the world."[2] He surely will help us to overcome everything, mightily, wisely and mercifully. In spite of all internal and external tests, my heart keeps saying: "I desire nothing, oh Lord, but Thy free mercy."

The 2nd of October. Because Mr. Lemke had to take care of other business affairs and Mr. Rabenhorst did not feel well, I was asked to hold school in town. Not only had our merciful Father in heaven, who knows what we need, given me sufficient strength to do it, but also so much blessing and pleasure with and among these lambs as if I were in heaven among the angels and the chosen children. I taught them some prayers for children in short, simple and unstructured rhymes which may well have been authored by the late Pastor Sommer. They memorized them quickly and practiced them under my simple instruc-

tion. Since they had given me so much joy with their good behavior, attention, and eagerness to understand God's word, I
wanted to reward them with some gifts of food that children like
very much and encourage them to do well and awaken other
children who were absent to come to school diligently, and I did
so after school. Since our dear God has started to gradually free
us ministers from our illnesses, we have decided in the name of
Jesus Christ, who was very fond of children, to restructure the
school in town in such a way that the oldest children on the plantations would consider it a good idea to attend the school in
town, by offering them in several subject areas more advanced
instruction here than in the plantation school.

For the first time since my latest illness, I had to go and see our
mills on business matters. When I saw them from a distance, I
was awakened to praise the Lord who had kept me alive,
strengthened my health, and let me see again the big works He
has built here with His hand. But most remarkable was the great
spiritual blessing He gave me through the company of our pious
and dear mill manager Hans Flerl and his like-minded wife. We
enjoyed and refreshed ourselves in a beneficial conversation,
and we prayed and praised our Father in the name of Jesus
Christ. Flerl did so with many tears, partly out of joy about the
many good deeds he had received from God's hand, and partly
because of the poverty of his spirit in recognizing his unworthi-
ness. It was easy to recognize from his prayers that he is committed with heart and soul to both the mill plant and the entire
congregation and its well-being.

The 4th of October. God also visited a serious illness on Peter
Hammer, an upright man from Saxony, who came with the second Swabian transport, and on his wife and three children.
However, He did not let them die, but made them recover, contrary to my and other peoples' expectations. For that we wholeheartedly praised Him on his plantation this morning and asked
Him on our knees for His continued blessing to carry out our
general and special duties.

They greatly enjoy the visit, encouragement, and prayer of a
minister and almost do not know how to express their joy well
enough in gestures, words, and works. They are patient and
content with God's taking care of them; and, in fearing God,

they seek to earn an honest living with their work. They showed me part of their blessings in the fields and acknowledged them as God's undeserved kindness and caring. There is one thing I am sorry to see these and several other good people in our community do and that is that they do their work at home and in the fields in the old German way and not in accordance with what the land requires. They follow the example of our old inhabitants, and much of their work is therefore in vain.

All weekly sermons in Zion Church are held at noon from 11 to 12 o'clock since that is the time when it is easiest for our listeners to leave their home and work and miss the least. Today I invited them all wholeheartedly and graciously in the name of Jesus Christ to attend these sermons on a regular basis and told them that we are now talking about the dear sweet gospel on the song: *Ja, Jesus nimmt die Suender an.* The benefits would be theirs. Also, with regard to the scheduled weekly sermons that are to be held in the winter and summer at noontime, it is imperative that one of us ministers live among those listeners. This is also a requirement for the school.

The 7th of October. On this 16th Sunday after Trinity I was the only one of the ministers who delivered a sermon. I did not take this job because I wanted it—given my continuing weak physical condition—but I preached in the morning and in the afternoon because I love God and His congregation; and hence God gave me extraordinary strength so that I became increasingly stronger as I kept working. Thus I again experienced what the end of today's epistle says: "God is able to do exceedingly abundantly above all that we ask or think, according to the power that worketh in us."[3] Be there praise for that in the congregation that is in Jesus Christ, from eternity to eternity. Amen.

In view of the fact that Mr. Rabenhorst is in Savannah today to preach to the Germans, we have asked him to also administer Holy Communion to our co-religionists so that we will not have to go down there later on for that purpose, but can, in our weak physical condition, serve our community and the people at Goshen, who also consider themselves members of our congregation. In his past fever attacks, dear Mr. Lemke has not taken care of himself and has kept working because of his love for Jesus and me, the most unworthy of all; and as a result he has lost more and more of his strength. May God reward him for his loyalty and may He give me enough strength to once again help him.

The morning gospel dealt with the important and extremely necessary issue of the very salutary application of our certain and general mortality. At the beginning I impressed, as best as I could, on my dear, frequently-meeting, eager listeners the verse of Sirach 18.22[4] on what true repentance really is and said that delaying it until one reaches ones sickbed and deathbed is very common but extremely dangerous. In the afternoon I made the sermon easier, much to my and my audience's edification, by reading from our very popular *Treasure Chest*[5] of which everybody has a copy, those verses and relevant complete applications dealing with true repentance and the very salutary application of our mortality. The beautiful songs we sang also contributed to our prayers and edification.

Praised be our triune God, Father, Son and the Holy Ghost, for all the spiritual and material benefactions He has shown to us this Sunday in this very nice fall weather! May He make us grateful from the bottom of our hearts, keep His word and the Holy Sacraments for us, and strengthen us, His poor servants, to do our work with diligence with the young and the old! He has given us willingness and He will also ensure that we accomplish what we wish to do.

The 8th of October. We have noticed for some time that some of our listeners are no longer quite as eager to attend the weekly sermons and evening prayers and that they have kept their children out of school for several weeks. I therefore thought it my duty to implore them in last week's prayer hour and weekly sermon in the name of Jesus Christ to come regularly and listen to His dear gospel reflected in the song: *Jesus nimmt die Suender an* . . . etc. and not to be distracted like sinners by cattle raising, farming, etc., for God would frown upon it. I repeated this friendly invitation yesterday, adding my request that they send their children to school on a regular basis.

I told them that our thoroughly gracious God had given them three ministers so that Christ's word should not live among them sparsely, but abundantly. However, if they hold His word and its servants in low esteem, He could easily take His servants away, making His word dear as it unfortunately happens in many

places in America. I told them that they knew what He was planning to teach in the summer and fall and that He would visit
illness on them all at the same time, so that they would not even
be able to work on their most urgent official tasks.

Yesterday, the 18th Sunday after Trinity, Mr. Lemke preached
a sermon at Goshen and administered Holy Commuion, while
Mr. Rabenhorst and I served our dear congregation with both.
We had 117 communicants. Today a man of the first Salzburger
transport confessed with tears of joy in his eyes, while praising
God, that Jesus Christ, the loyal Bishop of souls, had ensured
him during the sermon yesterday of his state of grace, freeing
him of all the scruples and anxieties he had been burdened with
in the past. He said his heart is filled with sweet peace and trust
in God through Christ, and he feels strong enough to walk
within the limits of Christianity and to fight as we are ordered to
do. Yesterday I heard of yet another example of a weak woman
whom our merciful God rewarded, like me and hopefully others, with grace and mercy through His word and Sacrament.

The 24th of October. Last year an unmarried man of the second Swabian transport by the name of Hekel[6] took in a brother
with his wife and four children among the third transport. Soon
after her voyage the woman died at Tybee, but the man, together with his children, of whom the eldest was 16 years old and
the youngest 7, moved up to Halifax, where he became a farmer
and had a very good crop. He[7] has now received the very sad
news that his brother died after a very brief illness, leaving his
children behind in very sad circumstances.

The worst is that the above-mentioned city is making arrangements to send, according to local custom, some of these children
for several years to Savannah Town to be raised there and placed
in service for many years. However, our tailor Hekel does not
agree with that, and he is right in doing so. I have promised to
contribute something to the education of the smallest child, and
he wants to follow my advice with regard to the other children as
well. A great many children are perishing in this part of the
world because they get no Christian education. Because they
were never given a firm Christian foundation, they fall prey to
all sorts of bad religious leanings as soon as they get to be among
other people.

We have tried very hard to find a good schoolmaster for the children on the plantations, but so far we have not been successful. Mr. Rabenhorst loves children. Because our dear God has now made both Mr. Lemke and me stronger in body and spirit so that we attend to all official matters in and around town and the plantations, we have offered him the job of teaching school (two hours a day at a time that is convenient for him), and he is willing to accept until our gracious God gives us an experienced and fatherly-inclined schoolmaster or makes it possible through the construction of a parsonage near the mill for one of us to move out there and, jointly with the schoolmaster, teach the children. How happy our Salzburgers at the Mill River will be to get dear Mr. Rabenhorst as a schoolmaster for their older and young children!

I received another friendly letter from Mr. von Brahm[8] in which he invites me to his plantation to see his sick wife, and we agreed on the week following the 20th Sunday after Trinity. Although it is true that I am still a bit weak and have much work and that the way to him is, as he himself writes, quite wearisome, I do plan on going because he has called me. May God bless this trip and my work with good results!

I saw a Negro woman at work, whose child was tied to her back, and in spite of its mother's moving all the time and working hard, the child was completely still and quiet. Sometimes, on trips on foot, Indian men carry their small children the same way, but if the latter are very small and their limbs not yet strong, the mothers tie them to a board that is carved out to fit the child's body and head and then carry them on their shoulders. They use thick and sturdy tree bark as a cradle in which to carry the child. It is hard to find a frail or bent Indian with a crooked limb or hunched back, which may have something to do with this care the mothers give to their children.

The 26th of October. Yesterday afternoon we received several letters from England and Germany from the ship. They had arrived with the ship that carried goods from Mr. Samuel Lloyd to Messrs. Harris and Habersham. Besides much sad news, we were pleased to read that our dearest Fathers and benefactors in London, Augsburg, and Halle are in reasonably good health, that they are praying for us, are feeling sorry for us in our manifold trials and, to the best of their ability, are trying to find solutions.

The 28th of October. The dear Court Chaplain[9] informs us that the very gracious Councillor Walbaum, who was very busy and experienced in God's service, has also entered the eternal peace and joy of his Lord, whom he loved so ardently and whose concerns he so faithfully tried to support in a truly Evangelical spirit, verbally and in letters, with distinguished and humble people at home and on travel. I met him personally in Halle as early as in 1728; and to this moment I have cherished, as a great blessing for me, our dear God's grace which was in him and inspired his entire life. The very anointed letters he often wrote to me were of great benefit to me and our listeners who were eager to be saved, and I expect the same to be true of the long, highly edifying and pleasant letter I just received, which he wrote after ending his recuperation trip and presumably shortly before his blessed death. May God be praised for the dear grace He bestowed on this faithful servant of his and, through him, on so many other souls nearby and far away, even in the East and West Indies. May He reward him when he comes face to face with Him and before His throne from eternity to eternity for everything, including the many material good deeds he sent us in the form of books, money, and many other useful things from dear Salfeld and Wernigeroda.[10]

For some time our wondrous God, who makes everything all right, has visited me with much inward and outward distress, and I have experienced in myself the words of our dear Savior: "Sufficient unto the day is the evil thereof."[11] But my Abba has not left me without comfort and has led me to His word and prayer so that I understand to some extent what David says: "The entrance of thy words giveth light; it giveth understanding to the simple."[12]

Today, on the 19th Sunday after Trinity, I experienced some unexpected sadness. When I opened my *Little Treasure Chest* on the page for today, i.e., the 28th of October, I found to my very great comfort among the Biblical words: "Abraham believed in hope against hope," (Romans 4:18, 21) the following Evangelical meditation: "Oh soul, unlike Abraham, you do not only have one, but many promises and many thousands of examples of faith before you. Therefore, you, too, stay with the word and faith, and even if there is no help, even if the evil becomes worse, do not weaken, rather be strong and happy because God's promises are fulfilled in such wondrous ways; and, since God is ready to help you when He seems least likely to do so, the opposite may take place. For whenever the distress is greatest, help is closest, and the reason is so that we do not, as we are always inclined to do, trust in what we see or feel, but only in words, which are the only thing we can believe in death. Therefore, even if it looks as if He does not want to . . . etc. Now Lord, may I work hard never to trust myself, but trust in you in everything!"

The 29th of October. The Salzburger Lechner, who lives on a remote plantation behind Abercorn, informed me through a friend of his mortal sickness and thanked me for all the good admonitions I had given him, at the same time, he asked me to encourage the congregation to follow the admonitions they receive. He and others thought it terrible that a dying woman in Abercorn had told her husband that they would never be saved after living the way they had lived. Lechner's wife and three children are also sick with fever. May our dear Lord help them, and may this punishment serve them in cleansing themselves and in finding a good basis so that they can make a good beginning! Tomorrow, God willing, my colleague Mr. Lemke plans to visit them, and that no doubt will be a great comfort to them and contribute to their recovery.

The 30th of October. Last evening we had a thunderstorm, heavy winds, and rain, while it turned very cold. So far we have had dry, very pleasant harvest weather, for which we will thank our gracious God and Father in the forthcoming harvest and thanksgiving sermon, which we will be held in three public places, i.e., in the Jerusalem Church, the Zion Church, and the assembly up on the Blue Bluff. Once again He has opened His charitable hand and filled everything with pleasure. We will also praise Him for all the blessings He has so richly bestowed on us in the fields and gardens.

Yesterday my colleague Mr. Rabenhorst started in God's name to teach school on the plantations, after he had graciously invited the children, as the lambs of Jesus Christ, on Sunday to attend. He could not hold school today because he felt somewhat indisposed and because the weather was so raw. Since I had to give the weekly sermon anyway, I taught school in his stead and, thank God, with such blessing for me and the children that I would not trade it for any earthly good, no matter how sensible that would be. The number of children who had come, even from the remotest areas, was about as large as yesterday, and the raw weather had not been a deterrent to them. From this I conclude that they will enjoy going to school with Mr. Rabenhorst.

I would consider it a special gift and dear act of kindness if God thought me worthy of teaching the children from the catechism and the Holy Scripture. But my two dear colleagues very much like to do it: Mr. Lemke in town and Mr. Rabenhorst now on the plantations, and I have my own work. From time to time, such as today, I will have the pleasure of helping out in school.

Currently I have to deal with many things that disturb me greatly. But in the church and in school I forget all my misery; and my spirit becomes bright and light, as if it had not been burdened before. The three verses from the 119th Psalm, to which the dear Samuel of our church, our fatherly Senior Urlsperger, referred to in the letters he wrote to me and my dear colleagues in April and May of this year, which we have just received, have greatly strengthened and edified me through the Holy Spirit, i.e., Verse 67: "Before I was afflicted, I went astray, . . . " etc. "It is good for me that I have been afflicted . . . " etc. and Verse 75: " I know, O Lord, that thy judgments are right, and that thou in faithfulness hast afflicted me."

The 31st of October. Highly praised be God and the father of our Jesus Christ for all His mercy and faithfulness, which He has shown unto me, my two esteemed colleagues, and the members of our dear congregation richly and daily during this month which is now ending. There are so many of these deeds that I am unable to count and describe them. In particular, He has restored our health and strength so that we can do our official work; and He has given us new courage and joy to save ourselves and our families by using the medicines properly, as the newly arrived fatherly letters from our dear Senior Urlsperger and the court chaplain again strongly encouraged us to do. They, like other faithful and dear servants of God, and our dear Fathers and friends, also have a great deal of suffering, but they are not

complaining. Rather they are content and do their work honestly, which impresses me very much, embarrasses me, and encourages me to do the same with God's grace.

While dear Mr. Lemke delivered today's weekly sermon on the
Blue Bluff, I substituted for him in the school in town. It turned
out that, according to Freylinghausen's *Golden A.B.C.*, the letters
S and T followed. That meant that a boy or girl disciple of the
Lord must endeavor to be gentle toward everyone and faithful
to the Lord Jesus Christ until death.[13] I myself have learned
some valuable lessons from these words and from the selected
passages underneath with regard to our pains and tribulations
that are also known to our dearest Fathers. May God not let me
forget them! Praised be His holy name from eternity to eternity.
Amen.

NOVEMBER 1753

The first day of this month has been a very memorable and
blessed day for me. I spent the day before His face with my dear
colleagues and other dear listeners, who, because of my many
physical ailments and shortcomings, assembled in the morning
at my home in order to remember, as a solemn memorial and
thanksgiving day, the many spiritual and material good deeds
we received from the Lord over the past twenty years. We wholeheartedly and humbly praise Him with all our heart for all the
help and blessings He has given us, also for the physical refresh-
ments He provided for the adults and children in the form of
bread, wine, etc. While enjoying the physical benefactions, we
read aloud the very uplifting letter from Councillor Walbaum,
our and the entire congregation's beloved friend, which he
wrote me a short time before his blessed end. It deserves to be
read often, and I would like our Reverend Fathers and friends to
know about it because it contains much wonderful and edifying
news about God's kingdom.

To come back to our extraordinary assembly today, we sang at
the beginning the beautiful song of praise: "*Ach, dass ich tausend
Zungen haette . . .* " etc. and read the relevant 103rd Psalm. I also
explained the reasons which made me spend this first day of the

winter month with humble people praising and praying to God, and at the same time with humility before His face: namely, on this day twenty years ago I was called to this Salzburger congregation. Afterwards, old and young fell on their knees; my two dear colleagues prayed forcefully and confidently one after the other. And I concluded the meeting with prayers, intercessions and giving thanks. Finally we sang the other half of the song mentioned earlier. To strengthen our faith, I read, prior to the benediction, the text from our *Little Treasure Chest* on page 305 under today's date: "When you began to pray, the command was issued . . . , etc." The meditation underneath it is very instructive and comforting. As usual we did not forget our Reverend Fathers, dear benefactors and friends in Europe in this threefold prayer. God will hear us and be gracious.

Apart from the great blessing of spiritual edification our true God gave us, as usual and through the letters from our dearest Fathers and friends, He put in the hands of our dearest Father, Senior Urlsperger, a material blessing of 300 florins. This sum is to be used to pay off part of our congregation's debts in London. Our dear benefactors have specified that some of the money be used for our own needs. We received it today with much joy; and we praised God and our dearest benefactors in V., in A., in M., in B., and S.G.[1] (from where the above-mentioned large alms came) for it, wishing them wholeheartedly in prayers, conversation, and letters God's blessing and true well-being.

I received the good news from the upright Salzburger Veit Lechner that he feels better now and is out of danger. He has a wife and four very young children, and it is therefore a great blessing that He is keeping this man and father alive for a while. This married couple is among those who thank God with all their hearts for leading them out of their errors, for saving them, and for bringing them to this peaceful place and His word.

The 2nd of November. I must incorporate in this diary, for the information and edification of our Christian friends, some *specialia* about my very dear benefactor and friend, the late Councillor Walbaum, and, in a sense, build him a monument. The dear Court Chaplain wrote me on July 27th:

Our dear Councillor Walbaum had already died before receiving the . . . For a year now, this Nathanael had suffered from
many physical and health-related problems. Then he suddenly
became ill with an *atonia* and passed away on Prayer Sunday in
peace and with the words: "He Himself, our Father, loves
you."[2]

"Those are words," the court chaplain writes, "to which one
can cling in death. Thus one after the other is leaving us. May
the Lord awaken others who can become the vessel of His grace
and the tools of His glory!"

The late councillor started his edifying letter of February
23rd of this year with these noteworthy and—to us—very welcome words:

Ebenezer! Until now, the Lord hath mercifully helped us. He
will continue to assist us; and, when the time comes, He will
help us enter His eternal kingdom, which Jesus Christ has won
and prepared for us, according to God's eternal loving counsel
over us. Hallowed be He forever!

Then he told us in a simple but very edifying way that he had
gone once more to see not only his old, dear and upright friends
ex ordine politico et ecclesiastico[3] during his visit, which his doctors
had advised him to take for health reasons, and that he had
strengthened himself with them in the Lord. He also wrote that
he had become aware to his great joy of many *Magnalia Dei eius-
que Regni*[4] in several countries and places and with various people. One of his old friends, Mr. von Charlot, Lieutenant in Wolf-
enbuettel's Mounted Guard, had taken leave of the world in his
presence in such a peaceful and joyful way that it seemed that he
was only leaving one room to go to the one next door.

Afterwards another proven disciple of our Lord Jesus and a
great carrier of the cross followed this gentleman with extraordinary refreshment from Jesus Christ's inexhaustible curative
spring. He writes:

Besides her, in my presence, two excellent sisters left this world
for joyful eternity and, after my departure, three more.
Among them was Mrs. Drost von Muenchhausen, who had
been graced with so many gifts and had remained faithful until she died.

In Hamburg he enjoyed the pleasant and stimulating company of several of the Lord's friends. On his way back he reportedly met in W. a very upright and cheerful major and his childlike, intellectually simple, and cheerful wife, with whom he and Abbot Steinmetz had already stayed the summer before. About the County of Ranzau and in the Holstein and Schleswig areas (if I understood him correctly), he said that the seed of God's word had been planted more abundantly there than in some other places and that God had thus won a good number of followers. Yet the Herrnhut epidemic has also been spreading, afflicting one and the other upright soul who had not been aware of its dangerous horror, and they are bewildered, if not upset, when somebody wants to tell them about it.[5]

To some of his old friends, he had to recommend Bogatzki's beautiful treatise *Warning of Relapse*,[6] and he made this strange comment:

> Reading this treatise has been a necessity and a blessing for me. Because the enemy[7] also seeks to trip and cause an ugly stench for us old and otherwise experienced and very blessed servants of the Lord through the evil that is still in us and often remains very active and through exterior circumstances, including even those God wills us into, so that the eyes of those who become aware of it may get filled with tears.

He also reports that, despite a marked recovery of his strength, our dear God had visited him soon afterwards with one physical illness after another, which caused him much pain and discomfort even while he was writing the letter. He continues:

> Among those just people who recently departed with blessings from this world is the rightly famous Prior Bengel. The death of this very honest, yet heavenly simple, very pure, pious-learned and learned-pious man before our very eyes is a great loss, not only for the entire church, but for the land of Wuerttemberg. Because he was a respected member of the consistorium there, he and those who helped him pray have watched with all his strength and with the greatest success that no hireling sneak into the vineyard. He believed that, while there continue to be many blessed awakenings through God's word in

that land and somebody had wanted to write to me about it some time ago, there was hardly any village left in that land which does not have at least one awakened soul.

Praise to the Lord!

Abbot Steinmetz was very pleased in Halle and testified to those from here who visited him:[8]

> In Halle he no doubt encountered much kindness, also among the students. The institutions there have remained, and continue to be, the blessed mother school, etc.

After thinking a bit about the scourge God sent the people in the Wernigerode region, not only through fire, but also through the livestock epidemic, he added:

> I hope the merciful purpose of our Lord, who uses such a scourge, will be recognized and will be successful! In the meantime, he believed in childlike submission! It cannot be any different here. The kingdom we share by the grace of Christ is a kingdom of crosses, but nonetheless it is a blessed kingdom in which only peace and salvation rule.

I will leave it at these excerpts, although the letter also contains many edifying details about some persons I know, and about other countries, including a princely person. There is one thing I would like to add though, and that is that the first respect was awakened in my heart for this dear councillor some 25 years ago in Halle, when a good friend of mine who knew him well said of him that this Mr. Walbaum was speaking more with God than with people. Therefore I am particularly impressed that His Lord and leader called him on Rogate Sunday, or the Sunday of Prayers.

The 6th of November. Our kind God gave us the joy of coming together to thank Him in both churches for the rich blessing in our fields. The harvest this year has been particularly good, although we have had much wet weather, which damaged some, although only a few, crops. Prices are beginning to fall. We talked in the Jerusalem Church about God's works as a mirror of his almightiness, wisdom, and kindness, according to the words in Psalm 104:24. As a starter, we covered the 9th and 10th verse from Sirach chapter 47.

This week the men had to work on the public roads. However, all those who worked close by came to church with their supervisor so that quite a few listeners were present to hear the harvest sermon. God also made me strong enough so that I could give them many a necessary lecture that could serve them in their work as a topic of useful conversation and something to think about, instead of futile gabbing that is usually done where many people are together.

The 10th of November. The Councilmen[9] in Savannah have permitted our inhabitants to do some other general work they would like to do during the six days they usually spend on roads each year. Thus some of them worked on the road and the long bridge between the town and the plantations near the mill river, while others cut wood for a house for a minister they would like to see live among them out on the plantations. Our churchyard close to town has particularly benefited from this permission since others fenced it well with shingles while expanding it at the same time.

Whatever they did, everything is very necessary and useful; and we are pleased that it could be done without special hardship for our parishioners and that it was also completed in reasonably good order.

The 13th of November. Our dear Mr. Boltzius has again been taken ill, but he seems out of danger today. If only our merciful Lord would leave him with us for a while, even if he no longer could do any work or only very little (as I would wholeheartedly wish him some peace in view of the great suffering, work and many worries he has endured). I would be content if we could benefit, if necessary, from his advice and instructions for some time to come.

Since we agreed today in the house of my above-mentioned colleague on how to use, to God's glory, the great gift of two pieces of cloth which a noble benefactress in Holland sent us at the request of her late husband, we were very happy in our homes and praised God, especially because the cloth is not only very fine and beautiful, but also in perfect condition despite the long time it has been in transit. There will also be many a poor person in our community who will enjoy receiving a part of this gift.

May the Lord graciously think of this dear benefactress and remember this incomparable alm to bless for ever!

We also had to admire God's providence, which knew how to help us so unexpectedly at the right time; it deserves to be glorified and honored for it.

Because Mr. Boltzius is weak and Mr. Rabenhorst has gone to Savannah in matters concerning the establishment of a plantation for his support, I held school and conducted the church service today on the mill river plantations. This was so easy for me to do with God's assistance that I did not feel tired at all, although I have not yet fully recovered from my most recent illness. In school I talked with the children about the late Pastor Freylinghausen's *Golden A.B.C.* and some of the verses underneath. That gave us an opportunity to do many useful exercises so that we spent almost two pleasant hours on them. In church we considered God's praiseworthy holiness, based on Leviticus 19:2: "Ye shall be holy, . . . " etc., which gave us much edification since I presented this material in an Evangelical way, without bypassing the Law.[10]

The 20th of November. Today a christening I had to perform gave me the opportunity to preach God's word from John 6:24 to the people at Goshen; in view of the rainy weather, not all those had come who usually attend. Since I was seven miles from Ebenezer, I visited the Salzburger Christian Riedelsperger, who offered me a friendly welcome. He has been in poor health for quite some time, which has forced him to neglect many things in his household. Still he is calm. Since I did not have much time, I could only cite him the words: "Like as a father pitieth his children, so the Lord pitieth them that fear him."[11]

Everywhere I went, people asked about Mr. Boltzius, and they seemed to be very concerned about his recovery, which I was glad to hear. On the other hand, I was very upset about a vicious lie I heard about him which is making the rounds in Savannah. Nevertheless I remembered that this is what usually happened to Christ's true servants, namely, that they were reviled by the world which, for them, is a better sign than being praised, especially if it is done by evil people.

However, because attending to worldly affairs, which we consider to be merely work of love and need, was at the bottom of the accusation referred to above, I was doubly anxious for our dear God to show me ways and means of how to get rid of these external matters with the help of an upright *Politicus*, or merchant, or other experienced *Oeconomus*,[12] so that our religious work, about which there were no complaints, would not suffer from it. While these things have frequently happened to Mr. Boltzius, occasionally people throw the two of us together and then have as many complaints about one as they have for the other. I heard another example of this kind which is especially worrisome, because it may include some people who seem to be our best friends and should have a better understanding. Oh Lord, do not hold this sin against them!

The 25th of November. On this last Sunday of the old church year we remembered the abundance of kindness, patience, and forbearance God has shown in the past toward both us ministers and our listeners. At the start of the morning sermon, and above all during our prayer hour, we were awakened to praise God for it; but we were also humbled by His greatness and we called on Him in the name of our sole intermediary to forgive us all misconduct, weaknesses, and faults, especially those which happened while His dear word and the other means of grace were preached, listened to, and used. In the afternoon, during catechism instruction, we were asked to give ourselves to the Lord with everything we have, even all our abundant sins, so that such talk would not leave anything behind. Otherwise our church service would only be hypocrisy, about which we talked in the morning sermon. According to the will of our Heavenly Father, our dear Mr. Boltzius has to continue to stay home and in bed, although he has started to feel better.

The 27th of November. This afternoon I had the pleasure of riding with an honest Salzburger from the mill to town, where I had to attend to some business matters, and of refreshing myself with him on the words: "He is gracious and merciful, slow to anger, and of great kindness,"[13] We came to speak of God's kindness, which we are enjoying every day in this desert, and this man could not find enough praise for them. Such people are of great comfort to us.

The 28th of November. Not only did I feel God's assistance during the sermon I preached today to the people on the Blue

Bluff and during the evening prayers in town, but He also showed my soul great mercy so that preaching His word was very edifying for me. In both places I found not only a good number of adults, but also children, with whom I could speak about God's truth, and that is something I enjoy doing.

DECEMBER 1753

The 2nd of December. We have many reasons to thank our true God, who let us start yet another church year and wishes to work on us anew through His word and Holy Sacraments; by so doing He showers us with one of the best blessings. May our dear God fulfil His loving final purpose, for which He makes use of His dear means of grace, on all those who did not want to be won over by Him last year!

In the morning I preached the regular gospel according to Saint Matthew about Christ's royal duties. We saw, first, what these duties were; and, second, we saw for whose sake Christ was performing them. At the beginning we read Psalm 29:10-11: "The Lord sitteth King for ever; the Lord will give strength unto His people; the Lord will bless His people with peace." And God lets us feel an abundance of His gracious help and blessing. My dear colleague Mr. Rabenhorst preached in the afternoon, again not without edification.

The 7th of December. Last Monday, the 3rd of this month, I had to travel to Savannah to take care of some affairs in connection with the plantation which Mr. Rabenhorst wants to donate to an institution that is well known to one of our dearest Fathers. I found the Councilmen[1] quite willing to do so. Not only did they order that the plantation near the new sawmill be surveyed, but they also permitted Mr. Hirsch to take up 100 acres in our community so that he can be our sawmiller, something no person of the latest Swabian transport has been allowed. Yesterday I returned with God's help, and today I resumed my regular work.

The 9th of December. Mr. Rabenhorst preached at the Jerusalem Church and I at the Zion Church. May God not leave the scattered seeds of His word without fruit for anyone of us! It is a great benefit to our congregation that they now have a third preacher, since it pleases our dear God to continue to keep our first minister in weak health. Otherwise we could not have public church services, and that would be of great concern to the people, because I find the Zion Church very crowded with children and adults whenever I have to preach there. Today I felt indisputable attention among my listeners; and one of the reasons is, as I have mentioned several times before, that we preach God's word in very clear, simple, and forceful terms and in good order. That requires the minister to prepare himself well in advance, or else he must be very well versed in God's truths and be in the proper frame of mind.

Today I dealt with waiting for Christ's future to pass judgment. To assist my memory, I have not only *divisiones* but also some, but few, *subdivisiones*; and I explain the sentences with a few words and immediately add the *Application* so that I can stop if there is not enough time to present everything. However, if the sentences hang very well together and I know that I have enough time for the dedication,[2] then I wait with it to the very end. Such an organization enables me to see my sermon from beginning to end, and this makes the delivery easier for me. I have to pray all the time: "Enter not into judgment with thy servant."[3] I also noticed during the catechization that this is the easiest way for the children to retain something. In this, my faithful colleague, Mr. Boltzius, has set a good example for me.

The 10th of December. Some children in our congregation have progressed to the point where they will soon be permitted to attend Holy Communion. For that reason I have started to teach those who live in town the parts in which they need more preparation. At the outset I am planning to teach them the most basic practical truths and am using the late Pastor Freylinghausen's *Golden A.B.C.* We always base our teaching on a number of specific books we have among ourselves so that the children have something in their hands; and, hopefully, it is easier for them to memorize certain things and to recall afterwards, to their benefit and with the help of these books, what they were told about the word of life.

The 11th of December. This afternoon I visited the family we hired to supervise the new sawmill. Together with them, I edified myself from the words Jeremiah 3:22: "Behold, we come

unto thee." And there is a joyous echo from the mouth of Jesus
Christ in John 14:18 "I shall come to you." Elsewhere it is recommended that we search for the Lord, and He in return assures us
that he is in search of us. Since both are involved in this search, a
welcome and blessed finding of each other and meeting with
each other is ensured. Oh, if only many, yes very many, our entire Ebenezer would set out to seek the Lord and to call out to
Him: "See, we are coming to you." This would cause joy in
heaven, and among God's children on earth. See *Golden Treasure
Chest*, page 345.[4]

The 14th of December. In today's preparatory session for Holy
Communion I talked to the children about the heavenly mind,
which differs from the earthly way of thinking. This is one of the
subjects that we in this country need particularly badly. In many
people, the earthly way of thinking dominates to such an extent
that they totally disregard heaven and eternity. For most people,
the only goal is to get rich; and they are restless and disen-
chanted if they do not succeed in their plan. How wonderfully
God's government is handling this by letting only a very few of
them be successful in their intentions. Consequently, God remains the one who makes people poor or rich and elevates or
humbles them. Somebody who thinks of heaven will always have
enough in this world, because he does not want anything else
except what our heavenly Father considers to benefit him; but
what he really wants, respects, and seeks and what he has his joy
in is heaven.

The 15th of December. The sweet names listed for God in the
145th Psalm, Verse 8, have been very important to me, ever since
I publicly dealt with the universal validity of God; and they have
been on my mind almost daily. This is why, today, I gladly seized
the opportunity, which presented itself to me during the preparatory meeting for Holy Communion prior to confessions, to
utilize it again for myself and my listeners in Zion Church. May
our true God bless my doing so!

The 16th of December. We have tasted and experienced Jesus
Christ's friendliness not only in His word, which we proclaimed,
but also during Holy Communion. This time we had 120 communicants, including some from other places, who came here

yesterday for that purpose. During the past church years, our catechistic instruction in the afternoon was based on the prescribed epistles for Sundays and special holy days. But, because we used to alternate with the Lutheran Catechism, we will now catechize about it at least every two weeks; and I have started to do so with God's help this afternoon. I felt that the Lord put a special, although seemingly small, blessing on it.

The 18th of December. Today I had to interrupt my work in town at the school and the preparation of the older children and instead hold school and church on the plantations. In town we have a schoolmaster so that, even if there is no religious instruction, the other lessons can be held. Out on the plantations we now need such a man as well. In church we derived much joy from the little verse: "Our God is in the heavens: he hath done whatsoever he has pleased."[5]

Now and again our experience with Negroes has been that, if one keeps them in good order, gives them enough but not too much work, feeds them at the proper time, treats them with seriousness but not in a rough and tyrannical way, keeps good order in one's house in front of their eyes, etc., an otherwise useless Negro may become useful. However, that cannot be accomplished through improper treatment and force. This also helps in some way to clear the way for Christianity in them.

We have hired a fine and quiet man to supervise the above-mentioned plantation near the new sawmill (we now call it appropriately "preacher's plantation"). If necessary, he can be stern, and he keeps good order. Together with his wife, he is God fearing. Also, when something has to be done with regard to the adoption by the Negroes of the Christian faith, he can be of great help to us. We hope to reap with God's assistance two-fold, i.e., spiritual and material, benefits from this plantation. Because God wants all people to be helped and to recognize the truth, He will not let our good intentions be entirely without results. This hopefully will bring joy and all the more blessings from God to our dearest benefactors of high and low standing, whose small contributions have enabled us to establish such a plantation, the primary aim of which is at this time to support our present third Ebenezer minister. Apart from the fact that

the congregation now has one more minister, such an arrangement can yield considerable future benefits in other ways, but I
do not want to go into details now.

The 23rd of December. Today, at Zion Church, I preached
about the twofold testimony which John the Baptist gave, partly
on his own and partly on Christ's behalf, in the gospel of John
1:19. That gave me an opportunity to point out the foolishness
of many people in this country who believe so much in human
testimonies, which they either bring with them here in writing
and misuse, thereby inflicting great harm on themselves, or
which they claim they received verbally, or which they believe
they have reason to supply about themselves. The best testimony
such a person can have is probably the one in Romans 8: "The
Spirit itself beareth witness with our spirit that we are the children of God." To this testimony Mr. Boltzius likes to add the *Testimonium paupertatis*[6] from the mouth of the late Doctor Anton.[7]
Cf. Saint Matthew 5:3: "Blessed are the poor in spirit; for theirs
is the kingdom of heaven."

27th of December. Praised be our loving God, who once again
allowed us in the past two days to celebrate our wonderful
Christmas with His blessings and in peace. Our first colleague
had to spend it in his room, because he continues to be physically
sick, but with the rich blessing God sent him through His son
from the Gospel. On each day Mr. Rabenhorst took care of the
public church services at the Jerusalem Church, where the entire congregation assembled the next day. On the first day I also
preached at Zion Church. After the afternoon church service I
rode my horse to Goshen to serve the people there with God's
word and Holy Communion. I had the necessary strength to do
this work, although I had felt weak the day before the holiday. I
arrived home safe and sound last evening.

It has become very cold, and this has made preaching at Goshen in an open hut somewhat difficult. Oh, may the sweet and
dear gospel on Christ's incarnation and birth we heard during
the past Advent and Christmas season be accepted by all, as it
should be! The comforting verse Isaiah 9:6 has been particularly blessed on me: "For unto us a child is born . . . " etc., as I
also heard from an upright Salzburger. And today I had the op-

portunity to recite it to an ill man on his sickbed in order to encourage and comfort him. May we humbly praise the Lord for
all His mercy!

In addition to the dear blessing of God's word which we abundantly enjoyed today in both churches, we had tonight, among
other pleasures, that of receiving some very dear and pleasant
letters from our benefactors and friends in Europe. Among
them were letters from our dear Doctor and Professor Francke,
Captain Krauss, Pastor Boltzius' son, who arrived safely with Mr.
Krauss in London, and some others which are giving us much
joy at the end of this year. It is very refreshing to us, who are
strangers here, not only in the spiritual, but also physical sense
and who live in this remote area, suffering for the most part
from all kinds of adversities, to have the joy of occasionally receiving a fatherly, brotherly, and friendly greeting by way of letters from Europe.

The letters we just received remind us strongly at the forthcoming turn of the year to praise the Lord humbly for pre-
serving our dearest Fathers and benefactors in this life and to
pray wholeheartedly for them, their life, and their well-being.
They also make us praise the name of the Lord for permitting
our dear friends, who left us early last summer, to complete
their voyage across the ocean to London in good health. Our
gracious God will continue to grant them His powerful protec-
tion for the remainder of the trip and take them to the final des-
tination of their journey.

The 30th of December. Today we are ending the old year,
which our heavenly Father, in His great kindness, has permitted
us to spend to its end. In school I also concluded the late Professor Francke's *Order of Salvation*,[8] consisting of five questions
and answers, which I had discussed with the children, at the end
not without benefit and blessing. But in preparing some of the
older children for Holy Communion, we are still considering the
late Pastor Freylinghausen's *Golden A.B.C,*[9] in which it says for
today: "Be sober when you pray. We cannot do without the so-
berness of a person who is very empty of the world" if we want to
be and remain willing and able to pray. Lord, help me to always
control my body (my senses, my desires) so that I will always stay

sober. Jesus, please help me so that I always will be sober like you.[10] In the late afternoon I spent a blessed hour with my colleague Pastor Boltzius, whose words of comfort were today: "Jesus Christ, yesterday and today, and the same also in eternity."

 *Daily Reports Of the Year 1754*

JANUARY 1754

The 1st of January. Last Sunday (which was the 30th of December of last year) my dear colleague, Mr. Rabenhorst, traveled to Savannah after holding Sunday morning and evening services at the Zion Church. Thus, he has spent the first day of this new year in Savannah and, we hope, to the benefit and blessing of the German people. In the meantime, I have performed the duties of our office here on my own; and today I have presented twice to the congregation God's counsel on human salvation in the manner dictated by Acts. 4:12 and the day's gospel. How clear and persuasive this advice and counsel are presented in the holy Scriptures! How sweet and pleasant are the truths dealing therewith! If only man were truly concerned with advice and help on how to extricate himself from his sin. But we must nonetheless not be astonished that many will not, and cannot, understand this advice and counsel; for the God of this world has blinded their senses so that they do not see the bright light of the gospel.

Yesterday a man came to our place and stayed with the manager of the mill, where he soon started discussing matters of religion, thus quickly baring the rotten core of his heart. Our manager, Flerl, answered him with much sense; and again he was convinced how necessary it is for the youth in this country to be well instructed in Christian doctrine. On such occasions the gospel of the Son of God becomes all the more sweet and dear to us.

The 2nd of January. The letters usually enclosed by our dear benefactors in their gifts contain much important and edifying news; and these communications are of particular benefit to us, the ministers. In particular, they strengthen us in our belief in many ways and awaken us to the need to pray warmly for our benefactors as is their due; and they provide us with much cause for joy and praise of the Lord as well as with many reasons why we should suffer our afflictions patiently and be content with our circumstances as these are the result of divine providence. Thus it has been with the letters that were sent to us with the gift accounts from our dear Halle through the benevolent care of our dear Dr. Francke. May our heavenly Father richly reward all our benefactors now and in eternity for their active love for Ebenezer, of which we now have had another clear and glorious sign.

The 6th of January. Today's Sunday, which we celebrated as the Feast of the Epiphany, has been a most important day. The great benefit that the Lord has bestowed on our forefathers by His word can be recognized by contemplating the blind heathen in this land, the Indians. Their condition is such that it might well move a Christian heart to prayer and pity. For they show us as in a picture how we would look without the means of grace. And we must note that these were not given to us because we are by birthright or nature better than the Indians; we must thank Jesus Christ and the Lord God and His mercy for them. We reminded our listeners in the Zion Church of this during today's service.

The 8th of January. There is little demand for cut boards these days, and therefore we have a large quantity stored at the mill. Tomorrow's shipment to Savannah is destined for Mr. Habersham and amounts to roughly 10,000 board feet. The latter has often rendered us service by taking on large quantities. We make little profit in these transactions, for the high wages and frequent repairs eat into all returns; however, our people have great use of these mills and they are quite indispensable to them.

The 9th of January. It would seem that some of our people are now quite ready to start lumber work and wood cutting and have become quite convinced of the usefulness of this type of work in this country. I heard this during my sojourn on the Blue Bluff (which is merely a name for the high land on the other side of Ebenezer Creek, which does not get flooded), and some people seem to have made a trial of this kind of work. Our people would be much encouraged in this matter if there were someone to buy the boards from them. For bringing them to Savannah on consignment without a firm buyer is not advisable, and our people cannot afford to wait long for payment since they need their money for their initial establishment in this country.[1] We as ministers cannot assume charge of this matter, for we have much more on our hands than we have time to manage, and are often ill judged if we get involved in external affairs.

It is surely comforting that God should assure His believers: "I will be with him in trouble, I will deliver him and honor him." Psalms 91:15.[2] Ebenezer has never been lacking in this and is not lacking it now. Among our sufferings, and I count in particular the illness of our oldest faithful minister,[3] the lack of a schoolmaster on the plantations, for we have not been able to find one here and now, and the physical want that still oppresses some among us. Also, there is a rampant cough and other maladies, which afflict the other two ministers so that they are prevented from following up on necessary tasks in the congregation, not to speak of the spiritual want that results from the lack of contrition and other offenses among our parishioners. But for all that we shall not want in courage, for the Almighty says: "I shall be with him who hath faith; I shall be with him in trouble, in his suffering and in all his pressing wants: I shall deliver him from all. For I am with you until the end of all days."[4] These comforts have been offered to us by today's weekly sermon and have strengthened the faithful among us.

The 15th of January. The first words of our beloved Jesus in His deepest humiliation, as they are recorded in the New Testament, namely: "Do you not know that I must be in that which is my Father's"[5] have strengthened me and others in our frailty. They have been further pressed into my memory by reading a funeral sermon delivered by our dear father in Christ, Senior Urslperger, which was sent to us recently. Today I had occasion with patients and other sufferers to press home these words in the very manner as in this edifying sermon. May God bless us in this effort.

The hut in which we customarily hold the prayer hour on the Blue Bluff was as crowded today as on several previous occasions; this gives us some hope that we may be able to work gradu-

ally on the hearts even of the people who live in this congregation. It is true that God has already spread His seed among
them, although it can as yet barely be seen.

The 18th of January. Zion church was badly in need of repair,
for not only the sills and transoms but in some places even walls
and the subfloors were rotted away. Much had to be done, therefore, to put in a new foundation and to repair walls and floor.
Since well-made pews have been lacking until now, these will be
put in at this time, as well as a convenient altar table. Our people
have worked on this task without pay, for the most part; but we
will have to assume payment of the carpenters, although we have
few funds available at this point. But we trust in Almighty God,
who is richer than those who pray to Him, and He will let us have
enough from His inexhaustible wealth through the agency of
benevolent donors or in other ways of His choosing, to pay for
these necessary outlays. True, our churches are poor, and our
listeners are poor, to wit, some have enough to live on, but
nothing to spare, and some must fight to make a living. Thus we
must look to the Lord for the maintenance of churches and
schools and must expect through Him the main part each time,
excepting some money that is given by some voluntarily.

The 20th of January. We are truly in a time of trial, for many
are affected by the cough and side-stitches, but God does not fail
to edify us from His word and comfort us, as happened today.
And when the hour comes, He will help us again, and until then
we shall be content if He eases our burden and sweetens it with
His strong comfort.

The 21st of January. Since the school on the plantations has
been lacking a schoolmaster for some time, and we have seriously been hoping to find one, we have offered the place to
honest Portz. He has now agreed to accept this service in the
name and with confidence in the Lord. He realizes that he is not
yet ready to be a model and guide our youth in every respect;
but we truly believe that he will prove a good man for the school
in the future, as we do not doubt his honesty and faithfulness;
we also consider that he is young and willing to learn what he
now lacks and in many respects is not unfit for this kind of work.
He is now being prepared by my dear colleague Rabenhorst, and
is not allowed to do much on his own but is required to watch and

observe how to treat children; here, he is receiving all necessary instruction.

The 25th of January. A few years ago, a man and his wife moved from Carolina to the Blue Bluff on the far side of Ebenezer Creek. This man seems to have a good mind and has made good arrangements for his plantation. He now has finished building a comfortable dwelling, and on his request it was consecrated last Wednesday, the 23rd of this month, with the word of the Lord and prayers at the time of our regular prayer meeting. On that occasion I learned that several people over there are ill and in bed, by which the Lord doubtless is preparing them for repentance.

Yesterday I resolved to travel to Goshen, but during the night I was struck with a high fever, followed by a sharp cough and the false side-stiches.[6] Today, I feel somewhat better through God's grace. Thus, things are in constant change, both inwardly and outwardly. The memory of the servants of Christ (Acts 14:22) serves us well in our suffering. It is part of the counsel of the Lord, given with grace and love and necessitated by our present unclean condition, that we shall pass to the Kingdom of God through much sadness. My dear frail colleague, who lives close by me, dropped in to see me this morning and encouraged me greatly by his advice to be quiet and resigned, following here the example of Christ, whose will is always subordinated to the will of His heavenly Father. It is a precious thing to be patient and hope for the help of the Lord. (*Lamentations* 3:26-33).

The 27th of January. Because of physical weakness, I was forced to let my dear colleague Mr. Rabenhorst carry the burden of this Sunday's work by himself. Praised be the Lord, who strengthened him in this task.

The 29th of January. Because I was able to visit a few families on the Mill River today, I stopped in with honest S. Reuter, who was sick, as was his wife. He is a living and active Christian, for whom the Kingdom of God lies not in words but in strength; thus, it was for good reason that, despite his great weakness, his mouth was full of praise. His material circumstances cause him no sorrow: he is constantly in communion with his Savior, although he has small children and almost no work gets done, since there really is nobody who can take care of the house. A well-intentioned young man, who formerly worked for us as a servant, attends on him on occasion and does his bidding. May God let him live just a little while longer, for such people are the support of our congregation, and their departure from this world causes me much pain, even if they truly are blessed thereby.

The 31st of January. At this end of the month, we have seen a sad example among us in a man who, even in Germany, had been in trouble with the authorities because of his evil conduct. Here, he continued in his ways, although not quite so blatantly. On this very morning, as he was about to depart on a journey, he fell ill and was dead by nightfall. We buried him today. At his funeral, we warned those present by his example not to defer repentance and conversion.

FEBRUARY 1754

The 1st of February. The weather has been so mild that we have even seen blossoms on some of the trees. We also had a thunderstorm this evening, but we fear that the cold may return. The Lord is regent, He will direct things in their proper way. If our listeners would only obey the voice of the Lord and accept good advice, how well off we would be!

The 8th of February. This afternoon I visited a few families. In one, I was asked to seek the reconciliation of husband and wife, and I found to my joy that they had in fact been reconciled. For this we thanked the Lord: "Blessed be the peacemakers, for they shall be called the children of God." In the next family, I was shown two children who have damaged their health by eating sand and clay.[1] Thus we find that this affliction has not passed from us. Both children have been well instructed and have realized that their eating of these materials is not right; but the older one, a boy, said that once the desire comes over him, it is so strong that it is impossible to resist. I instructed them how they should view this desire and how they should conduct themselves when it tempts and taunts them; and then we prayed together. The younger child wept and wished to be relieved of this pernicious appetite, which caused them so much suffering. It is hard not to be moved at this pitiable sight. May God help us here too.

The 10th of February. When I returned to the Zion Church for today's sermon, I found it restored to good condition and in some respects as well equipped as the Jerusalem Church; however, the windows are not yet as well fitted as here, because of our lack of funds and the fact that the other repairs have not yet been paid for. I was much pleased to see the church in its new state, and I felt moved to thank those who had worked without reward for their good intentions and their pains; here, the matter treated in today's sermon, namely the grace bestowed for good works originating in faith, Matthew 20:1 ff, offered me a suitable occasion. In the afternoon, we buried a young woman whom Mr. Rabenhorst had visited on several occasions during her illness and to whom she confessed her regret that during her healthy days she had postponed her conversion from one day to the next. True, she had been stirred and awakened during many sermons, but many things had set her back and distracted her, so that these awakenings had slowly disappeared. She would not or could not reveal to him what else had passed through her heart, for she was still very ignorant despite much instruction and necessary advice. This is yet another example to teach us that postponing repentance is a costly sin.

The 12th of February. The cold has returned with more force than during the entire winter months; this has destroyed the blossoms on the trees and, in whole or in part, such plants as do not tolerate the cold. However, the mulberry trees have not suffered any harm; for, although the sap had risen in them, there had been few green sprouts on any of them.

The 14th of February. It is truly to be regretted that many in this country who would be Christians, whether of our, the Reformed, or other religions, live in such blindness, conceit, and superstition. True, this is not often found at our place, and we would much regret that, but one need not travel far to find deep darkness. I have often wished that our circumstances would permit us to visit other towns on occasion and more frequently than now; but both time and resources are lacking. People do ask us to come and preach to them, but it seems that they just want to be polite; for, if we take them up and offer to come to them if only they will fetch us at an arranged time, it never works out as planned.

The 17th of February. The seed of the divine word has been richly sown among us on this day. If only it would fall on good soil everywhere! But there are still many things in this congregation which would cause this seed to be buried, lost, taken away, and smothered. Nonetheless, we are assured that we have not worked in vain and that there are those among us who resemble good soil and do not just hear the word but keep it with them and let it ripen into full fruit. May the Lord add to the number of those who believe and will be saved.

The 18th of February. In the family of Mr. M there is much sadness and tribulation. We have heard from her,[2] that she is a true follower of the Lord Jesus who is seriously concerned with the salvation of her own soul and that of her family. He too has made a good beginning, but he is not yet strong enough to meet his spiritual enemies head on and to withstand and vanquish their attacks.

The 20th of February. Today's prayer meeting at the Blue Bluff on the other side of the Ebenezer Creek treated of Ephesians 2:3-5. We used it to show our natural misery[3] and that we must recognize it before we can begin to set ourselves right. This is a difficult task with those who have considered themselves good Christians ever since their baptism, despite the fact that they have broken their baptismal covenant many times with deliberate sins. One might almost say that we have accomplished much if just one of them is ready to believe that he is worth nothing. Truly, we have found this often in our ministry.

When I went to the Minister's Plantation today, some men were busy repairing the dam in several places where the water had caused damage. For this task, they also used several of the Negroes who were bought for this plantation and who were not needed by the overseer. If the Lord should enable us to acquire some Negroes for our mills, they would yield some profit which we could invest in the congregation; for those Negroes are reliable, cheap, and industrious labor. True, they must be driven to industry, but this is true also for white servants, whom we dare not drive harshly for fear of losing them. We have tried every-

thing in our power to make do with white people. Had we suc-
ceeded, we would have been able to dispense with Negroes in
our town; but this will not be possible until this country is full of
people. For now, they all take up their own land, marry early,
and are good for nothing; thus, one loses both man and women
servants as quickly as one can get them.

The 24th of February. This Sunday our merciful Lord has
shown us His grace by His word, in that we contemplated with
our listeners the all-important history of the suffering and death
of our Mediator as recounted in Luke. In the prayer meeting,
which we now conduct during the day at five in the afternoon
and which every other day serves as a repetition lesson, I read
with some additional demonstrations the first instruction concerning the duty to remember the benefaction received from
the One who vouched for us; this is to be found in the second
edifying introductory sermon which our dear Senior Urlsperger had printed under the title: *Word of the Death and Life of
our Lord Jesus*.[4] Our dear Mr. Boltzius has been sufficiently
strengthened to attend today's sermon, which caused me much
joy.

The 25th of February. Today, Mr. Boltzius attempted to conduct the evening prayer meeting; and this, despite his persistent
weakness, proved more a joy than a burden to him. He based his
sermon on the delectable words: "The Lord will regard the
prayer of the destitute." Psalms 102:18; since he must still protect one eye, he intends to rely on well-known texts for the time
being. While I had to take over many of the prayer meetings,
I used the text of the late Professor Francke, *Brief Order of
Salvation*.[5]

I had previously learned on a number of occasions that some
of our listeners still lack proper understanding of the necessary
parts of the Christian faith; thus I assumed that our prayer
meetings would be a good opportunity to impart to them a summary of the order of salvation, as it is indeed stated on the title
page of the aforesaid work. I have often found it more useful
than many others, since it offers the truths necessary for salvation in a short, concise, edifying and sufficient manner.[6] I have
thus used this work with the children at school, in the preparation for Holy Communion and now most recently in prayer

meetings and weekly sermons, where I as good as chewed each truth contained therein for the children's better understanding and spoke to them of it in questions and answers. They have industriously attended school and church, and their parents seem to have insisted that their children should not miss any lesson. My major concern has been that they not only be offered those words that move and stir the will, for such stirrings disappear only too quickly for many of them. Rather I wish to impress and improve their understanding, so that they may receive well-founded and permanent knowledge.

In the meantime the aforesaid work by Dr. Francke has found so many readers that we have depleted our fairly large stocks; many ask for a copy, and people would be glad to pay for it if only they could obtain it. During these months I have so enjoyed catechizing my pupils that I wish I could spend my life at this task.

The 27th of February. Bächle on the Blue Bluff has had a new dwelling built which I dedicated today at his request with God's word and prayer. For the text, I chose the above-quoted precious saying from Psalm 102, verse 18.

MARCH 1754

The 1st of March. The wife of a former Frederica soldier has been close to death on several occasions and again is quite seriously ill.[1] At such times, she speaks much of her Savior and makes many good statements; but in truth it is difficult to reach the bottom of her heart and therefore I cannot trust in her even now. If we guide her to her sins and assure her that only those whose soul is pure and honest can gain forgiveness, she will readily admit being a great sinner, but then she wavers and talks of other things. It is truly difficult to help such persons. If we urge particular matters, they demand witnesses and one is just about in a court of law with them. This was almost the case with this woman on a previous occasion. With such people, it is better and more useful if we can find examples of similar conduct and demonstrate how such cases were set on the right path, without making it appear, however, that we are referring to them directly. It also is of good effect to give them an edifying book where their condition is clearly illustrated. Here, Ambrosius Wirth's book on communion has served us well.[2] We must wonder that there still are people like that in our congregation, for we do not hesitate to speak quite directly and frankly in our sermons; in this, thank God, we are quite free and unrestricted.

The 3rd of March. On this Invocavit Sunday, our faithful Savior has given us much grace from the story of His meritorious suffering and death. As it is said in today's message, the season of Lent is a most comforting time and a day of blessing. Many a soul has gathered a good store of salvation for eternity during this time, and we pray that our loving God may give us this grace again.

The 4th of March. It is our custom not to perform the rites of marriage until we have pronounced God's word for the day. Today, on one such occasion, we had the opportunity to listen to the comforting words of Hebrews 2:18. Because Jesus suffered and was tempted, He can help those who are tempted. This is a most suitable sermon for new spouses. For, while marriage is a state appointed by the Lord and much to be desired, we well know the temptations and trials that accompany it. Thus, pious spouses will receive these words as a great comfort.

The 6th of March. Yesterday a good friend from Savannah came here. In his house, the Ebenezer ministers have enjoyed much hospitality during their travel, and not only have we always been most grateful for these favors, but the Lord Himself has rewarded him in many ways. On his departure from Ebenezer this morning, we gave him a bundle of letters for Europe and a small box of nature specimens, which he will deliver to Mr. Habersham, who is loading a ship about to depart from Savannah.

Old Eischperger is among the truly poor in our village, and in part this is due to the frequent illness that strikes him and his family. For this reason they have much appreciated the benefactions that they twice received from charitable souls in Augsburg and Memmingen. They are otherwise well content with their circumstances and recognize that their trials are necessary to overcome their slovenly flesh; and yet they needed to be shown, during today's visit, the right way to vanquish the true enemy.[3] For this it is necessary to use constantly and industriously the word of the Lord, to engage in continuous prayer and in a constant vigil over mind and soul. If for lack of time they cannot do more, they should now and then recall or read a Bible verse and pray over it; they may then return to their work but note well what passes in their heart and mind, so that they will not forget everything right away but guard it in their aroused heart.

The 8th of March. The weather has been quite warm for the last few days, and green shows on every bush, including the mulberry trees. At the same time, the silkworm eggs could not be kept back anymore but yielded swarms of little silkworms. We notice a great joy in our congregation, for all approach the silk season with much enthusiasm.

The 10th of March. During last week's prayer meetings we have heard much through Luke 22:31 about the guile of one of our main enemies, which he[4] uses to select out the faithful by many harmful temptations. This is a matter that is most urgent in this free country, where there is much occasion for distractions and vanity, and where there is no barrier or defense against people from this and that sect.[5] And here we note with gratitude the merciful providence of the Lord for our congregation, which has been sheltered and protected from such people and around which the Lord has drawn a wall of fire, as He had promised His followers. We have used this circumstance to present to our listeners in Zion Church the words from Ephesians 6:18, where prayer is shown to be a means to salvation prescribed by the Lord Himself, by the constant and faithful use of which we can not only continue to share in these benefactions but also put on this spiritual armor against the enemy who is in our midst.

The 13th of March. Several among the congregation have declared their intention to participate in Holy Communion who have previously yielded to the vice of inebriation and have in part been punished for this by the civil authorities. We as ministers shall treat them in accordance with our duty and for their own best and that of others thus: Those who have caused open scandal shall be admitted only on the condition that they ask the whole congregation for forgiveness; but we will let a warning suffice for those whose transgressions did not become known. The explanations we receive on such occasions are quite good, so we hope the Christian discipline that we inflict will impress itself on their minds. Occasionally, we find that some say that they do not know how their drunkenness came to pass, and this should not cause much surprise with unconverted people; for the so-called rum is a dangerous potion in that its use cannot be forbidden altogether because experience has taught that it is of great benefit to health if taken in moderation.

True, it might be argued that weak beer could do just as well for this purpose, but beer is not easily available unless one makes it at home, as is the case in the house of the ministers and some other people. But, since this beer is made from unmalted corn and syrup, it is not the best and healthiest draught, although it serves us well enough. But for a number of reasons we would wish we could brew real beer at this place so that it could be sold at the taverns. For rum has two main faults: 1) It draws much money out of the country, and 2) it is the cause of many scandalous and disorderly events, which we would rather not describe in our diaries. If only all drunkards would consider that which is written in Galatians 5:21, that is, they shall not inherit the Kingdom of God.

The 17th of March. God's word was preached in both churches today, as was done a week ago. But, since tomorrow is our day of Thanksgiving and Remembrance and we will celebrate Holy Communion, the whole congregation will assemble in Jerusalem Church, and that is why we held today's services in two places.

The 18th of March. We celebrated our day of Thanksgiving and Remembrance today as follows: In the morning we opened the public service with a prayer, as is customary every Sunday. We then sang *Nun lob, Mein Seel, den Herrn*, etc., and then read the song of praise of Moses from Deuteronomy 32:1-44; this was followed by the hymn: *Sei Lob und Ehr dem höchsten Gut*. The sermon treated of Hosea 13:4-6, and we spoke to the renewed remembrance of the Lord's benefactions. The introduction was taken from Psalms 103:1, 2. We then sang another hymn, celebrated communion, etc.

In the afternoon, we first read a chapter from the Bible, as is our custom not only at the beginning but also at the end of each service, unless there is a large number of communicants or another important reason for omitting this step. After this reading, we edified ourselves with the congregation by singing two further hymns. In the intermission, several children repeated the 33rd Psalm, which they had learned by heart for this occasion. During the sermon, which was held in the form of a catechism, i.e., by question and answer, we learned first from 1 Thessalonians 5:18 the meaning of gratitude and what should lead us to it. We then encouraged each other to the praise of the Lord from Psalm 100, as the text for the day. Lastly, we sang the hymn written on this psalm: *Nun Jauchzt dem Herrn alle Welt.* During the evening prayer meeting we reminded ourselves of the many benedictions that the Lord has bestowed on us in this place. We ended with heartfelt prayer and intercession. Thus, on the very day and time when we made an offering of thanks and praise to our greatest Benefactor, we received all these new and great gifts from His benevolence. Hallelujah.

The 18th of March.[6] "Blessed be the Lord, who daily loadeth us with benefits, and the God of our salvation."[7] For this wonderful Lord has led me, Boltzius, close to death over the last four months, but then He took mercy on me and has so blessed the wishes sent to Him on my behalf by my dear colleagues and my pious listeners that my soul has received much blessing from this illness and my almost consumed body has received much strength over the last three weeks. I was able to resume my office in church, school, visitations, and others tasks. I cannot yet use my left eye for reading and writing because there still is a thin skin over my eyeball. For this, I am being treated by Mr. Mayer and am awaiting the help of the Lord in the manner which He has decided.

For there is much comfort in my heart from these words: "Thou shalt guide me with thy counsel,"[8] which has decided nothing but what brings me blessing. Even if it goes strangely at times, I still know that it will all come out well. And in this and other hours of trial, I have much appreciated the verse on which I plan to base my public sermon next Laetare Sunday, "For God is my King of old." Psalms 74:12.

On this our day of thanksgiving, which we are now celebrating for the 21st time since our arrival in Georgia in much peace and for the praise of the Lord and the edification of our souls, we have also celebrated Holy Communion with 132 persons.

The 19th of March. Hans Maurer's house has been visited by God with much sorrow for many years now, but this has caused much good to happen in his wife's heart. He is now down with fever and a serious illness in his leg. This has awakened him to seek earnestly the creation of grace in his soul. He asked for me and with humble words and flowing eyes made such a confession of the condition of his soul that I could clearly see in him the beginning work of grace of the Lord. His oldest daughter as well has been awakened to more seriousness in her Christianity and the seeking of grace by a burdensome illness. She and other grown children are being prepared for Holy Communion.

The 21st of March. A Reformed man from Purysburg asked me for a book of sermons so that he might edify himself with his neighbors during their Sunday meetings. I intend to lend him the sermons of the late Mr. Schade on the gospel for Sundays and Holy Days[9] and the related sermons by the blessed Professor Francke.[10] I have lent the latter's impressive sermons on repentance to a meeting of Lutherans and the Reformed people in Savannah.

The 22nd of March. Because our gracious Lord has strengthened our Mr. Boltzius, we shall be able to resume our visits to those of our confession who live farther away. Most importantly, these will be the people in Goshen, who exhibit far more serious concern for the world of the Lord than other people. They gladly contribute to the cost of travel and meet their ministers with much kindness; but we take nothing from them than the necessary food and drink during our sojourn; in addition, they pay for a travel companion, for one cannot travel alone.[11]

Today we preached a sermon of thanksgiving for them, too, for they have shared many of our benefactions and many of our trials, from which God has miraculously delivered them. They came in large numbers and listened with much emotion and stirrings of the heart to the sermon of thanksgiving: may God grant that it may go deeper than these transient feelings. We sang the edifying hymn, *Ich singe Dir mit Herz und Mund*.

The 23rd of March. A few weeks ago, our surgeon and justice of the peace[12] moved himself and his family to his plantation just before Abercorn. It would not have been profitable for him to pay an overseer for his three Negroes, for these men get at least

£ 24 sterling. But, if the owner of a plantation is not there to watch every aspect of the economy, there is much effort and money out but little to show for it. Both Mr. Lemke, and I, Boltzius, have learned this on our plantation, which was set up a little more than a year ago.[13] Neither of us can live there, because it is a good four hours from Ebenezer and we would not be able to serve our congregation as we can now. On the other hand, the Lutheran residents of Goshen would have more benefit from our office for their own instruction and that of their children if one of us could live there. For their houses and those of the residents of Josephs Town are close to our plantation; and Abercorn, where many German people have settled, is barely three English miles away.

Under the direction of my dear colleague, Mr. Lemke, a plantation for the support of the third minister has been set up close to the new sawmill, which is being worked with two Negro males, two females and one boy bought with the money sent to us for this purpose. We have hired a supervisor and manager, but Mr. Mayer and other knowledgeable men whose advice is much desired for this plantation have counseled that one of the ministers and his family will have to move out there if it is to serve its purpose. Mr. Lemke would be willing if the Lord were to show him more directly His will and intent. His office would not be affected, since this new plantation is at the southern end of the Salzburger plantations on the Mill Creek, and church and school are only two miles away.

The 24th of March. During my illness, our dear Zion Church on the plantations has been repaired with the help of the money that God has sent to us from London some time ago. We have been able to provide some convenient changes for both ministers and listeners. Today, this Laetare Sunday, I had the pleasure of preaching there for the first time and of presenting to my listeners the lesson on Christ's benefaction and our duty; and here I noted with much pleasure the help of the Lord and a right satisfactory attention on the part of my listeners. In the afternoon, Mr. Lemke took over from me, and he preached on a part of the story of the passion from Luke 22. Mr. Rabenhorst in turn has spread the seed of the gospel in the Jerusalem Church both morning and afternoon with preaching and catechizing. It pleased me much to see in church some of my old listeners who a few years ago moved to Goshen and Josephs Town for lack of good land around Ebenezer. They eagerly visit our sermons, although the journey out here and then back home takes several hours. Also, the distance is not thought too long for their wives after their six weeks of lying in, as we observed today for one of them.

The 30th of March. Among those being prepared for Holy Communion are some children who are well along in years but still most ignorant. They are a good example of the harm done if parents, or those who act in their stead, do not see to their children's instruction early on, but wish to teach them on their own although they are not fit for this task or in other ways neglect this work. When the time of admission to Communion draws near, as now, such children are finally sent into the preparation, but they cause us much inconvenience, for we do not know how to teach even the barest necessities of Christian faith in the short time allocated for their instruction. The above-mentioned children have come to our town only recently and many of them have not been brought up to do anything but a little reading.

We are now teaching these *praeparandis*[14] the catechism, both in town and on the plantations, and in the case of most our work is not without blessing, so that we do have some joy and edification in our work.

APRIL 1754

There are now a large quantity of white mulberry trees in our settlements and on all our plantations.[1] If God blesses our work, we shall have a good amount of silk prepared at our town. All of our families are showing great industry in this work, which is richly rewarded because silk still commands a good price. By contrast, some do not make the same profit from cattle as some years ago. The cows that wintered in the woods have lost much weight because of the wet season; some perished in the swamps and many have borne no calves. But God knows what is good for us.

The 6th of April. Whenever possible, we prefer to visit in their own house those people who work for wages; we do not only wish to avoid keeping them from their labors for long, but also like to use this occasion to speak to them from God's word according to their circumstances and pray with them, whereupon they receive their due wages. This procedure takes some of our time, but it is pleasurable and of considerable usefulness.

Today, some used this occasion to complain of their slowness in doing good and quoted some of the thoughts from our sermons that had impressed themselves on their minds or else not been fully understood. For the latter, we spent some time in simple explanation. Others considered it a great benefaction that their ministers would take time to awaken and remind them, and they added that the reading of good books is worthy and useful but cannot make the same impression as the sermon or advice of a minister. Also, their readings were not as clear and unequivocal as their ministers' words, etc.

The 10th of April. Things are getting much worse with the recently mentioned children who have hurt their health by eating clay and sand. In their great weakness, they have asked for a minister, and we gladly accorded them their wish and impressed upon them the words: "Even if we sin, we have an advocate," 1 John 2:2, whereby we led them to sin in general and in particular that by which they are harming their health and their life. We directed them to Jesus as their advocate, on whom, if they truly regretted their sins, they could count for sure. They listened to all this with much attention and much emotion.

The 13th of April. On the 10th, I had departed for Goshen in the evening, where I performed the following tasks. On the 11th, Maundy Thursday, I preached the sermon for Holy Communion and performed the act of confession after that. Before and after these tasks, I spoke separately with several persons, in seriousness and love, as required by their circumstances. The next day, I preached twice to the congregation, and Holy Communion was celebrated with 40 people. In this, our gracious Lord has much strengthened me. This morning I returned home, after having spent the night on the Minister's Plantation, and found my dear colleagues well. Mr. Boltzius, who is still a bit weak, has clearly felt divine assistance in his sermon on the cross, and this has given him enough courage and trust in the Lord to assume another sermon for tomorrow, the first day of Easter.

The number of German people of our confession has grown considerably in and around Goshen. Only a few people had come this time from Josephs Town, which is not far off, because there is much sickness there. Otherwise, the number of communicants would have been even greater. Since there is a nice number of children among them who need school and religious instruction, I had several matters to discuss with them. (1) They should think how to go about providing a larger and more comfortable place for public services, in particular for the instruction of their children. For this the narrow hut in which they have congregated until now will no longer do. (2) It would be necessary to choose a site roughly in the middle between Goshen, Abercorn, and Josephs Town, for these three places form a kind of triangle and thus would be suitable for forming one congregation. They immediately proposed a plantation which, although still unoccupied, has been surveyed and which they wished to buy so that their future schoolmaster could use the land for planting. This plantation abuts the preacher's land for the first Ebenezer minister, which land also lies just about midway between the above three towns.

(3) They should elect three elders with whom we could dispose of church and school matters, and who could charge themselves of these affairs and at the same time ensure that they conduct themselves worthy of the Gospel and admonish those who live a life of vexation or, if they cannot convince them, inform us accordingly. For, since there has been no arrangement for church discipline in this area, there have been many objectionable events. Those of good will much appreciated our proposals, and none raised objections. True, there will be hardly anyone who would not have his children instructed, if it is at all possible; and therefore we hope that we have met with everyone's approval. May our almighty God in His mercy for their immortal souls provide us with funds, so that we can realize all these good works.

They urgently need a schoolmaster, but where they shall obtain one and his support is known only to the Lord.

They have much hope to receive something from the new governor who is about to arrive, but this is most uncertain.[2] I trust in the Lord that we shall with His blessing receive enough income from the Minister's Plantation that we may use it for much good work here and in other places for the best of the Kingdom of God. True, the care of all matters related to these proposals requires thought, provision, inquiry, putting in order, prudence, calculation, and providence, all of which are a great burden; for there is hardly anyone here whom one could trust with the execution of such matters. Those who are trustworthy often lack skill; and the skillful lack trustworthiness. At least I have noted that those who take care of every trifle on their plantations can go far; among those who rely on others, however, many lose out. In order to provide some relief for myself in this work, therefore, I shall move with my family onto this plantation in accordance with the Lord's will. If God will only strengthen my heart and not lift His hand off me, things will go well.

We have done pretty well with our purchase of Negroes. They finish their daily work on time, so that we have no trouble with them on this account, in contrast to many others. They like it here, work happily, but are kept well for that. I think I can rest assured that none will try to run away. Recently, I caught a boy in lying; I reprimanded him and he was duly punished afterward. Since then he says he will not lie anymore for it is a sin; we heard the same thing when we examined him. I could report more good things about them, but will postpone this until another time.

Today and yesterday we celebrated Holy Easter. The three ministers were strengthened by the Lord to present the word of the Lord with blessing, on the first day in both churches and on the second in Jerusalem Church only. Since the first of these was forced under the Lord's will to spend last Christmas in his room and since his illness continued for a good while after that, we must praise the Lord that he has gradually regained strength sufficient to permit him to celebrate Easter in public and to testify to the strength of Christ's resurrection. Those who love the Lord's word have pleased us with their careful attention to our sermon; the only difficulty was a heavy rain this morning which prevented them from coming but which much blessed our fields.

The 19th of April. The work on our silk is proceeding well, and God is giving us temperate weather.

The 24th of April. In traveling to the Blue Bluff (now called Bethany), I noticed a strange plant with a yellow flower, which I had not seen before and shall describe in greater detail elsewhere.

The 30th of April. The Lutheran inhabitants of Goshen, Josephs Town, and Abercorn have elected three church elders in accordance with our plans and have decided to fence in a large and convenient place where they can hear the Lord's word. They have therefore felt the need to discuss this matter with me in greater detail, and I traveled there on the 27th, although on that day I continued my ride as far as Dr. Graham's house. I was much astonished by the beautiful stretch of land between his domicile and Abercorn, but all this area has been surveyed. My intention on this trip was to have a look at indigo production, for this is well developed at his place. We are therefore resolved to try this in our fields as well, and it may well be that God blesses this work as he has done for our silk.

I, Rabenhorst, have returned by God's grace from Savannah, where I preached and dispensed the Lord's Supper. Upon my return, I found that God has placed a new cross on my frail help-meet. I therefore prepared for the passion week and thought to myself, who knows what the Lord has decided for me? A year ago I was in much sadness because of the illness of my wife, which was so severe that she thought she would depart for heaven on Good Friday. But the Lord helped me then, and He is helping us now gloriously. And here I cannot but help mention that the Lord had awakened some good friends in Holstein to provide us with several good medications, among them a precious essence, some of which was given to me for my house. And God so blessed this remedy that after I had twice given my wife several drops in a glass of wine, she was completely restored with these drops and a *pulvis vitalis* from *Halle*. "Bless the Lord, O my soul, and forget not all his benefits."[3]

The 30th of April.[4] This past month, the Lord has bestowed much blessing on ministers and listeners, body and soul. The word of the Lord, thank God, has been publicly and abundantly preached to the whole congregation. And, while the Lord does not at this point let us notice much of the benefit from the sowing of His word among the adults, we much enjoy witnessing it among the children, ten of whom have been prepared for Holy Communion through teaching and admonishment. I have been in charge of seven and can say of most of them that our faithful Savior has instilled in them, through His word, spirit and life and set a good Christian beginning in them.

MAY 1754

The 2nd of May, I was called to a sick woman, with whom I talked of the important preparation for a blessed death, that is, that she must first of all recognize her sins and believe in Him who redeems them. I led her to examine her behavior and obedience toward the richly proclaimed Word of the Lord and the blessing emanating therefrom through the Holy Spirit, etc. She confessed she had nothing but bad conduct to report in this regard, and I left after giving her the necessary instructions.

The 4th of May. Today ten of the children we have been instructing have been confirmed among much emotion on the part of the children themselves and their elders. I had all of them come to me for an hour prior to the *actu confirmationis*,[1] and I catechized them on the words: "Know that ye were not redeemed with corruptible things, as silver and gold, etc.,"[2] I showed them their vanity or that they walk empty of all true good, and emphasized above all the word "Knoweth," showing them how this is a most important part of true faith, etc. Then I prayed with them and dismissed them from my presence.

The same took place on the 5th, before the sermon and before they went to take Holy Communion, when I spoke to them of the first love, and quoted also Isaiah 43:4, "and I have loved thee," etc. My dearest oldest colleague preached the sermon of confirmation, for both children and adults, from 2 Corinthians 1:21, 22. The dear children gave us all much joy, and how could we but rejoice at their fine answers in response to Mr. Lemke's examination, their attention to the act of confirmation, and their remorseful hearts? They took a sad leave from me, who had instructed them on the plantations, and now we trust in the blessing of the Lord and desire to see them become ten fruitful vines and living stones on the walls of the house of the Lord in this time of grace.

The 5th of May. If we have reason to say with Jacob, "We are not worthy of the least of all the mercies, and of all the truth, which thou hast showed unto us,"[3] how much more true is this in view of today's happenings, in part because of the rich edification which we have received from the preached words of the Lord, from the wonderful hymns sung, and from our common prayer, and in part because of our rejoicing at the incomparable love feast bestowed by our dearest savior, and by which He has abundantly delighted our souls.

Of the children who have heretofore been instructed in the town and on the plantations, a total of ten, that is three boys and seven girls, have been admitted for the first time to the Lord's Supper. Their conduct until today may well serve to shame some among their elders in terms of conduct and their recognition of the truth. Prior to the confession, they were examined from the catechism, and thereupon they were confirmed with much emotion on their part. This occasion prompted our senior minister to preach an impressive confirmation sermon in the morning and with great benefit. He used for this sermon the text of 2 Corinthians 1:21–22, "Now he which stablisheth us with you in Christ, and hath anointed us, is God; who hath also sealed us, and given the earnest of the Spirit in our hearts."

Prior to the conclusion of this sermon, each of the ten children received a letter from the *Golden ABC* of the late Pastor Freylinghausen,[4] and each promised publicly to become a fervent follower of the Lord Jesus, that is to say, to conduct himself or herself in accordance with the content of such a golden letter. This was done without even the shadow of constraint; instead, there was a general emotion among all. At this point I will not go into our hopes for each of the children, if God so wills it, nor that which He may plan for them.

The names of the ten children are as follows: Johannes Remshardt from Langenau; Christian Steiner, first son of the pious deceased Ruprecht Steiner; Jacob Bechle from Langenau; Hanna Elisabeth Gronau, a deserving daughter of the late Christian Israel Gronau, whose memory is still bestowing much blessing among us; Maria Rosina Hammer from Lausnitz, in Saxony; Maria Kogler, the oldest daughter of our sawmiller; Ursula Unsold, from Giengen; Barbara Schneider, from Trimbach; Anna Maria Zuercher, whose father died in this country, but she was born in Purysburg and has a miserable fellow for a stepfather, who knows well that he is walking on the broad path to hell but will not become sober and free himself of his own will from the snares of the devil in which he is caught. Her mother, however, is of good character, and this Anna Maria, her daughter, gives us much hope. Anna Maria Haefner; her father, too, died here, that is, in Savannah. Her stepfather's name is Straube.

They all give us much hope. In addition to these, others have received instruction who, while old enough, could not have been admitted this time. But, if they are industrious and obey the word of the Lord, we shall admit them the next time and meanwhile continue with them in their instruction.

The 6th of May. In yesterday's sermon of confirmation, Mr. Boltzius demonstrated that there are many, also among the adults, who are not capable of confirmation, since they have learned nothing and in all other respects give no proof of anything good in which they could be confirmed. He pitied such people and, since there are several of those among us, he offered them an hour or so of instruction on Sundays, if they so desired, for their work will not permit time during the week. Today I learned from two young men that this remonstration had left a deep impression on them and that they lamented their misery with many tears and sighs; they would much like to see a minister, but one of them feared he was no longer capable of learning. However, we will be glad to condescend and speak to them in a simple fashion, so that this obstacle can be overcome.

Today I met an old man of fifty and some years, who is also very ignorant but must listen well to the sermons, for he remembered having heard in them some of the things I told him today. It is truly pitiful that we must hear from such people that instruction was so very poor at their homes in Germany when they were young. All they had to do was learn some things by rote, and then they were straightway admitted to the Lord's Table. One of them said he wished he had never received the Lord's Supper, for they had left him in great ignorance; and he would now be all the more ready for instruction. One is truly shocked at such news, if one considers their fate on the last day of judgment. As they themselves admit, however, it is not always the

ministers who are at fault, but rather worldly parents and superiors who do not give enough time for instruction to their children and subordinates. Thus, the teacher is forced to speed the
lessons, much against his wishes, an experience which we have
also had in this country.

The 7th of May. I was forced to travel to Savannah for some
urgent business, from which I returned on the evening of the
9th with God's help. We had left the night before and, because it
was dark before the moon rose, we missed the right way and the
strong current drove us aground on a small island in the river so
that the bow of the loaded boat was wedged in the sand. After
much heavy labor, we were adrift again, but the men were forced
to row against the current with all their strength so as to avoid
being caught in the tree stumps at the upper end of this island.
We barely navigated around these obstacles, and we must thank
the Lord for having torn us from this danger. Traveling on the
Savannah would be good if it were not for these tree stumps
which dot its course.

The 10th of May. The gentlemen of the Council traveled to
the Ogeechee together to lay out the plan for a future town.[5] In
Savannah, much is being done to clean out brush and weeds
which are found here and there.

In Savannah, we encountered some Indians, who gallivanted
about in their atrocious manner, which caused one of them to
lose his life in a cruel accident. Nobody even so much as looks at
them, so as to avoid renewed quarrels, to which they are easily
disposed because of their suspicious nature.

May the 12th. Today, at the end of the morning sermons, it
was publicly announced in both churches that we shall begin
with the instruction of those who fell behind in the course of
their lives. After the afternoon sermon, a goodly number of
them assembled in the first minister's house for this purpose,
and we spent a good and pleasant hour with them. May our
faithful Lord bless this work in all of them, so that they may see
the truth and be helped, if this is His blessed will.

The 14th of May. Last Sunday, examination of the ninth and
tenth commandments led us to the glorious words "Delight thyself in the Lord; and he shall give thee the desires of thine
heart."[6] Psalms, 27:4. We took this word home with us for fur-

ther reflection; and today, when I held the weekly sermon in the
Zion Church, I chose this for my text. From this, our faithful
Lord gave much edification, and I praise His glorious name.
Our listeners derive the greatest satisfaction from these well-
known verses, a fact that we have noted often. They know the
words, and therefore our teaching stays with them all the better
and can thus work more strongly in their hearts. The word of
the Lord is a rich source: the deeper we dig, the more richly
flows its spring, and this we note with regard to such beautiful,
often taught words, "This is a true saying."[7]

I cannot omit another well-known verse, which Mr. Boltzius
examined last week in the prayer hour for our renewed edification. We find it in 2 Corinthians 5:14, 15: "The love of Christ
constraineth us; because we thus judge, that if one died for all,
then were all dead; and that he died for all, that they which live
should not henceforth live unto themselves, but unto him which
died for them, and rose again." What deep words these are! God
be praised for the bountiful treasure that lies hidden in these
words. For how well we are fed on our pasture in this desert by
the Lord, our shepherd. The word is true, "I will allure her, and
bring her into the wilderness, and speak comfortably to her."
Hosea 2:14.

The 16th of May. A sick woman sent word to ask for my visit,
and I found her in a most impressive state of mind. She suffers
much but is quite resigned as befits a true disciple of Christ, to
which her husband testified with several instances. He also declared that they had both subjected themselves entirely to the
will of the Lord but, if He were to listen to their prayer and help
his wife regain her health, they would make this their lesson for
the rest of their lives and eagerly serve the Lord with a faithful
hearts.

The 17th of May. As I am now committed to hold the weekly
sermons at Zion Church, I am continuing to attempt to impart to
our listeners a summary understanding of the order of salvation. I myself am feeling a good effect of this, and I hope the
same for my listeners. I have never found it as important as I do
now, for it is an order fully in accordance with the wisdom, holiness, and grace of the Lord: an order which could not be better
constituted for its intended purpose, which is to return man to

his lost salvation without offending the honor of the Lord. I thus feel much aggrieved if people show me books which claim to have been written for this purpose but where I can hardly find a trace of this order. In some instances, it is merely named, but not explained; and this causes many disadvantages to some.

The 26th of May. We truly suffer from the fact that many to whom God's word has been preached for many years insist on remaining unrepentant.

The 27th of May. Today I called on Michael Schneider, whom I found hard at work in the field despite his age. His hair is gray, he is not far from being seventy, but always healthy; in truth, he has not seen much illness while in this country. He lives at the far end of the plantations on the Mill River and has much opportunity there to raise his cattle, which is his main source of income.

The 31st of May. At the end of this month and after a long wait, our friendly God has edified us with letters from our dear benefactors and friends in Europe, for which gift may His name be praised. We gather from these letters that they are all still alive and well and that we are remembered in their prayers and blessed by their friendship. May the Lord strengthen them all and keep them alive for many years and continue to let them support us in their dear letters with advice, comfort, and joy at times of need. We consider these an inestimable benefit in our pilgrimage.

JUNE 1754

The 1st of June. In the evening prayer meetings in preparation of the feast of Epiphany, Mr. Boltzius used these important words as the basis of our edification: "If ye then, being evil, know how to give good gifts unto your children; how much more shall your heavenly Father give the Holy Spirit to them that ask him?" Luke 11:13. This gave me occasion to read once more the important sermon of our dearest Father in Christ, Court Chaplain Ziegenhagen, on these words, and to draw much benefit from them.

The 3rd of June. Yesterday and today, we celebrated the Feast of the Epiphany with much blessing and joy. It was not only pleasant but also highly edifying to see our listeners come in

large numbers to our sermons and listen to them with such attention as if they wished to say: "Now therefore we are all here
present before God, to hear all things that are commanded thee
of God."[1] Thus, we cannot but believe that the Holy Ghost and
His power of salvation is here among us. On the first day, Mr.
Rabenhorst celebrated the word of the Lord in Goshen as well,
and today he helped the first minister in Jerusalem Church.

The 6th of June. After catechizing my listeners at Zion
Church, I returned to our recently developed Minister's Plantation where, after a brief delay, I had the pleasure of receiving
our dear colleague Mr. Boltzius on his return from Savannah.
He brought several additional letters from our dearest Fathers
and benefactors from Europe, which Mr. Whitefield had delivered to him. Of the latter, he recounted several pleasant instances, among them his continuing friendship and generosity
towards our congregation, and his continuing disposition to
help us in material matters as well.

Since this 6th day of June is also the anniversary on which Mr.
Rabenhorst received his call to the ministry in Halle, he used this
occasion, together with several friends, to awaken and edify but
also to humble himself before the Lord for all the faithfulness
that He has shown him.

The 15th of June. We hear from Halifax[2] that many new settlers are arriving there from North Carolina, Maryland, and
Virginia; this is also reported from the area of the Midway River
between Frederica and Savannah. As a result crops, which have
until now been quite reasonable, have risen in price.

The 16th of June. Today, the example of Lazarus and of the
rich man in Luke 16 has served to recall to us our mortality. For
from both of them it is said: "He died". And thus it will be for
any and all of us, whether sooner or later, and this has served to
awaken all those who have been lacking so far in true repentance
and to prepare themselves for a blessed death. We have held
Holy Communion with 125 persons.

The 20th of June. In addition to our normal work, we have
been busy for several days in responding to our recent letters
from Europe so as to expedite them shortly. It is a great relief to
us in our afflictions to be able to write so fully and openly about

our needs and concerns; I regret, however, that they still have much trouble with our material needs, although they bear this burden gladly.

The 26th of June. Upcountry and in a northerly direction, in the vicinity of the Mississippi River, a beautiful terrain has been discovered which has aroused the interest of both the English and the French. The former, we hear, have started to take possession, while the latter have built forts in several locations to expel the English. We do know that the governor of Carolina has sent a troop of men in this area in order to interfere with the French in their endeavors. It may well be difficult for the English, at least initially, to subsist in this remote part of the Mississipppi, because they have difficulties in transporting provisions there. But they seem to be able to weather these difficulties, at least in part. As long as they are able to keep themselves supplied with rum and sun-dried meat, which is easily obtainable here by hunting, they can subsist until they get better provisions. I have tasted such dried buffalo meat and find that it has a pleasant taste and is strong and nourishing.[3]

It is such people, who can help themselves and make do with little, who are suitable for this country; but those who arrive in the belief that they can pretend to be gentlemen from the outset, as has been true of many Germans, will not do well here. But those who work hard, do not fear hard work, and are content with what they have can in good time very well become gentlemen in this country. I can easily supply a list of such persons if it would serve a purpose. The most important thing is to settle on good land at the outset, and here the Salzburgers failed, because they did not know the land; there is little that can be done to change this now.

In particular, people who are knowledgeable about lumber can make a good living, provided they have learned to economize. For they can earn as much as three to five shillings per day, and this goes for wheelwrights, carpenters, cabinet makers, masons, and others. But they must not be headstrong and think that they know it all, but accommodate themselves to the manners of this country. This is not difficult, for here they seek no great artisans but desire simple and durable products, because these can be made in a shorter time. I know somebody who at first cut boards himself and has now become a great gentleman, while still gaining most of his profit from lumber.

On the 27th, we again received much joy from a letter of our dearest Father in Christ, our beloved Senior Urlsperger. In particular, I, Rabenhorst, much enjoyed my ordination sermon and the enclosed excerpt from *God's American Husbandry*.[4] May my Savior be praised for arranging everything so well. May He repay his servant for his care and trouble and let your[5] plans succeed under the blessing of His hand.

Until now, the people in Goshen have shown great hunger for the word of God so that I, Lemke, have arranged with my dear colleagues to teach the word of the Lord to them every third Sunday if one of us can be spared.

The 28th of June. In the catechetical hour, I talked to the children about the glorification of Christ, which has benefited us as much as His humiliation. The greatest blessing we derive therefrom is the intercession which our Mediator, the right hand of the Lord, undertakes on our behalf and the bestowal of the Holy Spirit. As is our custom, this lesson took place in the form of questions and answers, so that one question followed the other in good order, but never too fast; and, if God will bless us, there were no other questions than those which were to the heart of the matter and for our improvement. In this way, we keep the children's constant attention and encourage them to think and speak.

In church, we heard the comforting lesson of justification through faith, which was presented from the word of the Lord in such a manner that it cannot lead us to false security but only to salvation.[6] This lesson is such that, despite being industriously applied, it cannot be fully and correctly and beneficially understood until we experience it personally. We have often found this to be true among our congregation. Souls which are first becoming concerned about their salvation often cling to the law and good works; it is difficult to make them see that forgiveness of our sins must be accepted and desired from faith alone, and it is only from that condition that good works can flow.[7]

We thus seize every opportunity to challenge the faith of all those who are troubled and burdened, and we have just experienced this in our evening prayer meetings as conducted by the first minister, when we contemplated the beautiful song: *Nun bitten wir den heiligen Geist* and its second verse, which the late Master Sommer had specially couched in terms of questions and answers by the congregation.

JULY 1754

The 3rd of July. My dear colleague, Mr. Rabenhorst, will preach in Goshen next Sunday and dispense Holy Communion. Today, he held a preparatory sermon there and at the same time inquired into the previous life circumstances and actions of the parishioners. This was to make sure that, if penance or reconciliation were necessary, it could be taken care of prior to Sunday; but it seems that he found a fairly orderly state of affairs among them.

The 28th of July. The content of the fourth petition in our Lord's prayer, which we examined in public this afternoon, was most appropriate to today's gospel of Mark 8:1, etc. Through both the blessed Lord has strengthened us in our belief in Him, the almighty Creator and Lord of heaven and earth. In particular, the dear promise in Hebrews 13:5 has been blessed in a number of our listeners. Today's Holy Communion was attended by a large number of people; and we conducted it as if we were close to death, singing a number of mourning songs during the ceremony. The preparation was held yesterday, in similar manner, in both churches.

The 29th of July. Today, an honest Salzburger told me with a heavy heart of several men, largely among the unmarrieds, who yesterday frivolously missed the afternoon sermon on the day of the Lord; this despite their recognition of the letter of the Lord, who must thus know that the violation of the Sabbath and the contempt of the means of grace is a serious sin. We agreed to use the necessary seriousness in dealing with such people and agreed that we would rather not have them in our congregation than to suffer their impious ways.

The 31 of July. We have now passed the second month of the summer in health and peace. We recognize this as a blessing and all the more so with much gratitude as it recalls to us the season when our miraculous Lord, a year ago this summer, found it necessary to chasten us with illness, from which affliction and trial He has by and by mercifully delivered us. As I recall, only two people in the community are ill. In Purysburg, death made a clean sweep of it last spring, which has much disturbed the people there in their silk manufacture. Here, however, we have produced more than 2,000 pounds,[1] a quantity never reached before. Since every year a new stand of mulberry trees is planted and the older trees increase in size and strength, it is to be hoped that in a few years we will produce a goodly amount of silk. The poor people here benefit much from the profits to be made in this undertaking, for they have nothing else with which to provide for their clothes.

Next to silk, indigo is one of the most profitable enterprises and may well be preferable to silk in this respect. One acre can well yield three times the crop necessary for a hundred pounds of this plant, and the work takes barely a few days. The pound brings 4 shillings or more. We do not have much knowledge and experience in indigo production here, for else we would have a larger trade in it. We have not had any except for what has been tried this summer on the Minister's Plantation.

AUGUST 1754

Since I now live closer to Zion Church, public service will be held there more often for as long as God keeps the three of us healthy. Our dear colleague Boltzius as well preaches there every third week, as happened today; and he brought us rich edification.

The 18th of August. Last Friday, or the 16th of this month, the herdsman and overseer of the community cattle ranch, Johann George Lamprecht, rode from the woods into town and from there left by way of the first sawmill. By that time, night had fallen and a strong thunderstorm had come up, causing pitch black darkness such as we have not observed for a long time. Nonetheless, the aforementioned man did not want to stay at the mill, despite all cautions to the contrary. Instead, he set out to return to the town, but on his way across the large bridge close to town, he slipped and fell into the water with his horse. Today, he was found dead in the bushes. It is strange that this sad coincidence should have happened just before the 10th Sunday after Trinity, when we read the story of the destruction of Jerusalem. This gave the first minister a good occasion to illustrate today's sermon with many admonitions. Further, we note that said Lamprecht was among those of whom we had occasion to list serious complaints on June 29.

The awakened spirits among us are making much progress on their path, and some of them are very serious about their salvation. Sometimes these are joined by a few others, although there are not many of them. We cannot write about what the Lord may do here and there in secret, but there is no doubt that even now things may well come to pass as at the time of Elias, of which Paul reports in Romans 11. May the Lord therefore strengthen His poor servants with courage and strength.

SEPTEMBER 1754

The 1st of September. With this new day the Lord has also bestowed upon us the first month of autumn, and at the same time His word has prepared us in our hearts for the impending trials. He has assured us of His good intent for all times, and we shall therefore rejoice in this now as in all previous and future times, regardless of the suffering that may await us. The Lord is faithful, and He shall make sure that we will not be tempted.

The 7th of September. Those preparing for Holy Communion have been confirmed today to the edification of all present. We wish them much forgiveness from the Lord, the Father of our Lord Jesus Christ, so that they may be faithful and carry out their good promises every day of their lives. As the names of the children involved have always been noted, I shall list them today, too:

Benjamin Friedrich Staehli from the Wurttemberg region, who now lives with his parents in Goshen; Johannes Gruber, the only living son of a deceased honest Salzburger; Johann Jacob Heinle, from Gerstaetten; Hanna Flerl, the oldest daughter of a Salzburger who is our faithful mill overseer; Maria Kalcher, the second daughter of our dear and honest Salzburger, the now deceased Kalcher; Elisabeth Maurer, who also benefits from the fact that she is the daughter of two pious Salzburgers; Anna Margaretha Rosch, born in Purysburg, who now lives in our town. Her parents recently died. Elisabeth Gnann, from the Ulm region; Maria Elisabeth Schwarzfelder, an orphan who was born here;[1] and Angelica Heckel from Langenau.

The 9th of September. Last Sunday, we received some letters from Europe, and today we jointly read and considered their content. We are happy to learn of the continued well-being of all our dear Fathers. May God keep them in their health for many years so that we may continue to enjoy their love. The rest of the content of these dear letters may serve us well to humble us and teach us caution and prudence.

The 16th of September. Master Altherr, who married the girl Amalia[2] who served in my house, sent his men and his boat to fetch me to Savannah, where I preached the word of God before him and others. May God think well of him; I remained there until the 21st and admonished them of the will of the Lord. May God bless these teachings. For then I shall not remain without hope that the Lord's spirit is working in many a soul.

My dear older colleague recently began basing our daily evening prayer hours on the beautiful and edifying question section of our catechism. From this, our dear Lord has bestowed much grace upon us. Mr. Boltzius commenced this exercise in such a way that everyone should be awakened to serious consideration and to pray heartily for him as well, for he declared that he did not know whether he would be able to finish it. His body is consumed with the work of his life and often creaks with weakness, but God gives him strength to keep up despite many trials. I truly rejoice that God has led me here during his lifetime and I can hear how he delivers the word of the truth.

For many reasons, the establishment of the Minister's Plantation is one of the most important undertakings in Ebenezer. For without such an institution we would not know how to support churches and schools and the ministers and teachers in them. It would be of little use to demand such support from the congregation for, even if they were able to contribute, it would be difficult to force them in this free country. And, if the honest souls among them are willing, their good will will not suffice when others stand aside. And, if we look at the entire congregation, there are no means to continue the present church and school establishment.

If it has pleased the Lord to help our congregation through the aforementioned institution, our desires and prayers are that He, our almighty God, should in the future continue to awaken beneficent souls who will support us and the Minister's Plantation with their fruitful contributions so that the several important purposes referred to may be fulfilled. They may rest assured that the opportunity and the location for this important work is most suitable, and that we have secured it by a timely act of God's special grace.

At the site there is land for growing corn and indigo, and in particular there is a large tract which can be flooded at will and can thus be turned into a good rice plantation. We have made the first installations for this purpose, and thus only need to keep it up and prepare the land. The only thing we are missing is sufficient labor, which we must secure by the purchase of several Negroes. If the dear Lord should give us the means, as He has already done for the beginning of this work, there is little doubt that Ebenezer, and other places, will benefit greatly from the completion and extension of this useful work.

On this plantation, there is a sawmill which has already yielded some profit; but, since we have had to find day laborers (who are difficult to obtain) and the wages are high, our profit has not been as large as one would have expected from this type of enterprise. But if we could run the sawmill with our own people, its profit will surely be doubled. The current overseer on the plantation also takes care of the sawing, which is a great relief in regard to costs. But we also need our own teams for transport, for which we have neither men nor money. True, a family could make a good living from supplying transport for the sawmill but, since the establishment is to benefit the entire town, we must make sure that none be excluded from the profit. Together with my colleagues, I am therefore seriously considering how we can help and contribute to this work, and we shall support it with our joint effort as much as is within our means.

Since the often-mentioned plantation is within the Ebenezer district, one of the ministers can live on it and thus exercise careful supervision, which will ensure proper administration.

The 22nd of September. From today's gospel, Matthew 6, we see what the true servants of the Lord can expect from their Master with regard to their material well-being. If all those in Ebenezer were true servants of the Lord, many would have better incomes and sustenance; for our Savior has assured us that all those who yearn for the Kingdom of God shall be supplied with their necessities; and this shall indeed be the case, let unbelievers think and say whatever they wish.

The 23rd of September. Since a number of our parishioners have again formed the notion of returning home, for reasons which I shall explain shortly, Mr. Boltzius used yesterday's sermon to demonstrate in love to his listeners how the Lord can and will supply people even here, in Ebenezer, and how for this reason none will have to leave. He did this so that those who undertake such changes without call and against the will of the Lord will have no excuse when things turn badly for them. That this is in fact true, and that all those who know how to go about their business can do very well here, particularly if they fear the Lord and enjoy His blessing, will be quite clear to every one who has occasion to inquire with creditable people into the circumstances of those who are leaving. I shall let others take the word here and quote the testimony of some to whom I have spoken. A knowledgeable man said only a few days ago in my presence that he could not see how strangers might believe that there was no living to be made in Ebenezer, since the people who do leave on occasion generally take a good batch of money with them, even though they arrived quite penniless.

Another stated from his own experience that this is a country for poor people who will be content with the poor fare from their plantations and in addition put their work into cattle raising. It was also mentioned on this occasion that, if two people from this town marry, however poor they may be, they will be quite well off in two or three years if only they work hard and keep an orderly household. This, surely, is not often to be found in Europe. We could quote many more examples if this were practical. This man had nothing when he arrived; he now has a well-equipped plantation and about forty head of cattle; and he would not wish to sell his property for a thousand ducats. But, since some, however well they may be off and whatever they may have achieved, cannot be content but must look for something better, they move away from here and go elsewhere. The old Adam has become greedy and cannot satisfy his desires here; so it is said: "Off we go, for here and there we could find this and that," and so forth.

Some dislike our insisting on the word of the Lord and true fear of Him; and they say they do not wish to be inconvenienced and to live under this yoke. See Malachi 3:14.

If such reasons were to be believed, fear of God and virtue would count for nothing. And who will believe that?

The 27th of September. We now have good weather for harvesting; and our people are beginning to bring in their rice, Indian peas, pumpkins, and corn. The latter has been ripe for a month but has not been picked; instead, its stalks were bent and they are not being picked with the peas planted underneath the corn. These peas continue in bloom once they start in the spring, and they keep on developing new pods which must be picked once they are ripe, yielding several harvests. Similarly with cotton, indigo, and similar plants.

A little while ago a Negress on our Minister's Plantation killed a turtle, which is eaten as meat by these people and some of the whites here. This animal had a large and gray stone encased in a thin skin on one side, behind the back leg. The stone was not quite 5 inches long, about 2 and a half inches thick and 3 and a half inches wide. It had the shape of a closed shell, and thus these dimensions must be understood to extend from the farthest to the farthest point of its circumference. This stone is a most unusual occurrence, and that is why we mention it here. I have kept the stone and shall send it to Europe at a convenient time.

OCTOBER 1754

The 1st of October. Venetian theriac has been found a good remedy against dangerous snakebite; one of the Salzburgers has made several trials with it and recently cured a boy who had been bitten. We have no stock of this remedy, however; and, since it has a number of good uses, we would wish for some supply. The Indians cure snakebite as follows: They make an inci-

sion into the wound so that the infected blood can be drawn out
quickly and as profusely as possible. Then they hold a glowing
ember or some other red hot object close to the wound so as to
extract the poison. In this manner, they cured a young man in
Old Ebenezer about a year ago.

This summer we have killed some terrifying rattlesnakes of
considerable size. Their fat is said to be a good remedy against
sick or dull eyes. It is therefore extracted from the carcass of the
snake, rendered, and stored apart, but we do not know how to
apply it correctly.

The 3rd of October. Some of the children now come to my
house so that I can teach them in the absence of a schoolmaster
on the plantations; I much enjoy this task, as always, and also
save time and strength if I do not have to make the two-mile ride
to the Zion Church every day. On Tuesdays and Fridays, however, lessons are held there, since I conduct prayer meetings in
the church.

The 4th of October. We have now tried indigo for the third
time and, while the first two trials went badly, this one has come
off well. It is not a difficult task in itself, but several details must
be well arranged if the work is not to be for naught. Several of
our people have now been encouraged to follow us in the planting of indigo if the Lord grants them life and health.

The 5th of October. Today we received news that a governor
for Georgia has been named in London and that the present
counselors are to remain in office, but their number increased to
twelve. This has caused much rejoicing. May God remember us,
and listen to our prayer and entreaties, and may He give the
country a magistrate in His mercy.

The 10th of October. Cutting down the indigo plants has increased the young shoots so that we have double the amount for
cutting than before. Since we do not have much equipment for
preparing indigo, we have had to repeat the procedure this
week, which serves to instruct and confirm us in our work.

This and other work on the Minister's Plantation required
much of my time and strength last summer, although it has not
yet yielded any profit for me, nor could it have. If with the blessing of the Lord we should slowly reach a stage where this establishment can benefit the community, in addition to providing for

the third minister, I might then share in the benefit; I ask for nothing else. I look upon the Lord in this matter and am assured that He will be pleased with my disinterested work, carried out in faith. This will be my reward. I am convinced the aforesaid establishment will serve for the glorification of His name, the spread of His kingdom, and the comfort and edification of honest souls; all these are reasons to encourage me to avoid neither trouble nor labor until the intended purpose is obtained with the blessing of the Lord.

The 11th of October. In visiting our listeners, the *Golden Treasure Chest of the Children of God*[1] serves me well, particularly the most recent edition, which contains an excellent new feature. Under every date of the month, that is to say, for every day of the week throughout the year, there is an edifying verse with edifying comments and little rhymed verses. When I visit our people in those houses that have one of these *Treasure Chests*, I like to inquire for the saying of the day, and I find their minds well prepared for what I tell them for closer application. By this means, the Lord causes much edification and provides us with necessary and welcome material for prayer.

Yesterday, at their house, the wife of an honest man wanted to talk to me and lamented her condition. However, the noon heat was getting worse and I had another four miles to travel from the mill to my house and business to take care of on the way with shoemaker Weitmann. I therefore promised her to come back soon, and this morning I returned to her house. God is making her recognize and feel her lack of faith and other terrible ballast of sins drifting around her. She needs instruction and guidance so that she will not remain under the law and attempt to improve on her own and by her works, but rather come to Christ as a bent and burdened sinner.[2] She said that she likes to hear strict sermons on the law, and that she needed those, but that she could not do much with the gospel. I then showed her what she could apply to herself from the gospels even now and what she would learn in the future if she would be faithful. I opened the *Treasure Chest* at page 280, "He who is born of God," which contains a beautiful instruction on how to reach faith and vanquish the world both inside and out. We then prayed to Jesus as the beginning and the final consumption of all faith and called upon Him from our hearts to prove Himself thus for this sinner, so that it may be said of her pious husband that "he believes and with all his house,"[3] which is the content of his prayer morning and night. I then showed her the verse over which we prayed in the *Treasure Chest*, p. 73.

There are goodsized pomegranates in our area, although little work is spent on the trees, or rather shrubs, that bear them. We do not know how to make use of them, else we would pay more attention to their cultivation. Many of the trees here bear fruit, but we have neither time, nor people, nor means to tend them and guard them with fences against cattle and hogs. Everyone here is concerned only with growing enough for food and clothing on their plantations, for clothing is very dear here; the rest goes for paying the doctor and having some relief during illness. Everything else is let go, particularly since nothing can be turned to profit but is consumed here. This also goes for cotton, which grows well and abundantly on fair land and would yield more than flax and sheep. But the trouble with this plant is that the kernel or seed is firmly attached to the fiber and takes much work to separate.[4] Further, we fear that, in comparison with the cotton that is brought to Europe from the West Indies, our product would be held for little and bring a poor price.

On the next boat that sets sail from Savannah to London, I plan to dispatch a few pounds of our cotton to a noble benefactor who wishes to promote the well being of Ebenezer by all possible means.[5] I shall consult him on the amount we should pay here per pound and whether it is permitted to ship it to Germany. For the English do not let the people in the American colonies trade with certain goods.[6]

If we were not so far removed from this German benefactor, and if the freight by water and land were not as dear, we would also send him some sesame oil for his opinion. The English here call it benne seed oil, and the seed grows well and abundantly. It is said to yield far more oil than other seeds or kernels. If not used right away, the oil from stored seed is said to be not inferior to olive or similar oil. This would be a good crop for our people, for it grows even on poor land, which is most of the land here, and we could easily build an oil press near the mills. But here too, someone will have to set an example, as was the case for silk.

We lack the means, and we are often blamed for taking care of outside matters, although we have with God's grace never neglected the duties of our office. In this respect and that of promoting the physical well-being of our dear listeners, we can only say: "The love of Christ constraineth us."[7]

The 12th of October. The good Lord has given us favorable weather for the harvest, so that all crops have been given time to ripen and be brought in before the rains. The crops have turned out well, although the rain during the summer has kept back peas and pumpkins planted on the rich low land; some were even spoiled in the bud. There is much rice and corn, as well as hay and grass, and an abundance of fodder for the cattle. Those who must work their land with white labor have the least profit from their gardens and fields and suffer much from the laborers' lack of loyalty and their bad habits.

The 13th of October. Oh how miserable it is in a certain house.[8] Father and children are poor lovers of church and school, although they have leisure for both. They may soon lose all opportunity for edification. May God have pity on the poor parents, who subvert the order of Christ: i.e., "Seek ye first the Kingdom of God,"[9] and prefer this kingdom to that of heaven, following both the spirit and the example of those who disdain the Lord's Supper. This reprehensible attitude is imparted to the children by example and teaching, and with some there is no changing this by admonition, entreaty, or threats from the law or the gospel.

Today, I went to several plantations near by and told both parents and guardians of several children that, God having begun to restore our health, I intend to hold again the preparation for the older children and that our dear colleagues and the schoolmaster will instruct both large and small children in the fundamentals of the Christian religion and in reading, as well as in other necessary and profitable matters, if only the children will be sent to school more frequently than has been the case in the past.

Our physician, Mr. Thilo, has again been quite weak and can therefore not attend prayer meetings and sermons, despite his deep love of these occasions. He had me fetched this afternoon so that he could talk to me from God's word for the edification of

his hungry soul; we spent a good time of true and heavenly pleasure in conversation. If our listeners will not just be content with
coming to church and listening to our sermons, but instead seek
private conversation with their ministers as much as their time
permits and use their counsel and help in their prayers, then
they will fare as is written in Greek in Galatians 6:6, and thus
they will truly be saved. May God render all our listeners quite
simple and hungry for their salvation.

The 14th of October. One of our pious Salzburgers, whose
plantation is located behind Abercorn, came in last night for the
prayer meeting. When I saw him this morning, I told him how
much I would like for him and others of our old listeners who
have moved to Abercorn because of the good land there to come
into town on Saturdays and attend the prayer meeting as a preparation for the day of the Lord. I would gladly arrange for quar-
ters in our silk facility if they should lack shelter because there
are few houses left in our town. He thanked the Lord with a glad
mouth and happy face for having come to this prayer meeting
and for having listened to the dear gospel of Jesus Who accepts
the sinners. He felt, he said, as if he had been in heaven and
would have liked to listen all night without sleep.

We have now completed our consideration of the gospel in regard to the beautiful song: *Jesus nimmt die Sünder an*; we have
seen witness after witness of God's word in this who all testify,
with heart and mouth from their own knowledge, to the eternal
and well founded truth: "Jesus accepts sinners." May God be
praised for this eternal and dear truth, to which several of the
members of our congregation can testify. With the help of the
Holy Spirit, the Biblical verses that are listed below each strophe
of this song have brought us much insight into the counsel of the
Lord concerning our salvation and, at the same time, much
edification.

To the praise of our Savior I can speak thus, "For me this word
is a lily, a sweet gospel, yea, pure milk and honey."[10] Since my
dear colleague, Mr. Lemke, is ill and dear Mr. Rabenhorst has
traveled to Tybee Island on the sea to improve his health
(whence he returned in good health this afternoon, thank the
Lord), it was necessary for me, regardless of my continuing

feebleness, to preach both morning and afternoon last Sunday and to conduct prayer meetings and weekday sermons as well as performing other tasks of my office. Praise the Lord, this has not impaired my health, rather my strength has gained with His blessing while I labored, and this I ascribe entirely to the high priestly intercession of my faithful Shepherd and Savior, and to the pious prayers of His servants and children, both here and elsewhere.

Our faithful Lord has also lightened my labors and rendered them pleasant by His gospel, which I presented both in the weekday sermons and in the prayer meetings on the basis of the aforesaid song, and the sweetness of which I was thus the first to relish. Where God benefits the soul, the body will often benefit as well. On this 17th Sunday after Trinity, my dear colleague Mr. Lemke has found himself so much strengthened that he resumed his edifying catechization in the afternoon on the beautiful epistle; and this has truly lifted my spirit. Tonight was the first time, as the days are getting shorter, that we lit candles for the repetition of the comforting lesson that we poor sinners have a pious Lord in Jesus Christ.

Today is also the anniversary of the consecration of our comfortable Jerusalem Church several years ago, and for this reason we led our listeners at the beginning to realize the many benefits and their duties as implied in the words of Psalms 25:8. And I thanked the willing and industrious among them and wished them the Lord's blessing as a recompense, for it is they who helped us repair the church this year and improved it in many ways. I took the occasion to request my listeners to lend a helping hand also for the Zion Church, which is badly in need of repair and should be fixed, as well as the fences of the two cemeteries. I assured them that the Lord would not leave those who help us without reward. For here, too, those who have pity on the poor churches and schools in fact make a loan to the Lord (for these edifices are His scaffolds for the structures of the spirit), and He will repay them for their good deeds (which He will do without difficulty, for He owns heaven and earth).[11]

The 15th of October. In Savannah our dear colleague, Mr. Rabenhorst, received a package of letters for me, Mr. Lemke,

Captain Krauss, and Mrs. Rabenhorst. These letters were sent to
me through Mr. Samuel Lloyd in London by a distinguished
benefactor in Europe, who is always concerned with improving
the good name of Ebenezer and our welfare with word and
deed. These letters contain much that will improve our faith,
praise the Lord, and renew our courage to introduce or continue several new and useful ventures. In addition, they contain
some loving corrections, for which we praise the Lord and ask
Him for generous reward. We have had neither letters nor news
from our other European Fathers and friends, but we expect to
have news with the ship which is expected in Savannah in a few
weeks with winter stores from Mr. Lloyd.

Mr. deBrahm also wrote me a pleasant letter in which he reports on his many material and spiritual trials and requests my
prayers. His wife is ill and requests my presence for spiritual advice and conversation at their plantation, which is at a considerable distance from Savannah. However, I am still too feeble
to undertake such a long journey, and today I informed Mr.
deBrahm of this and offered him the services of my experienced
and faithful colleagues.

The 16th of October. Yesterday I, Lemke, had to travel to Goshen, whence I returned today. I was not able to preach a public
sermon there because I wished to visit several people, particularly in Abercorn, who had previously lived in Ebenezer but
moved away for lack of good land and who still are professed
members of our congregation. Truly, they are lovers of God's
word, and the family men among them often come to us to listen
to our sermons, which the women and children are prevented
from doing because of the distance, which is a fact that much
troubles them. They seek edification from Arndt's *True Christianity*,[12] the summary explication of the gospel by Inspector
Rende, which they have obtained from us, and other useful
books. They read a few chapters from the bible and attempt to
put their Sundays to good use with this and other exercises.
They are much aggrieved that their children must miss school;
they do their best so that they may not remain entirely ignorant,
but lament that the progress is not sufficient.

With regard to their material circumstances, it is now three
years from the date of their move, but they are already so well

established that it is easy to see the difference between good and poor land.

The 17th of October. While I was gone, another bundle of letters arrived from our dearest friends in Europe, for which may the Lord be praised. I therefore rode into town to my dear colleagues, who were just then assembled to read a report of the emigrants, which was very noteworthy and should rightfully inspire us to pray for our brothers in the faith and for the growth of the Kingdom of God.[13] Oh, if only all our Salzburgers would recognize and never forget the great benefaction that the Lord is bestowing on them by giving them the free use of the means of salvation and by maintaining them in this state. May He render us all thankful.

Since my good Savior is now strengthening me day by day both in body and in mind, I have begun to visit my listeners even on the remote plantations. Nonetheless, it would be much easier for me if I myself were to live on the plantations, which I would much like to do. Today I visited the sick N. N. In this illness God has made her feel her sins, and I find in her reliable signs of a true and unfeigned repentance. Both spouses are now of one mind, and they much edified me with their words and their conduct. This example again taught me not to give up hope with our young people, even if they do not right away accept the good instruction for a true salvation. The word of the Lord often lies in them a long time, hidden as in the field, and it will finally sprout when God sends a tribulation.

I only pity those who came to our place as adults and without sufficient instruction. Even when threatened by trials and death, they let things go on as before, using the means of salvation and performing their good works, but they have no concept of the order of salvation, which is the only assurance of a blessed death. How much we would like to teach such people from the catechism and in private, if they would only consent. A woman showed me a sackful of beautiful cotton which was picked off the seed. She said that her three children, of whom the oldest is nine years old, had separated twenty-five pounds of cotton from the seeds, which is the most difficult work with cotton, as the fiber is closely attached to the seed.

The wife of a sickly Salzburger recently received, for herself

and her household, a share of the money which our dear Lord
bestowed on the congregation through the offices of the esteemed Society. I met her three times today; and on each occasion she showed me her joy at this welcome gift and blessed me
most heartily, while I deflected her blessings to the unknown
worthy benefactor and his family. But I do consider myself
blessed to be the feeble tool which distributes these welcome
blessings among orphans, the sick, and poor lying-in women,
who then offer me their prayers and their good wishes. However, I must also suffer the disaffection and accusations of favor-
itism from those who cannot participate in these gifts, as is often
the case.

The 19th of October. It has rained all day long. Nonetheless,
the parishioners congregated in the plantation church to hear
the weekday sermon; this gave me much joy and reason for rejoicing. God graciously gave me, and I hope them, the gospel for
a new revival to come to Christ so that we can preach John 5
tomorrow. It is not easy to travel from town to the plantation
church in the rain, especially as there is no place for changing
clothes out there. The heat of the sun is equally hard, in particular when we leave the church for home at noon. Extremes of
heat and cold easily bring about fever and other untoward conditions in this country. For this reason it would be good if one of
us were to live among the Salzburgers on the Mill River, for then
the preacher and his flock would have but a short ride to the
church.

I consider it a special blessing of the Lord and entirely equita-
ble that our sickly and overworked Salzburgers, and their feeble
women and children, whom they sorely need for their house-
work because of the lack of servants, should have three ministers. These will not only share in the burden of the office but
make it easier for these feeble people to attend church and enjoy
the blessing of communion if one of their ministers lives among
them. Then they will not be obliged (if God should strengthen
our health) to travel into town on Sundays and holidays, regardless of the weather. Instead, they will have a service at the Zion or
Plantation Church on two consecutive Sundays and Holy Communion every six weeks; and on the third Sunday they and their
minister will join us in town at the Jerusalem Church, where

Communion is to be held for those who live in town, the nearby plantations, and on the Blue Bluff across the Ebenezer Creek.

True, we ministers are as one in the unity of the spirit, and each one of us looks upon the entire congregation as his own and works on each and every member both in public and in private. It will nonetheless be most useful if *ob curam specialem et specialissemam*[14] we should share among ourselves our dear listeners in sickness and in health, such that one will care mostly for the Salzburgers on the Mill River, the other, that is our dear Mr. Lemke, will have charge of the townspeople and the plantation owners around the town, and dear Mr. Rabenhorst will look after the people on the Blue Bluff. The latter is, of course, still an inconvenient location, since a bridge and clearly marked paths are still missing.

The 20th of October. Our oldest colleague was so strengthened today by the Lord despite his current weak constitution, that he was able to edify our souls richly with the treasures of the gospel, in part basing himself on the text for today and in part on Psalms 130:7, 8. May the Lord be blessed for His merciful assistance!

Last week about thirty Indians, not counting women and children, arrived in Old Ebenezer. When the supervisor of the cattle ranch there did not or could not give them what they wanted, they tied him up and taunted him in their manner; they probably would have robbed him but were prevented by two Englishmen who happened by. When we learned about this incident, several men rode off on horseback and dispersed the Indians. These blind heathens easily take offence, and then they can only think of revenge. Further up, on the Carolina border, the French Indians are said to have killed several people and abducted some more.

The 31st of October. Last night we heard cannon fire at our place; and today we had news, brought by our dear first colleague on his return from his last voyage, that the recently nominated governor of Georgia had arrived. He considers it a heavenly blessing that he was detained longer than expected for want of transportation, for else he would have been forced to return promptly in order to offer the governor his respects. The latter's arrival has caused much joy everywhere.

NOVEMBER 1754

The 4th of November. According to the letters received from our dearest father in Christ, Senior Urlsperger, our generous Lord has prompted benevolent hearts from all places, near and far, to contribute a rich material blessing for the poor and for widows and orphans in Ebenezer. For this we praise His glorious name most humbly, for He thus shows clearly that He remains the father of the orphans. Mr. Boltzius is distributing these gifts with many blessings on the benefactors, and it is in fact a good time because some will be able to buy necessary clothing.

Today the congregation has commenced, with joint labor, to build the long-planned bridge across Ebenezer Creek. We hope that this, too, will yield a benefit for the kingdom of God; for those from Bethany who wish to visit our service will no longer have to travel by water, and the children will be better able to attend school. Our school here in town has already taken in four children from the second Swabian transport.[1] Also, those who pay little heed to the Lord's word will have all the less excuse.[2]

The 9th of November. With God's help, and without any injury or other accidents, the bridge has been advanced to the point that the planks can be laid. True, we must still throw up a high causeway so that we can reach the bridge at high water despite the deep mud. This will probably not be done this year, but it can now be scheduled more conveniently, for this is labor for which not everyone is fit.

The 13th of November. Today in Jerusalem Church, as we did on the plantations yesterday, we have revived ourselves from God's word and humbly offered thanks to our dear and charitable Lord for the rich harvest which we have brought in this year. The words on which our oldest colleague, Mr. Boltzius, based his thanksgiving and harvest sermon are in next week's Sunday text, Matthew 22:21, which he advised the children to understand thus: "Render unto God the things that are God's." From this, he presented (1) God's beneficence to us; (2) our duty to Him.

For the first point, it was demonstrated that God is not only our creator but also maintains us in His mercy and has given us in both material and spiritual respects so much and so much more than others. In regard to the second matter, our listeners were admonished in an evangelical manner to give back to God 1. their soul, 2. their bodies, 3. their time, particularly on Sundays, 4. their temporal goods to poor orphans and widows and to churches and schools, 5. the parents their children. We finished with prayer and song. We noticed in some of our listeners afterwards that the spirit of the Lord had come close to them and convinced them. May the Lord, who gives us His word and our material sustenance, be most humbly praised. May He strengthen His word and His charity in our midst so that we shall witness our joy at His grace, not only in some but in all our listeners. Amen.

The 17th of November. Toward evening, we had a blessed hour dedicated to prayer. So that we might all agree on the subject of our prayer, my dearest older colleague gave us material from his rich treasure. For our pleasant and gracious Lord has arranged it that in our recently arrived letters we received news of the oppression of our Protestant brethren here and there, who would gladly give up house and farm and all their belongings to gain freedom of conscience and the freedom of practicing their faith. We insist on this point with our Salzburgers so as to awaken them, for else they might have received their miraculous delivery in vain and rather to their great detriment. And since one or the other among them might in fact have worsened despite the rich word of the Lord, our oldest brother admonished us to pray for these so that God might work even this to their improvement.

We then prayed for these and for our oppressed brethren in the Lord, so that God might save them according to their will and deep longing, just as He saved the people of Israel, as shown in the book of Exodus, which is now being read in church. We also prayed that He might let this work redound fully to their blessing, for a true change in mind and improvement in their lives, and give our dear listeners grateful and repentant hearts and praise His dear name all over Christendom in all schools, both high and low. Our dear and faithful Fathers in London, Augsburg, and Halle, our dear benefactors and friends and intercessors, wherever they may be, are all in our poor prayers and entreaties, upon which God will nonetheless smile because of Jesus Christ.[3]

In Savannah, a Parliament will be held shortly in which our town will have two members. One of these, however, will be elected by this place and one will be taken from among our congregation in Savannah. These members must be honest patriots who are truly concerned with the country's welfare.

My dear oldest colleague received two letters from Savannah recommending two persons who are said to be inclined to represent our congregation, and one of them will surely be chosen. There is much interest in these positions in Savannah, because it is a high honor to be a member of such an assembly and to speak to the English liberties. May God consider this matter His own and choose such people as are honest and truthful and a truly concerned with the welfare of this country. In such assemblies, people are burdened with unpleasant matters. We shall therefore instruct our representative to suggest a collection to contribute to the bridge which is now being built and the projected causeway through the swamps, which will have to be a good eight feet high for much of its course. We suggest a collection because this bridge and its approaches will constitute the public highway to Carolina and Augusta and thus bring much trade and commerce to this country.

N.N., a man from the Swabian transports, is being chastised harshly by the Lord. He is among those who brought a large family with him. He quickly lost his wife and three children, among them his two oldest daughters; we hear of the last daughter that she is right miserable. Now his hut has burned down and he only saved the bedding and his old clothes which he was wearing.[4] He came and asked for old clothing, which we gave him with the admonition that he should now start repenting. He could see how heavily the Lord's hand was resting on him in punishment. He said there was no comfort for him. But I responded to this that it was this very comfort which he used in vain and which had gone, and that God treated him so harshly that all false comfort would leave him. He should turn to the Lord from the bottom of his heart and he would soon be comforted.

According to the recently received letters from our dearest Father in Christ, Senior Urlsperger, the blessed Lord has collected in his hands a material blessing flowing from many places and destined for the poor, the widows, and the orphans in Ebenezer. For this, we praise His glorious name in all humility, for He is actively showing that He remains the Father of the orphans. Pastor Boltzius is now distributing this gift among these poor people, calling for many blessings on our dear benefactors. This gift has come just in time for them to procure some needed winter clothing.

The work on the causeway and bridge was ended to day; the bridge has been brought as close to completion as we had hoped. No accidents have occurred, for which we thanked the Lord jointly in our evening prayer meeting.

The 18th of November. Our governor has been installed by solemn proclamation, yesterday in Savannah and today in Ebenezer. In this connection, I remember what we read last Sunday from I Timothy 2: 1–2 concerning our prayers for the government and its final purpose: Namely, that we might lead a peaceful and quiet life, safe in God, and with due regard for our fellow man.

The 19th of November. When I returned home from Zion Church today, I was much taken by the many beautiful acorns that lined my path in the woods. We had a strong wind which shook them off the trees and onto the ground. Some people gather these for their cattle as fodder for the winter; they are said to do well on acorns but will get sick if they eat too much. The hogs were left to forage for acorns more than a month ago; they will swim through creeks and ponds to get at them, but then they run the danger of being devoured by wolves, bears, or lynxes or, as they are called here, tigers.[5] The last two kinds of predators have in fact caused some damage among the cattle and the hogs during the fall. For a while, a tiger frequented our area in the vicinity of the other sawmill. No hog was safe from it until a few of our men hunted him with their dogs and chased him off.

Glaner has been much impressed by the death of his child and recognizes the need for a change of heart. When he announced the child's death to me, he said with deep feeling: "Oh yes, we must become as children, for else we will not enter the Kingdom of God." I and others confirmed him in this.

For my exordium on the 24th, I dealt with the words of Luke,

5. "The power of the Lord was present." After this I then preached from the gospel concerning the overwhelming power of the Lord Jesus Christ, which (1) is proven from the gospel and other words to strengthen our faith; and (2) can be shown to have worked for our salvation. Dear Jesus, let us experience thy overwhelming power in us and in our congregation, both among the awakened souls and those who sleep in their false security.[6]

The 26th of November. Today, we married two pairs of our youngest workers. Johann Renz married Barbara Unselt and Georg Michael Weber married Maria Magdalena Greiner. For the first two, I used the oppportunity to show them the blissful estate from Ephesians 4,23–24 and how they could reach it and remain in it. May our merciful Lord render them so new that we see nothing of their old estate in their new being. He is now running the tavern, and I therefore used the 4th and 5th chapter of this wonderful epistle to instruct them with the help of the Lord.

The 29th of November. God be praised, our dear Mr. Boltzius has safely returned from Savannah. He can hardly find enough words to praise the fact that he is back in Ebenezer, where the dear Lord offers us much good every day in body and especially in our souls.

DECEMBER 1754

The 1st of December. The last week of the church year also was a week of preparation for Holy Communion. It was held today with much edification and much blessing, a goal towards which we had directed all sermons on the Lord's word throughout the week. Prior to administering Holy Communion, our first minister spoke to the entire congregation on the power of our heavenly King, Jesus Christ, and His guidance of our souls for the purpose of our salvation. As an exordium we showed our listeners from the recent past how our almighty Lord has guided benevolent minds of high, middle, and low station towards Ebenezer, who wish to strengthen our spiritual and material well being; we should use this to show gratitude for past benefactions and to strengthen our faith for the future. In the afternoon, and with the merciful assistance of the Lord, I catechized the children on Sunday's text, a practice we have followed throughout this church year instead of using the catechism.

The 6th of December. Among the children we confirmed last year, two came from Black Creek, an area close to Savannah; these much pleased us, their teachers, and others by their industry and obedience to the word of the Lord. After their confirmation, we had testimony from their neighbors that they had turned out well and had become a guiding light among these people. We now repeat and stress this testimony for the boy Jacob Bechle after his death, which occurred quite suddenly from a sudden attack of epilepsy.[1] May the Lord refresh him for his brief but, as I hope, honest life of imitation of Jesus Christ. It is such examples that strengthen me to continue to pasture these sheep, even if labor and trouble often appear to be in vain. But we are all plowmen who labor in the hope of the Lord.[2]

The 8th of December. On this second Sunday in advent I have, with the aid of the Lord, presented to our listeners the last future of our Lord Jesus Christ. I preached here in town, both in the morning and the afternoon, from the gospels and from the word of John: "whose fan is in his hand," etc.[3] and showed how sad will be those on the day of the Lord who are but chaff or whose Christianity is based on false repentance and on faithlessness and infidelity but who nonetheless wish to comfort themselves in Jesus Christ, and who thus are of a light and frivolous Christianity.

According to Romans 11, they are lacking repentance, with a hard and sullen heart. According to 2 Thessalonians 1:8-9, they are disobedient to the word of the Lord Christ. These shall suffer from fire and misery, fear and pain, and fiery embers and revenge. Oh God, among these people almost none will believe; one would rather accept this from whores, profaners, thieves and such rabble. But we have shown the repentant and the faithful what has been prepared and given to them with the word of the Lord. May the Lord Jesus place his blessing on this, as on the word that my dear colleague and all servants of the Lord have preached today, which is a day of repentance and conversion of all wicked or worldly honest and hypocritical sinners.

The 13th of December. We have now sold the small quantity of indigo which we grew as a trial crop, and we were told in Savannah that it was of the best kind. We would much like to grow a full crop on our Minister's Plantation, if we could only afford it; for this establishment still requires much work to be fully equipped. I have been much surprised to learn that a prudent Englishman last summer invested £ 1500 Sterling in his plantation without having any return on it this year. He is convinced that it will amply return his investment, however. This shows that money so invested should not be considered lost. For the purpose of such an establishment, as we have learned, can be best and soonest realized if a sufficient capital investment is made. And, since only about a third of the above-named sum has been put into our plantation, we much hope that our heavenly Father will continue to let His well run over for our benefit.

The 15th of December. Through the grace of God I have let myself resolve again today to lead my parishioners, whom I had before me in Zion Church, to Christ with all my strength if it is possible and to create a path for Him in their hearts. If I had to believe that it was in vain, this would hurt me very much, since I am seeking not my own but their good, in which I am driven by love alone. I believe this, and it is the reason why ministers should be the servants of Christ according to the profound verse of our Sunday epistle, which we contemplated in the exordium.

The people in Goshen, as also in Josephs Town and Abercorn, have made a beginning toward a schoolhouse, in which church is also to be held. They will put it on Mr. Boltzius' glebe land, which lies in the midst of them. Because they will need help in this, they will submit a petition for it in the coming Assembly. This makes it appear that they wish to make themselves into a regular congregation.

Several among them have advanced so far that they have been able to acquire plows and horses, and they are beginning to cultivate the land. One of them said that he had never thought while on the sea that he would ever achieve such a condition again, since he, along with the others, had lost all his possessions to the Spaniards.[4] From this one can see that people who wish to support themselves regularly here can succeed very well.

The 22nd of December. This morning I held the confessional first. The preparation for it was on the words in 1 John 2:3. After this I spoke in the sermon concerning the lack of knowledge of Christ among Christians, using the gospel of St. John 1:19 ff., and afterwards I held Holy Communion. In the afternoon I remained with the said material and spoke of the causes and sources from which flows the lack of knowledge of Christ. During this I cordially thanked God for His assistance, which did not let my soul lack for strength and refreshment, even though my body was tired.

The 25th and 26th of December. In the two days of Holy Christmastide, the gospel of the birth of our dearest Savior was proclaimed by us ministers with good physical and spiritual strength, and our parishioners paid diligent attention. Divine service was held in both churches.

On the first day of Christmas I drew my listeners during the morning sermon in town to two great benefactions, in accordance with the beautiful introductory verse, 1 John 1:2. I then proceeded to consider, for the edification of our hearts, the gifts of salvation which have been shared with us through the birth of our Immanuel. I based the afternoon sermon on the same text; in particular, I demonstrated how the precious grace of the Lord, which was obtained by Jesus Christ and given to us through His intercession, acts on people who partake of this high treasure in the proper order of salvation. My two dear colleagues conducted the service out on the plantations.

The 26th of December. Today and yesterday our dear Lord let us rejoice in the Christmas holiday. Ministers and listeners have been strengthened by Him in their bodies so that they congregated in both churches for the reading and the reception of His glorious gospel and other edifying exercises. May His name be praised for this.

I ended the celebration of this holy day by reading the word of the Lord on the text for today. May our charitable and gracious Lord turn this into a living seed which will bring much fruit here and in eternity. May He also give to our oppressed brothers in the faith ample room and let them partake of the good which we and other evangelical Christians living in freedom of belief can enjoy. Amen.

The 29th of December. Mr. Lemke preached on the plantation, and the first and third colleague preached here. In the
morning, the congregation was instructed in the beautiful verse
from Luke 2:21: "And behold, there was a man in Jerusalem."
etc.[5] Those who listened were convinced that, since they were
men, they could become such as Simeon, in the order of a true
conversion; for Simeon also was a man, lived in a rotten place,
that is the large city of Jerusalem, where even the clergy was rotten. May our dear Lord convince all that they need to become
such a man and that for all of us there is only a single way, which,
however, to the praise of the Lord, can be found everywhere in
the Holy Scriptures.

Among our gifts we also count this, that we have been sent a
governor this year who is showing a kindly and pleasant disposition toward our congregation. We have often recommended to
the Lord our dear magistrates in this country, and we have offered prayers for the best of the whole country and in particular
for our congregation, all of which may the Lord grant us in His
mercy. He has also maintained in life and health the three ministers and, according to His wisdom, has given us strength and
opportunity to carry out our tasks in church and school, in days
of sickness and health. And He has given much to our congregation, quite apart from the great benefaction of the rich lessons of
His holy word and the exercise of the ministry.

It is only just to list material peace and external quiet first. If
some may not like it that the Lord has led us from the noise of
this world, many others recognize this as a great gift. We also
learn that some who thought that their work here was too difficult and that they could find better opportunity elsewhere
would love to return, if only it could be done easily and without
great cost. Our material blessings have flourished under the
blessing of the Lord so that none of us lack for bread or have to
depend on others for sustenance. In addition to the silk, which
turned out well, our people had good crops of Indian corn, rye,
potatoes, and so forth. The wheat has failed again, but some had
good crops of barley.

We have also improved our trade with cypress boards, lumber,
double staves, and similar things, which has lightened our
burden.

With this I finish the incomplete and poor report for this year, with the humble wish that God bless us in body and soul and remember us and all our friends our benefactors at the end of the old and the beginning of the new year.

Appendix I

EXTRA DIARY FOR APRIL 1753

The first few days of this month have been very cool, and we can hardly expect any more hard night frosts. Some of our inhabitants have the peasant rule[1] (or perhaps it is an empty fantasy) that the cold weather is not entirely past as long as the corn bird is not heard.[2] May God graciously protect the European grains, which have a nice appearance everywhere and of which the rye has almost finished blossoming. May He grant a good harvest to the poor, whose food has been rather sparse this year. To be sure, we have helped some to the best of our weak ability, but we cannot help them all. May God give them faith!

If these and those people (as it is often said to them here clearly enough and frequently, as it pleases many of them) would penitently recognize their overhastiness and worldly purposes as well as the disobedience against God's word they showed in their fatherland and become true Christians through true conversion, then they would become orderly and useful; and then there would be no doubt that they would earn their physical subsistence and be pleased with their tribulations. For with Godliness is contentedness; and, if anyone has dedicated his heart to God, He will let him be pleased with His ways and guidance. Those who are thus, or those who wish to become so through the rich preaching of the divine word, they are very much at home in Ebenezer.

The others like to complain, ascribe their fatalities (as they call them) to the *causis secundis*[3], choose all sorts of questionable means, make perforated wells,[4] request help from people, especially from their ministers; and, if they don't find what they are seeking, they cry out against the ministers and the congregation and even the entire country, especially when they return to Europe. It is surely a great sorrow for us and it causes us much trouble when we see our parishioners, either young or old, in hardship, danger, or want and still cannot help them. If only they wished to become children of God, adapt themselves to the country, and seek the kind of work that brings in money here, then our wise, kind, and almighty God, who is honest in His fulfillment of His promises, would surely grant their needs.

All of our parishioners, and even our enemies and enviers, are convinced that we are seeking not our own good, but the good of the congregation, the glory of God, and the extension of Christ's kingdom. It is well known to everyone inside and outside of our community that in our behavior we reveal the word of the Lord that to give is more blessed than to receive, and therefore better to receive no gift in even the smallest things but to pay cash for everything, to make do with the most extreme frugality, and to rejoice when we can give our parishioners an opportunity to earn something.

The fact that we wish to have the land we have received from God's hand and care cultivated according to the wish of the authorities is among other reasons, because we hope through God's blessing and the Negroes' work to proceed so far that we will no longer be so burdensome to our worthy Fathers and benefactors with regard to our inadequate salaries and that we will accomplish something from which we can give to the needy. It is very useful if ministers are in a condition to come to the aid of their parishioners not only with advice and comfort, but also with real help. We have no calling to gather anything for our children: God will surely provide for them if they fear, love, and trust Him above all else. At the same time, we are not forbidden to administer in a Christian and conscientious way what has been rightfully given and to apply everything correctly at its time.

At about the middle of this month Mr. Habersham wrote me that his ship had arrived with twenty-six Negroes, large and small, and he requested me to announce it to Mr. Mayer and others of our inhabitants. They are to be sold at a public auction. Since peace came, Negroes have been scarce and expensive. That is why we have wished since January to establish a plantation at the advice and with the help of our worthy patrons, indeed, at the desire of our authorities (who do not wish to have given us such good land to have it lie fallow). However, we have had to carry out all the early work with white people. Because we must now buy some such Moors, we are imploring God that, through His providence, He will grant that such will come to us who are willing to work and to receive Christian instruction. For our chief purpose is the saving of their souls.

I am taking two knowledgeable and cautious men from here along with me and will also use some upright friends who are experienced in the Negro trade to use all possible caution in the purchase of these poor slaves. Whenever a ship full of Negroes from Africa or the West Indies comes to Charleston, it must be kept in quarantine for some time and the Negroes are examined by the doctors and surgeons to see whether they have brought any infectious diseases.

Otherwise it is not usual for new Negroes to be sold at public auction, rather everyone has the freedom to choose the ones he wants and to agree on a price with the merchant. One buys no cheaper at auction than in the regular way. For not only does the auctioneer set the first price for the object or the Negro who is to be sold, but the owner of the Negroes or objects has his friends there to buy back for him those things that would be sold too cheaply.

Two kinds of Negroes come from the West Indian sugar islands: new Negroes, whom the slavers have brought there from Africa, and previously used ones, who do not wish to work and are being transported to other colonies like the malefactors in England. In general they are treated very harshly there and therefore commit excesses. Perhaps they will do better if they receive merciful masters. As far as I have understood from descriptions and word of mouth, the Negroes who have been brought to Savannah are of the latter kind, and therefore more caution will have to be used with them. Necessity is forcing us to this, otherwise we would not trouble ourselves with it. If even one among many is converted to Christ, then the risk and the money would be well applied.

On the 18th there was an auction of such Negroes or Moorish slaves that had been brought to Savannah from St. Kitts or St. Christopher. There were twenty-six of them, large and small and both male and female. Most of the children had to leave their mothers behind, which must have been just as painful for them as it was for an old Negress at the auction who had to see her children sold to different masters. Soon after their arrival in Savannah they had looked miserable and starved, but, when they had rest and more food and had dressed themselves as cleanly as possible for the auction, they all had a good appearance and found enough buyers, even though they were only sold for cash.

In addition to these twenty-six Negroes from St. Christopher, a few were brought from Port Royal and sold. Among them was a Catholic Christian, a handsome, strong, and modest man of twenty-six years, who was sold to me at £28 Sterling for our plantation. Besides him I bought two other men and two women. Dr. Graham showed me the kindness of buying these black servants inexpensively and with great caution and with the judgment of our friends.

In Savannah a ship had come from Mr. Lloyd to Messrs. Habersham and Harris, which brought a packet of pleasant letters, a chest of books for the congregation and a friend in Savannah Town, and a bell for our Zion Church. The bell was a gift of the minister Whitefield, who is still our friend and benefactor, even if there is no lack of people who are attempting to turn him against us. He wrote to me in a very friendly way and is requesting me to write to him at the first opportunity. He is attempting to help us get some Negroes; and he wishes and hopes that they can be lead to the Lord Jesus. His heart is ever inclined to Georgia, but he cannot come here until the large church that is being built in London under his auspices is put into condition. His orphanage and the surrounding land is now becoming well established, and I believe that it will gradually become (as it has been until now) a real Bethesda and a house of mercy.[5] Much is being done with the help of his Negroes.

In the English and German letters, we have received much matter for joy and for the praise of God, but also matter for sympathy and intercession. What brings us joy in the edifying letters we have received and arouses us to the praise of God consists especially in the following: our merciful God has noticeably strengthened the health of His dear servant, Court Chaplain

Ziegenhagen, and of his intimate colleague and has especially blessed their intercessions and loving efforts for us so that we are gradually being freed from our debts in London.

In former times I have, according to my duty, mentioned the cause of this debt in London and of another in Ebenezer; and, God be praised,! we have hope to be freed from them. Our merciful God has again raised up our dear Samuel and Father, Senior Urlsperger, from a physical weakness and granted him not only new strength but also great joy to submit an intercession for Ebenezer to high chiefs and men of rank, which our loyal God has so blessed to our astonishment and joy that a lovely gift has come together as capital for the support of Ebenezer's third minister. May the Lord give counsel and wisdom to invest this capital in such a way that the desired and unexpected use can be accomplished by it, namely, the support of our very worthy brother and colleague.

We are therefore asking him, and we have also spoken publicly to the members of our congregation about it, not only to praise our merciful Father in heaven for this new, exceptionally beautiful evidence of His gracious providence over our congregation as well as to implore Him for wisdom and gracious governance for a right safe and useful investment of these moneys. Because our dear Senior Urlsperger, Court Chaplain Ziegenhagen, another prominent and worthy benefactor, and many others in Germany and England found it good that this money should be used as a capital in Ebenezer and its interest or usufruct should be used to support Mr. Rabenhorst.

Therefore I began to consider this important matter with some pious, clever, and experienced Salzburgers as to how and in what manner this capital could best be applied to increase it and provide the interest customary in this land. Mr. Habersham offered to borrow £500 Sterling at 8% interest for three or four years and to invest it in his business, and he does not doubt that in that time he will earn so much that he can pay the capital and the interest in cash. Next to that, the safest and most useful way to win good interest in an innocent way would be to buy a number of slaves and to establish, in the local manner, a plantation on which one would not only cultivate corn, beans, rice, and other crops as well as indigo but also raise cattle and s.v.hogs and train the Negroes to cut cypress boards and produce other kinds of woodwork. The above-mentioned crops always bring a good price and one does not have to worry about buyers, except in time of war, when shipping is unsafe and expensive and the insurance rates are very high. Indigo also brings a right good price, and woodwork is exported to the West Indies almost as fast as it is taken to Savannah.

Appendix II

HYMNS SUNG BY
THE GEORGIA SALZBURGERS
IN THE YEARS 1753 AND 1754

All identified hymns are reproduced in Albert Friedrich Fischer—W. Tumpel, *Das deutsche evangelische Kirchenlied des 17. Jahrhunderts* (Gutersloh, 1916, reprinted Hildesheim 1964), and their authors are listed in Friedrich Fischer, *Kirchenlieder-Lexikon* (Gotha, 1878, reprint Hildesheim 1967).

Ach, dass ich tausend Zungen hätte . . . (Oh, if only I had a thousand tongues), by Johann Mentzer. This hymn sometime begins *O, dass ich*. I wish to thank Pastor Hartmut Beck for this and several other identifications. p. 148

Alles sei dir übergeben . . . (May everything be surrendered to Thee), unidentified. p. 12

Auf, o Seele, preise deines Schöpfers Güte . . . (Up, oh soul, praise the goodness of thy creator), unidentified. p. 47

Du meiner Augen Licht . . . (Thou, light of mine eyes), by Johann Georg Kehl. p. 134

Es ist nicht schwer, ein Christ zu seyn . . . (It is not difficult to be a Christian), by Christian Friedrich Richter. p. 10

Ich singe dir mit Herz und mund . . . (I sing to thee with heart and mouth), by Paul Gerhard. p. 171.

Ich quäle mich mit keinen Grillen . . . (I vex myself with no fancies), unidentified. p. 46

Ja, Jesus nimmt, see *Jesus nimmt*

Jehova ist mein Hirt und Hüter . . . (Jehovah is my shepherd and guardian), by Johann Anastasius Freylinghausen. p. 24

Jesus nimmt . . . (Jesus accepts sinners), by Erdmann Neumeister. pp. 140, 142, 198

Kind des Höchsten lebe, lebe . . . (Child of the Highest, live, oh live!), unidentified. p. 40

Mein Herz sey Gottes Lobethal . . . (May my heart be the valley of God's praise), by Aemalia Juliana, Gräfin von Schwarzburg-Rudelstadt. p. 86

Mein Vater, du hast mich erwählt . . . (My Father, thou has chosen me), by Friedrich Michael Ziegenhagen. pp. 2, 47, 49

Nun bitten wir den heiligen Geist . . . (Now we beg the Holy Ghost), by Martin Luther. p. 187.

Nun jauchzt dem Herrn alle Welt . . . (Shout with joy to the Lord), possibly the same as *Nun jauchzet alle Land*, by Michael Müller. p. 170.

Nun lob, mein Seel, den Herrn . . . (Now praise, my soul, the Lord), by Johann Gramann (Poliander). p. 169

Seelenbräutigam, Jesu, Gottes Lamm . . . (Soul of the bride, Jesus, Lamb of God), by Adam Drese. p. 121.

Sei Lob und Ehr dem höchsten Gut . . . (Praise and honor be to God), by Johann Jacob Schütz. p. 167.

So Kommet vor sein Angesicht . . . (So come before His countenance). This is from a hymn beginning *Sei Lob und Ehr dem höchsten Gut* by Johann Jacob Schütz. p. 86

Notes

NOTES TO JANUARY 1753

1. vv. 23-24.

2. Bonaventura Riesch had ministered to those Salzburgers who first found refuge in Lindau and had remained their benefactor.

3. Boltzius is playing on the name Samuel, that of the Old Testament judge and of the Senior in Augsburg.

4. Samuel Urlsperger, *Wort vom Tod und Leben Jesu Christi, als göttliche Kraft und Weisheit, in 10 Fasten- und Osterpredigten abgehandelt.*

5. The senior member of a Lutheran Ministry, like Senior Urlsperger.

6. Deuteronomy 33:3; John 316.

7. The temptation to lose faith in Christ in times of tribulation.

8. *Kinder, die der Vater soll ziehen zu allem Guten,* and *Bin ich denn nun Gottes Kind, warum wollt ich fliehen, etc.,* both verses from the hymn *Schwing dich auf zu deinem Gott, du betrübte Seele,* by Paul Gerhard. I wish to thank Pastor Hartmut Beck for this and other identifications.

9. Martin Luther's *Tabula Oeconomica.* While preaching the equality of all believers before God, Luther nevertheless upheld the class system as economically necessary; and he resisted all communistic movements, such as that of his friend Carlstadt.

10. Boltzius is referring to the land at Halifax. Although only a few of the third Swabian transport settled there, many other Germans did.

11. The third Swabian transport of 1752.

12. Christian Riedelsperger. See entry for 22 Jan. Riedelsperger probably went along to buy goods for his store in Ebenezer.

13. Revelations 2:5.

14. From the President of the Council, now Dr. Patrick Graham. The local government of Georgia consisted of a President and five Assistants, whom Boltzius called "Rathsherren."

15. He had come over with them.

16. *die kurz gefasste Ordnung des Heils in* 5. Fragen und Antworten. Halle, many printings.

17. Johann Anastasius Freylinghausen, *Ordnung des Heyls, Nebst einem Verzeichnis der wichtigsten Keren-Sprüche.* Halle 1724.

18. *Jesus der wahrhaftige Sünderfreund,* unidentified.

19. Boltzius, or the typesetter, put Grimmer, but that name did not exist in Ebenezer. Johann Caspar Greiner, with family, arrived with, or simultaneously with, the third Swabian transport.

20. Psalms 6:3; Hebrews 10:36.

21. *Geht es gleich durch manch Gedränge, sihst du doch den Ausgang schon,* from a hymn.

22. Jeremiah 10:24.

23. This means that Schrempf is beginning to turn from the fear of the law taught by the Old Testament to the grace taught in the New.

24. *allerunseligste Unveränderlichkeit,* perhaps the unwillingness to advance in Christianity.

25. Psalms 13:5-6.

26. *ich will, ich wills thun, ich will kommen,* Isaiah 46:4. The King James version differs.

27. 2 Corinthians 5:21.

28. *Nichts kann ich vor Gott ja bringen, als nur dich mein höchstes Gut: Jesu! es muss mir*

gelingen durch dein rosenfarbiges Blut. From the hymn *Eins ist Not! Ach Herr,* by Johann Heinrich Schröder.

29. The *Ausführliche Nachrichten.*

30. They were both Lutherans.

31. The ricebird or bobolink is a song bird in the north, but a pest in the ricefields.

32. The bobcat (*lynx rufus*) is a lynx, but the much larger mountain lion (*felis concolor*) was a panther, from which the Georgians got the word "painter." Elsewhere it is also called a cougar or a puma. "Painters" are now extinct in Georgia, but a few endangered ones survive in the Florida Everglades.

33. Only twenty years later an old Negress was burned alive for attempting to poison the Rabenhorsts.

34. This building material, called tabby, has lasted for two and a half centuries.

35. "Life and fame walk in step." Although Boltzius uses the word *Ambition,* he must be equating it with *Ehrgeiz,* which originally meant "greed for fame."

36. Boltzius does not state whether this was an English or a German society. The small number of members suggests the latter, in which case it would have been the Friendly Society, which is still active.

37. Boltzius writes that the woman died *mutwillig s. h. in ihrem eigenen Blute.* The *s. h.* is not explained. Sometimes *s.h.* appears to refer to fecal matter, possibly humorous, from *Scheisshaus.*

38. Capt. Isaac was the master of the ship *Success,* which had brought the Bornemann party to Georgia in 1752. He was then sailing for Harris and Habersham.

39. Boltzius did not see fit to mention that he had sat for a portrait by the Swiss painter Jeremias Theus, an engraving from which appears as the frontispiece to Vol. II of this series.

40. Psalms 100:3; see also 1 Kings 8:60.

41. Revelations 14:13; Isaiah 3:10.

42. John 13:7.

43. 1 Timothy 115; Luke 19:10.

44. *Sehet, aus der Schaar der elendsten Sünder, macht der selige Gott selige Kinder,* from a hymn.

45. This would appear to be Magdalena Lackner (Lechner), wife of Veit Lackner (Lechner), who died in 1742.

46. Ephesians 5:14.

47. 1 Timothy 1:15.

48. Matthew 11:28.

49. Veit Lemmenhofer.

50. It is not indicated which of Johann Anastasius Freylinghausen's many publications is being referrd to.

51. Samuel Urlsperger, *Passions- und Osterpredigten.*

52. See note above.

NOTES TO FEBRUARY 1753

1. *Sie werden nicht anders, und fürchten Gott nicht.* Psalms 55:20. In the King James version it is 55:19.

2. *Lass dich Gottes Geist in Zeiten, doch zur wahren Busse leiten, wohl zum Tode zubereiten.* From a hymn.

3. *Sicherheit* was a Pietistic term for a false sense of being saved.

4. Psalms 149:4.

5. Genesis 1:19, 17.

6. *Höre Tochter, schaue drauf,* etc. Psalms 45:11. I wish to thank Pastor Hermann Winde for this and many other identifications.

7. The *Extradiarium* for the month of April, which followed that month in the regular diary, is found in Appendix II.

8. He was a Lutheran.

9. *Der Herr hat alles wohl bedacht, und alles, alles recht gemacht, gebt unserm Gott die Ehre,* from a hymn by Gustav von Mengden, which usually begins *Gott hat alles. . . .* This is typical of the theodicy of the time, which received a jolt two years later from the Lisbon quake.

10. Matthew 25:35.

11. *Sie werden nicht anders.* See note 1, above.

12. *Wo ich nur mein Aug hinkehre, find ich, was mich nährt und hält.* From a hymn.

13. By "current" (*Courent*) Boltzius means South Carolina pounds, which had about a seventh of the value of Sterling.

14. See note 9 above.

NOTES TO MARCH 1753

1. *des Herrn Carl Gottlob Hofmanns Christliches Denkmahl.* Unidentified.

2. The word *Haushalt* denotes the family's entire economy, including homestead, fields and livestock.

3. Genesis 3:17; Psalms 90:10; Job 14:1; Sirach 40:1.

4. He had great pleasure *an den Passionspredigten des Herrn Sen. Urlspergers, und Herrn Hofpredigers Ziegenhagen, von dem grossen und schweren Seelenleiden Christi.* Unidentified.

5. The Halle typesetter mistakenly typed 14th.

6. Boltzius and Capt. Krauss.

7. It was a favorite tenet of the Pietists that no one can win salvation on his own merits but only through the grace of God through Jesus Christ.

8. Boltzius was right. Dependence on maize was a major cause of pellagra.

9. "His" naturally refers to Lackner, not Boltzius.

10. This was Johann Paul Francke, whose story is told in *Detailed Reports* Vol. IV.

11. *Herrn Schützens einfältige und fassliche Catechismus-prüfungen.* Unidentified.

NOTES TO APRIL 1753

1. A German settlement southeast of Ebenezer.

2. Probably Savannah, the one town Boltzius and Urlsperger spared from criticism.

3. Her husband was either Bartholomäus or Martin Botzenhardt, two brothers who failed in Georgia and returned home to Germany, where they wrote scathing denunciations of Georgia to ingratiate themselves with the authorities.

4. A settlement up the Savannah River where the third Swabian transport had intended to settle. Only a few members did so.

5. Boltzius means, of course, the Lutherans.

6. *Wenn schien alles zu zerrinnen, ward doch deiner Hülf ich innen. Tausend, tausendmal sey dir, grosser König, Dank dafür.* Probably from the hymn *Jesu, meines Lebens Leben* by Ernst Christoph Homburg.

7. *Herrn Pfarrer Starkens Communionbüchlein.* This may not be the title.

8. Isaiah 43:24.

9. Matthew 28:6, Mark 16:6, Luke 24:6.

10. John 12:32.

11. We do not know who this "third person" was. Perhaps he had been sent to manage von Münch's enterprizes.

NOTES TO MAY 1753

1. Lamentations 3:22-23.

2. *Jesus kommt als ein Gerechter und ein Helfer.* Pastor Hartmut Beck suggests that this

may be an allusion to the words *Er ist Gerecht, ein Helfer wert* in the hymn *Macht hoch die Tür, die Tor macht weit!* by Georg Weissel. The verse is based on Zechariah 9:9.

3. *des Herrn Sommers kurze Reimgebethlein von Weyhnachten und Pfingsten.* Boltzius is referring to the *Güldenes ABC Büchlein,* which was a popular Sunday school primer.

4. He is referring chiefly to Heinrich Melchior Muhlenberg, Johann Peter Brunnholtz, and the Rev. Handschuh. See entry for May 7.

5. The Francke Foundation had been supplying ministers for Lutheran missions in Tranquebar, Madras, Cudulur, and elsewhere in India. See entry for May 7.

6. "Bond of Christian brotherhood."

7. *der 5ten Fortsetzung der pensylvanischen merkwürdigen Nachrichten.* Reports sent by the Pietist ministers in Philadelphia to their superiors in Halle.

8. Psalms 115:9.

9. 2 Corinthians 6:17.

10. John 11:4.

11. John 16:24.

12. *Schriftmässiger Unterricht für Kranke und Sterbende.*

13. See note 3, above.

14. Matthew 18:20.

15. Constappel has not been located.

NOTES TO JUNE 1753

1. The meaningless, but clearly typed letters *Laern* must be a typographical error. The context calls for a word meaning contributions or dues.

2. It was common at the time for pious people to send Bible verses to each other, either written out or just numbered.

3. She must have meant, "I, with my children, have sent . . . "

4. *Anfechtungen* were the temptation not to believe that Christ, through His merits, can save even the worst sinner if he is truly penitent.

5. *Der schöne Traktat des Goodwins,* unidentified.

6. Christian Friedrich Richter, professor at Halle.

7. Romans 8:32.

8. Boltzius and Gronau had been ordained at Wernigerode.

9. John 11:40.

10. *Eine ernstliche Vermahnung des Herrn Jesu, den Vater zu bitten um den heiligen Geist.*

11. In Pietist parlance "misery" (*Elend*) meant "alienation from God" or sin.

12. Stückhauptmann Krauss, an artillery captain who accompanied the third Swabian transport but then returned to Europe.

13. Matthew 7:11.

14. Galatians 5:6.

15. *Des Blut zeichnet unsere Thür, das hält der Glaube dem Tode für, der Würger kann uns nicht rühren, Halleluja.* From the hymn *Christ lag in den Todesbanden* by Martin Luther.

16. *Angefochtene,* see note 4, above.

17. *durchbrechen* (break through) was a Pietist term meaning to achieve the realization that Christ, through His merits, can save sinners.

18. Since this makes no sense, the word *finden* may be an error for *hindern,* to hinder.

19. See May, note 15.

20. Siegmund Jacob Baumgarten, professor at Halle.

21. See May, note 7.

22. Matthew 6:33.

23. By "wild cats" (*Wildkatzen*) Boltzius usually means raccoons.

24. While somewhat dormant all winter, malarial chills and fever recurred every summer.

25. See Jan., note 14.

26. At this point Urlsperger has added the following footnote: "This can and will not happen, since the salaries are so moderate that they will not maintain a household."

27. Boltzius means, of course, among the Negroes.

28. Matthew 10:30-31.

29. *Betrachtung der göttlichen Vorsehung über die Menschen*, unidentified. The verse that follows is based on Romans 8:28.

30. *Dass wir denen. die GOTT lieben, Alle Dinge zum Besten dienen*, from a hymn.

NOTES TO JULY 1753

1. Karl Heinrich Bogatzky, *Güldenes Schatz-kästlein der Kinder Gottes* Halle, many printings.

2. The word "Ebenezer" was sometimes translated "the Lord hath helped so far."

3. "For pious purposes."

4. Luke 23:34.

5. "To kill two birds with one stone" or, literally, "To whitewash two walls with one pot."

6. Boltzius is not implying that the Savannah River is small. He means, "other rivers, which are small."

7. Psalms 11:7; Revelations 16:7.

8. See May, note 4.

9. An error for 3 July.

10. Boltzius, or the typesetter, erroneously calls this 1 Timothy 4:15.

11. Psalms 55:22.

12. Psalms 73:28.

13. Matthew 18:7.

NOTES TO AUGUST 1753

1. In the *Ausführliche Nachrichten* this and the following entry are erroneously given as July. This explains why there are two entries marked the 16th.

2. Ruth 1:16-17.

3. Boltzius does not give the symptoms of *Seitenstechen*.

4. This date is incorrect. See note 1, above.

5. Georg Koegler. It is unclear why Boltzius is using the dialect form this one time.

6. Psalms 68:19.

7. Psalms 37:5.

8. *Er tut uns alles Gute*. Possibly a reference to Micah 6:5 in Luther's translation, which differs here from the King James version.

NOTES TO SEPTEMBER 1753

1. Psalms 145:19.

2. The Society for Promoting Christian Knowledge, the Georgia Salzburgers' chief patron in England.

3. Secretary of the above-mentioned Society.

4. This list, if it was written, has been lost or misplaced.

5. "An agency through which the state works indirectly." Lemke had taken over many secular tasks from Boltzius, such as managing the mills.

6. *Diess Leben wird hier in dir angefangen: und wenn du in der Zeit es mit Beständigkeit behältst, so wirst du ewig darinn prangen*. From the hymn *Du meiner Augen Licht*, by Johann Georg Kehl.

7. See July, note 1.

8. "Through difficulty to the stars."

9. The Book of Wisdom (*Sapientia*) is found in the Apocrypha, but in neither Luther nor the King James version.

10. This is Ephesians 3:20.

11. Lamentations 3:22-23.

NOTES TO OCTOBER 1753

1. "Spiritual and church matters."

2. Revelations 5:5; John 16:33.

3. Ephesians 3:20.

4. Sirach is a book of the Apocrypha.

5. See Sept., note 7.

6. Johann Haeckel.

7. "He" obviously refers to the previously mentioned bachelor brother.

8. Johann Wilhelm Gerhard von Brahm, the leader of the second Swabian transport.

9. Friedrich Michael Ziegenhagen, chaplain to the King.

10. These cities are now written Saalfeld and Wernigerode.

11. Matthew 6:34.

12. Psalms 119:130.

13. *S* stood for *sanftmütig* (gentle) and *T* stood for *treu* (loyal).

NOTES TO NOVEMBER 1753

1. V., A., and M. are probably Venice, Augsburg, and Memmingen, all sources of frequent gifts. B. may be Berlin, while S.G. could be St. Gall.

2. Cf. John 16:27.

3. "Of the political and ecclesiastical order."

4. "The great deeds of God and His kingdom."

5. The Halle Pietists were then feuding with Count Ludwig Zinzendorf and his Herrnhuters or Moravian Brothers.

6. *Warnung vor dem Rückfall*, by Karl Heinrich Bogatzky.

7. In German, the "enemy" (*Feind*) often means the devil.

8. The Halle typesetters may have been in error regarding quotation marks, since the preceding statement appears to have been made by von Wallbaum rather than by Boltzius.

9. See January, note 14.

10. Although this was an Old Testament verse, Boltzius treated it as a gospel verse.

11. Psalms 103:13.

12. Statesman or businessman.

13. Joel 2:13.

NOTES TO DECEMBER 1753

1. See Jan., note 14.

2. It is not clear what Boltzius means by the "dedication" (*Zueignung.*)

3. Psalms 143:2.

4. See Sept., note 7.

5. Psalms 115:3.

6. "The testimony of poverty."

7. Paul Anton, Pietist professor at Halle.

8. *des sel. Prof. Frankens Heilsordnung.* This comes as a surprise, since the more popular book of this type in Ebenezer was Johann Anastasius Freylinghausen, *Ordnung des Heyls,*

Nebst einem Verzeichnis der wichtigsten Kern-Sprüche. Halle 1724. The "late professor" was the very prolific August Hermann Francke.

9. See May, note 3.

10. *Jesu, ey nu, hilf mir dazu, dass ich stäts nüchtern sey wie du.* Apparently from a hymn.

NOTES TO JANUARY 1754

1. Boltzius is alluding to the last three transports.

2. Luther's translation differs considerably from the King James version.

3. This term will be used often for Boltzius.

4. The Luther translation differs markedly from the King James version.

5. *Wisset ihr nicht, dass ich seyn muss in dem, das meines Vatters ist,* unidentified.

6. *unächte Seitenstechen,* not identified.

NOTES TO FEBRUARY 1754

1. Clay-eating is a symptom, not a cause of Ancylostomiasis, which is caused by hookworms.

2. Mrs. M.

3. The Pietists used the word *Elend* (exile or misery) to mean alienation from God, therefore, sin.

4. See Jan. 1753, note 4.

5. *Kurze Ordnung des Heils.*

6. This best-seller was sent from Halle in quantities for distribution and sale.

NOTES TO MARCH 1754

1. This woman from Wurttemberg had married a soldier named Dod or Dodd at Frederica.

2. *Beicht- und Communionsbüchlein.*

3. See Nov. 1753, note 7.

4. The "he" (*er*) probably refers to God, who uses the devil to tempt and test man.

5. Baptists from Virginia were active at the time around Augusta.

6. This is the second entry under that date, perhaps by another hand.

7. Luther differs greatly from the King James version: *Wir haben einen Gott, der da hilft, und einen Herrn Nerrn, der vom Tode erretet.*

8. Psalms 73:24.

9. Johann Caspar Schade, *Geistreiche Predigten über die Sonn-Fest- und Feiertags-Evangelia durch das ganze Jahr,* etc. Frankfurt/Leipzig 1731.

10. This was probably August Hermann Francke, *Kurze Son- und Festtags-Predigten.* Halle 1694 ff.

11. The area around Goshen was still sparsely settled and had few well marked paths.

12. (Johann) Ludwig Mayer.

13. Boltzius and Lemke each received 300 acres on 5 August 1749, but these plantations had no names. On 21 August 1750 Boltzius received a plantation he named Good Harmony.

14. Those preparing for confirmation.

NOTES FOR APRIL 1754

1. The date of this entry is not given, but it is probably for the 1st.

2. John Reynolds.

3. Psalms 103:2.
4. This entry bears the same date as the preceding one.

NOTES FOR MAY 1754

1. The ceremony of confirmation.
2. 1 Peter 1:18.
3. Paraphrased from Genesis 32:10.
4. See May 1753, note 3.
5. Hardwick, a short-lived seaport.
6. Psalms 37:4.
7. 1 Timothy 3:1.

NOTES FOR JUNE 1754

1. Acts 10:33.
2. A settlement up the Savannah River from Ebenezer. The third Swabian transport had intended to settle there, but they found it too remote.
3. Boltzius seems to be describing pemmican.
4. *Das americanische Ackerwerck Gottes*, the title given to the Ebenezer reports after April 1751. Urlsperger probably sent this copy to advise the Ebenezer ministers what things he preferred to have suppressed in future entries.
5. Rabenhorst is now speaking to Urlsperger.
6. See Feb. 1753, note 3.
7. This is Luther's belief that we can be saved by faith alone. The Pietists taught that good works, even civil respectability (*bürgerliche Ehrbarkeit*), cannot win salvation. Belief that one can achieve one's own salvation is a snare of the devil.

NOTES FOR JULY 1754

1. Of cocoons.

NOTES FOR SEPTEMBER 1754

1. An error for Schwartzwälder. The Schwartzwälder family had moved from Old Ebenezer, where they had been servants at the cowpen.
2. Amalia Schiermeister.

NOTES FOR OCTOBER 1754

1. See July 1753, note 1.
2. See June 1754, note 7.
3. Allusion to John 4:53.
4. This problem was solved nearby only a few decades later by Eli Whitney.
5. Surely Chrétien von Münch.
6. For diplomatic reasons, Boltzius complained less than most colonials about Great Britain's stifling mercantilistic regulations, which were soon to lead to independence.
7. 2 Corinthians 5:14.
8. See Feb. 1754, note 3.
9. Matthew 6:33.
10. *Dies Wort ist mir ein Lilium ein süsses Evangelium, ja lauter Milch und Honig*, apparently from a hymn.

11. This seems to contradict the dependence upon faith alone. See June 1754, note 7.

12. Johann Arndt, *Vier Bücher Vom wahren Christenthum*. Halle 1731. By far the most popular Pietistic treatise of the time, also published in America.

13. Apparently the Salzburger exiles in East Prussia, with whom the Georgia Salzburgers maintained a correspondence.

14. "For the sake of special care and most special care."

NOTES FOR NOVEMBER 1754

1. When the bridge is completed, they will be able to come to school on foot instead of only by boat.

2. To come to church.

3. At this point Urlsperger has appended the footnote: "For these are the drafts which they send ahead of us to heaven and which, if we will only believe, are never rejected."

4. At this point Urlsperger has inserted the footnote: "How often the Biblical passage in our prayer of repentance proves true: Thou hast stricken them, but they have not grieved; thou has consumed them, but they have refused to receive correction." (Jeremiah 5:3)

5. Boltzius is referring to mountain lions (cougars, *felis concolor*), now extinct in Georgia but surviving in the Everglades, which are actually panthers. Poultry and small animals were endangered by bobcats (*lynx rufus*), a true lynx that is still prevalent around Ebenezer.

6. See June 1754, note 6.

NOTES FOR DECEMBER 1754

1. The word *Epilepsie* was used of any paroxim, usually a symptom, not a cause, of illness.

2. Boltzius is using the metaphor of God's husbandry, of which he is one of the workers.

3. This is not John, but Matthew 3:12. The word *Wurfschaufel* in Luther is much clearer. It refers to the winnowing fan with which the Lord will separate His wheat from the chaff.

4. He was among the passengers who arrived in 1737 on the *Three Sisters* with Capt. Hewitt. This party had departed on their own from Rotterdam but had been captured by two Spanish corsairs, robbed, and taken to Bilbao in Spain, from where they were ransomed by the British.

5. This not Luke 2:21 but Luke 2:25. This was Simeon, who recognized the Christ child as the Messiah.

NOTES TO EXTRA DIARY 1753

1. *Bauern Regel*. Boltzius is referring to ancient customary rules by which the German peasants determined their time of communal planting.

2. Since German birds differed from American birds, we do not know what American bird the Germans identified as a *Kornvogel*. Sometimes such identification missed the mark greatly. The British, finding no robin in America, gave the name to a russet breasted thrasher, which was larger than the robin and ate worms rather than berries.

3. "secondary causes."

4. "leaking arguments."

5. George Whitefield had named his orphanage near Savannah Bethesda, which meant "house of mercy." It was the name of the curative pool in John 5:2.

Index

ABC books, see Sommer.

Abercorn, village near juncture of Abercorn Creek and Savannah River, mentioned, 62, 172, 175, 177, 198, 200, 210. Lutherans reside there 63, "behind Abercorn" = Goshen.

Abercorn Creek (Mill River), branch of Savannah River, mentioned 99, 161, 172, 183, 202, 203

Acorns, being gathered 207

Agriculture, see Crops.

Albinus, Samuel Theodor, court chaplain in London, letter from 35, 37, 96, package from 35

Altherr, Master Johann, fr Purysburg, sends boat 190

Animals, wild: bears, lynxes, wolves, tigers, dangerous to livestock 207; Jan 53, n. 32

Anton, Paul, Pietist professor, author of *Testimonium Paupertatis* 154, Dec 53, n. 7

Arndt, Johann, Pietist, author of *True Christianity*, 31, 83, 88, 93, 200

Assistants, see Council.

Augsburg, city in Swabia, benefactors in, 69, 167

Augusta, city up the Savannah River, mentioned 42, 78, 103

Ausführliche Nachrichten, source of *Detailed Reports*, mentioned 17

Bacher, Christina, Salz, w Matthias, sick 15, dies 16, 17, 24, a prudent midwife 24

Bächle, see Bechle.

Baptisms 148: Negro girl 105, schoolmaster's daughter 127

Bauern Regel, customary peasant rules, Extradiary n. 1

Baumgarten, Dr. Siegmund Jacob, benefactor 93

Bears, dangerous to livestock 207

Beaufort, town in South Carolina, mentioned 18, 19

Bechle, Jacob, fr Langenau, confirmed 179, dies 209

Bechle, Swabian, house consecrated 166

Beer, being brewed 168

Beicht- und Communionbüchlein, see *Confession* . . .

Beiträge zum Bau . . . , see *Contributions* . . .

Bell, donated by Whitefield 85, 218

Benefactions, source of, see Augsburg, Halle, Holland, Holstein, London, Memmingen, Leipzig.

Bengel, Prior, righteous man, dies 145

Bethany, village on Blue Bluff, mentioned 177, 204

Bethesda, Whitefield's orphanage near Savannah 218

Birth control, understood by Negroes 106

Black Creek, German settlement southeast of Ebenezer, mentioned 56, 209. Lutherans reside there 63

Blue Bluff, new name of Uchee land across Ebenezer Creek, mentioned 6, 13, 34, 53, 67, 68, 73, 74,, 92, 105, 140, 158, 159, 164, 176, 203,

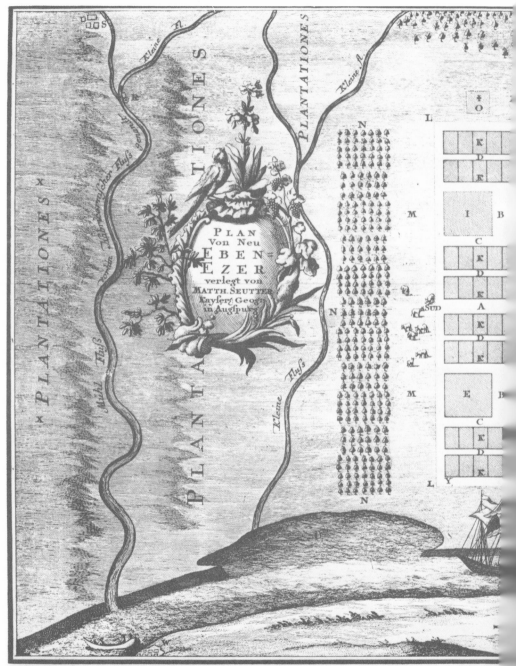

PLAN
Von Neu
EBEN=
EZER
verlegt von
MATTH. SEUTTER
Kayserl: Geogr
in Augspurg

A. Haupt Straßen. B. Marckt Platz. C. Mittle Gaßen. D. kleine Gäßlin. E. Store Hauß. F. Pfarr Wohnungen. G. die Kirchen
rer ein jeglicher Zehen Wohnungen faßt; So in einem Hauß Hof ü: Garten bestehet. L. ein Schindel Zaun Sechs Fuß hoch
welcher ebenfals eingezäunt. P. Hölz. Q. Eigenthumlichs Land einer kleinen Nation Indianer. R. die Mühl. S. Fabricor:
Land wo die Saltzburger ihre Vieh Ställe haben. Y. Sind 20 Hauß Plätze zwischen drey Straßen, so Hr: General Ogleth:

This plan of Ebenezer first appeared in Urlsperger's *Ausführli*
A tinted copy is in the De Ren